MOBILE EDGE ARTIFICIAL INTELLIGENCE

MOBILE EDGE ARTIFICIAL INTELLIGENCE

Opportunities and Challenges

YUANMING SHI
ShanghaiTech University
Shanghai, China

KAI YANG
JD.com, Inc.
Beijing, China

ZHANPENG YANG
ShanghaiTech University
Shanghai, China

YONG ZHOU
ShanghaiTech University
Shanghai, China

ELSEVIER

ACADEMIC PRESS
An imprint of Elsevier

Academic Press is an imprint of Elsevier
125 London Wall, London EC2Y 5AS, United Kingdom
525 B Street, Suite 1650, San Diego, CA 92101, United States
50 Hampshire Street, 5th Floor, Cambridge, MA 02139, United States
The Boulevard, Langford Lane, Kidlington, Oxford OX5 1GB, United Kingdom

Notices

Knowledge and best practice in this field are constantly changing. As new research and experience broaden our understanding, changes in research methods, professional practices, or medical treatment may become necessary.

Practitioners and researchers must always rely on their own experience and knowledge in evaluating and using any information, methods, compounds, or experiments described herein. In using such information or methods they should be mindful of their own safety and the safety of others, including parties for whom they have a professional responsibility.

To the fullest extent of the law, neither the Publisher nor the authors, contributors, or editors, assume any liability for any injury and/or damage to persons or property as a matter of products liability, negligence or otherwise, or from any use or operation of any methods, products, instructions, or ideas contained in the material herein.

Library of Congress Cataloging-in-Publication Data
A catalog record for this book is available from the Library of Congress

British Library Cataloguing-in-Publication Data
A catalogue record for this book is available from the British Library

ISBN: 978-0-12-823817-2

For information on all Academic Press publications
visit our website at https://www.elsevier.com/books-and-journals

Publisher: Mara Conner
Acquisitions Editor: Tim Pitts
Editorial Project Manager: Naomi Robertson
Production Project Manager: Kamesh Ramajogi
Designer: Miles Hitchen

Typeset by VTeX

Contents

Part 3. Edge training

List of figures

Biography

Yuanming Shi

Yuanming Shi received the B.S. degree in electronic engineering from Tsinghua University, Beijing, China, in 2011. He received the Ph.D. degree in electronic and computer engineering from The Hong Kong University of Science and Technology (HKUST), in 2015. Since September 2015, he has been with the School of Information Science and Technology in ShanghaiTech University, where he is currently a tenured Associate Professor. He visited University of California, Berkeley, CA, USA, from October 2016 to February 2017. Dr. Shi is a recipient of the 2016 IEEE Marconi Prize Paper Award in Wireless Communications and the 2016 Young Author Best Paper Award by the IEEE Signal Processing Society. He is an editor of IEEE Transactions on Wireless Communications and IEEE Journal on Selected Areas in Communications. His research areas include optimization, statistics, machine learning, signal processing, and their applications to 6G, IoT, and AI.

Kai Yang

Kai Yang received his B.E. degree in electrical engineering from Dalian University of Technology, Dalian, China, in 2015. He received the Ph.D. degree in Communication and Information System from the Shanghai Institute of Microsystem and Information Technology, Chinese Academy of Sciences, Shanghai 200050, China, in 2020. He was advised by Prof. Yuanming Shi and Prof. Zhi Ding during the PhD program. He was a visiting student of University of Toronto, Toronto, Canada and advised by Prof. Wei Yu in 2019. Kai Yang is currently an AI researcher in JD.com, Inc. His research interests are designing efficient systems and optimization algorithms for machine learning, federated learning, and their applications in financial risk management.

Zhanpeng Yang

Zhanpeng Yang received his B.S. degree in electrical engineering from Xidian University in 2020. He has joined the School of Information

Science and Technology, ShanghaiTech University, in September 2020. His research interests include blockchains, federated learning, and their applications in mobile edge AI systems.

Yong Zhou

Yong Zhou received the B.S. and M.E. degrees from Shandong University, Jinan, China, in 2008 and 2011, respectively, and the Ph.D. degree from the University of Waterloo, Waterloo, ON, Canada, in 2015. From November 2015 to January 2018 he worked as a postdoctoral research fellow in the Department of Electrical and Computer Engineering, The University of British Columbia, Vancouver, Canada. He is currently an Assistant Professor in the School of Information Science and Technology, ShanghaiTech University, Shanghai, China. His research interests include Internet of things, edge computing, and reconfigurable intelligent surfaces.

Preface

With the availability of massive data sets, high-performance computing platforms, sophisticated algorithms and software toolkits, and artificial intelligence (AI) have achieved remarkable successes in many application domains, for example, computer vision and natural language processing. AI tasks are computationally intensive and always trained, developed, and deployed at data centers with custom-designed servers. Given the fast growth of intelligent devices, it is expected that a large number of high-stake applications (e.g., drones, autonomous cars, industrial IoT, and AR/VR) will be deployed at the edge of wireless networks in the near future. As such, the intelligent wireless network will be designed to leverage advanced wireless communications and mobile computing technologies to support AI-enabled applications at various edge devices with limited communication, computation, hardware, and energy resources. This emerging mobile edge AI technology is envisioned to promote the paradigm shift of futuristic 6G networks from "connected things" to "connected intelligence".

In the first part of this book, we present the foundations of machine learning and convex optimization for developing mobile edge AI frameworks, followed by a brief overview of mobile edge AI categorized according to different system architectures. To fully unleash the potential of network edges to support intelligent services, the mobile edge AI will rely on the characteristics of different AI models and optimization algorithms to learn the models. To design efficient mobile edge AI systems, it is challenging to coordinate a number of edge nodes and allocate available resources for performing edge training or inference tasks. In practice, there are often various physical constraints due to the heterogeneity and limited resources of edge nodes and regulatory constraints out of privacy and security concerns. Therefore we propose to jointly design computation, communication, and learning across various system architectures.

The second part mainly focuses on the inference process for an edge AI system. We present three representative methodologies of edge inference, including model compression for on-device inference, coded computing for on-device cooperative inference, and edge computing for edge-server cooperative inference. Specifically, to deploy deep neural network models at resource-limited devices, model compression approaches have attracted numerous attentions to reduce the model size and computation complexity, for which we present a layerwise network pruning method in Chapter 5. In Chapter 6, we show that mobile devices can perform the inference task cooperatively through a wireless-coded computing system, which is particularly suitable for large-size models that are infeasible to be deployed on a single mobile device. For computation intensive inference tasks, in Chapter 7, we further investigate the alternative computation offloading approach for edge inference, where the inference tasks are uploaded and executed by edge servers via wireless cooperative communications.

The third part focuses on the training process of edge AI with emphasizing on a collaborative machine learning paradigm termed as federated learning, which enables deep learning model directly training over a large volume of decentralized data residing in mobile devices without uploading clients' private data into a center server to keep data privacy. In particular, we provide three promising technologies to improve the communication efficiency in federated learning, that is, over-the-air computation, reconfigurable intelligent surface, and blind demixing approaches. Specifically, over-the-air computation provides a principled way to exploit the waveform superposition property of a wireless multiaccess channel, thereby achieving fast global model aggregation of federated learning, which is presented in Chapter 8. As a smart radio environment wireless technology, reconfigurable intelligent surface is further leveraged to achieve fast yet reliable model aggregation for over-the-air federated learning by reconfiguring the reflected signal propagations, which is demonstrated in Chapter 9. To avoid the high signaling overhead of obtaining channel state information, in Chapter 10, we further provide a blind demixing approach for simultaneous channel estimation and model aggregation in wireless federated learning.

Distributed machine learning over wireless edge network provides a promising way to reduce the network traffic congestion, preserve data privacy, and enable real-time decision. The aim of this book is to present recent advances in wireless technologies and nonconvex optimization techniques for designing efficient edge AI systems with a comprehensive coverage including problem modeling, algorithm design, and theoretical analysis. Through typical case studies, the powerfulness of this set of systems and algorithms is demonstrated, and their abilities in making low-latency, reliable, and private intelligent decisions at network edge are highlighted. We hope that the discussions of mobile edge AI through this book will enlighten more designs of mobile edge AI and attract more researchers into this novel and intriguing field.

Acknowledgments

We express our gratitude to the support of National Nature Science Foundation of China under Grants 62001294 and 61601290. We also would like to express our sincere thanks to Dr. Zhi Ding and Dr. Wei Yu for their valuable contributions to the related works presented in this book.

Yuanming Shi
Kai Yang
Zhanpeng Yang
Yong Zhou

PART ONE

Introduction and overview

CHAPTER ONE

Motivations and organization

1.1. Motivations

Artificial intelligence (AI), namely the intelligence demonstrated by machines, has made unprecedented achievements in a wide range of applications, such as searching and recommending commodities in e-commerce, content filtering in social networks, autonomous vehicles, unmanned aerial vehicles, and so on. Compared to the global gross domestic product (GDP) of 2018, AI is expected to add about 16% to it by 2030, which is around 13 trillion dollars [1]. The advancement of AI benefits greatly from the rapid growth of data. The upsurge of mobile devices accounts for much of the data growth, for example, smart phones and Internet-of-things devices. As predicted by Cisco, nearly 85 Zettabytes of data will be generated by all people, machines, and things in 2021 and are four times as much as the traffic of cloud data center (21 Zettabytes). Therefore, we are witnessing and taking part in the paradigm shift of AI from "cloud intelligence" to beyond.

Ubiquitous AI services for mobile devices are putting increasingly high requirements on low-latency, privacy, security, and reliability. In many applications, mobile devices are the target users and also the data provider, whereas a traditional cloud AI engine is not able to meet these requirements. Therefore it is increasingly emphasized to push AI engine to network edges [2], which are physically located closer to the data sources. A representative example is the EdgeRec [3] recommender system developed by Alibaba to achieve real-time user perception and real-time system feedback for mobile Taobao, which is one of the most popular e-commerce platforms. However, network edge nodes, including edge servers at wireless access points, and edge devices such as mobile phones and wearable devices are usually equipped with limited computation, storage, and communication resources. Unfortunately, it is generally infeasible to directly deploy AI models on resource-constrained devices because of the large model size and/or high computational costs. It is thus critical to design novel system architectures to exploit distributed computing, storage, and communica-

Mobile Edge Artificial Intelligence
https://doi.org/10.1016/B978-0-12-823817-2.00010-3

tion resources across a fleet of edge nodes. This motivates a new research area, termed *edge intelligence*, *edge AI*, or *mobile edge AI* [4,5].

Performing AI tasks at network edges differs from cloud intelligence in many senses:

- **Heterogeneous and limited resources.** There is a fundamental difference between edge and cloud on the available resources of each participating node. Edge nodes are usually equipped with limited computation resources, whereas the cloud servers possess a large number of extremely powerful processing units. The power of edge nodes is much more limited than that of cloud servers. In addition, edge nodes are often wirelessly connected, and hence the limited communication bandwidth becomes one of the main bottleneck for exchanging information in mobile edge AI.
- **Data availability structure.** Due to the limited communication bandwidth and storage in network edges, the access to decentralized data across nodes severely slows down the efficiency of edge AI. Therefore the system design strongly depends on the specific data availability in different applications, which is barely considered in cloud intelligence systems.
- **Privacy and security constraints.** Traditional cloud AI engine requires collecting all input data from end users. However, there emerge a number of high-stake applications in intelligent IoT with privacy and security concerns such as smart vehicles. Furthermore, stricter regulations for protecting data privacy are enacted by operators in recent years, for example, General Data Protection Regulation (GDPR) by the European Union [6] and Personal Information Security Specification issued by China's National Information Security Standardization Technical Committee (TC260).[1]

It is a challenging mission to enable efficient mobile edge AI via coordinating a fleet of resource-constrained edge nodes with different data availability and privacy/security constraints. The mission challenges the existing mobile communication system and leads to its paradigm shift of *connected things* to *connected intelligence*. In addition, it is also mission critical to adapt optimization methods of training an AI model to mobile edge AI system structures in different applications. Therefore mobile edge AI is an emerging area requiring interdisciplinary knowledge of machine learning, optimization, communication theory, and so on.

[1] https://www.tc260.org.cn/upload/2018-01-24/1516799764389090333.pdf.

1.2. Organization

To provide the readers with thorough understanding of mobile edge AI, we organize this book in the following structure:

1. In the first part, we present the primer on AI and optimization methods and an overview of mobile edge AI.
2. In the second part, we present the methodologies of model compression for on-device inference, coded computing for on-device cooperative inference, and computation offloading for edge cooperative inference.
3. In the third part, we introduce an important paradigm of edge training termed federated learning and present over-the-air computation technique, reconfigurable intelligent surface technique, and blind demixing technique for fast data aggregation of federated learning.
4. In the final part, we conclude the book and present discussions on the future directions.

References

[1] J. Bughin, J. Seong, Assessing the economic impact of artificial intelligence, ITUTrends Issue Paper No. 1, Sep. 2018.

[2] J. Zhang, K.B. Letaief, Mobile edge intelligence and computing for the Internet of vehicles, Proc. IEEE 108 (Feb. 2020) 246–261.

[3] Y. Gong, Z. Jiang, Y. Feng, B. Hu, K. Zhao, Q. Liu, W. Ou, Edgerec: recommender system on edge in mobile Taobao, in: Proceedings of the 29th ACM International Conference on Information & Knowledge Management, 2020, pp. 2477–2484.

[4] Z. Zhou, X. Chen, E. Li, L. Zeng, K. Luo, J. Zhang, Edge intelligence: paving the last mile of artificial intelligence with edge computing, Proc. IEEE 107 (Aug. 2019) 1738–1762.

[5] Y. Shi, K. Yang, T. Jiang, J. Zhang, K.B. Letaief, Communication-efficient edge AI: algorithms and systems, IEEE Commun. Surv. Tutor. 22 (Jul. 2020) 2167–2191.

[6] Regulation (EU) 2016/679 of the European Parliament and of the Council of 27 April 2016 on the protection of natural persons with regard to the processing of personal data and on the free movement of such data, and repealing Directive 95/46/EC (General Data Protection Regulation), Offic. J. Europ. Union L 119 (Apr. 2016) 1–88, https://eur-lex.europa.eu/legal-content/EN/TXT/HTML/?uri=OJ:L:2016:119:FULL&from=EN.

CHAPTER TWO

Primer on artificial intelligence

2.1. Basics of machine learning

Machine learning (ML), as a subfield of AI, is a category of algorithms that are able to learn knowledge from data samples and history experience. The hidden mapping patterns between input features and output labels are expected to be explored by effective models and learning algorithms. Through continuous exploration and attempt, the ML algorithms pervade a wide range of applications, including image recognition, speech processing, semantic segmentation, automatic control, and so on [1–3]. Particularly, the wireless systems utilize ML algorithms to facilitate channel estimation, resource allocation, and system optimization [4,5]. In this section, we demonstrate the most trendy ML algorithms with an intuitive understanding.

Generally, ML algorithms can be roughly divided into three categories: *supervised learning*, *unsupervised learning*, and *reinforcement learning*, depending on the characteristics of data samples. The supervised learning algorithms require the samples to have input features and output labels, and learn a generalized function that maps from features to labels, so as to predict or classify the samples. The unsupervised learning algorithms learn the structure of unlabeled samples that only contain input features, and discover the hidden patterns among the features. The reinforcement learning algorithms have no data set required but interact with a dynamic environment to maximize the cumulative reward by taking appropriate actions. An overview of each ML algorithm is presented as follows.

2.1.1 Supervised learning

The supervised learning algorithms train models from input features and output labels to produce an inferred function to predict or classify new samples. To conveniently represent the mathematical model and training process, we first define some notations. We denote the input *features* by $\boldsymbol{x} \in \mathcal{X}$, where $\mathcal{X}$ is the *input space* containing all possible input features $\boldsymbol{x}$. The output *label* is denoted as $y \in \mathcal{Y}$, where $\mathcal{Y}$ is the output space. Generally, there is an unknown inherent mapping function $f : \mathcal{X} \rightarrow \mathcal{Y}$, which is expected to be estimated by proper algorithms. By defining a *dataset*

https://doi.org/10.1016/B978-0-12-823817-2.00011-5

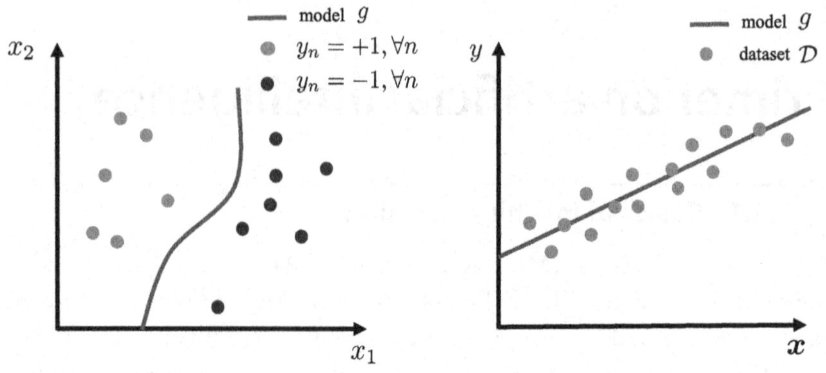

Figure 2.1 Illustration of classification (left) and regression (right) models.

$\mathcal{D} = \{(\boldsymbol{x}_1, y_1), (\boldsymbol{x}_2, y_2), \ldots, (\boldsymbol{x}_N, y_N)\}$, which consists of N pairs of input–output samples, the function represents $y_n = f(\boldsymbol{x}_n)$, $n \in 1, 2, \ldots, N$. The goal of supervised learning is to utilize the dataset $\mathcal{D}$ to produce a mapping function g, which approximates the ground truth f as accurate as possible.

The primary tasks of supervised learning include *classification* and *regression* [6]. The classification algorithms are utilized in the case of discrete labels, that is, the output space $\mathcal{Y}$ is a finite set. On the other hand, the regression algorithms are applied when the labels are continuous and $\mathcal{Y}$ is infinite. The main differences are illustrated in Fig. 2.1.

2.1.1.1 Logistic regression

Logistic regression is a variant of linear regression, which is widely used in binary classification problems. Given the input feature vector $\boldsymbol{x} = \{x_1; x_2; \ldots; x_d\} \in \mathbb{R}^d$, where x_i is the ith feature of $\boldsymbol{x}$. The linear model attempts to learn a formula as a linear combination of features, that is,

$$g(\boldsymbol{x}) = w_i x_1 + w_2 x_2 + \cdots + w_d x_d + b = \boldsymbol{w}^\mathsf{T} \boldsymbol{x} + b, \tag{2.1}$$

where $\boldsymbol{w} = [w_1, w_2, \cdots, w_d]^\mathsf{T}$ is a weight vector, and b is a bias. For dataset $\mathcal{D} = \{(\boldsymbol{x}_1, y_1), (\boldsymbol{x}_2, y_2), \ldots, (\boldsymbol{x}_N, y_N)\}$, $\boldsymbol{x}_n$ is defined as before, and $y_n \in \{0, 1\}$ denotes the label of classification. The $\boldsymbol{w}$ and b can be estimated by learning algorithms to minimize the mean squared error as

$$(\boldsymbol{w}^*, b^*) = \arg\min_{\boldsymbol{w}, b} \sum_{n=1}^{N} (g(\boldsymbol{x}_n) - y_n)^2. \tag{2.2}$$

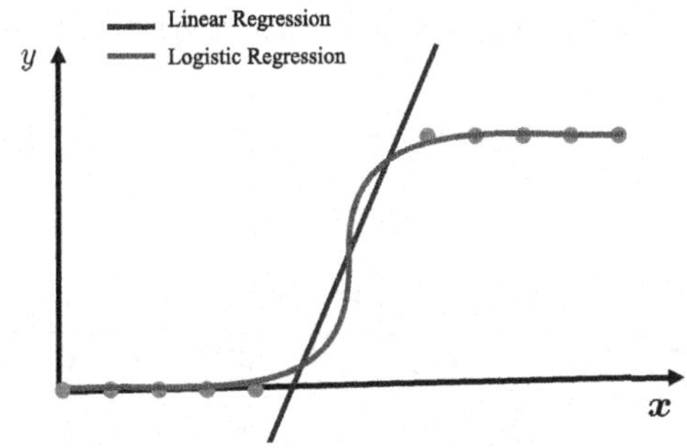

Figure 2.2 Linear regression and logistic regression.

Problem (2.2) presents the formula of linear regression in Fig. 2.2. Obviously, it cannot be directly applied to solve the classification problem. Therefore, the *sigmoid* function is used to approximate the step function, which is similar to the unit-step function to output the class of either 0 or 1. The calculation formula can be expressed as

$$\sigma(z) = \frac{1}{1+e^{-z}}. \tag{2.3}$$

If we define $z = g(\boldsymbol{x})$ and substitute it to the sigmoid function, then the approximate mapping function with respect to $\boldsymbol{x}$ is given by

$$g'(\boldsymbol{x}) = \frac{1}{1+e^{-(\boldsymbol{w}^{\mathrm{T}}\boldsymbol{x}+b)}}, \tag{2.4}$$

where $g'(\boldsymbol{x})$ presents the predictive class of $\boldsymbol{x}$. By denoting $y = g'(\boldsymbol{x})$ to simplify the equation, the equivalent transformation of (2.4) is

$$\ln\frac{y}{1-y} = \boldsymbol{w}^{\mathrm{T}}\boldsymbol{x} + b, \tag{2.5}$$

where y can be regarded as the possibility that $\boldsymbol{x}$ is a positive example, and $1 - y$ can be regarded as the possibility that $\boldsymbol{x}$ is a negative example. Hence, we have

$$\ln\frac{p(y=1|\boldsymbol{x})}{p(y=0|\boldsymbol{x})} = \boldsymbol{w}^{\mathrm{T}}\boldsymbol{x} + b. \tag{2.6}$$

Obviously, from $p(y=1|\boldsymbol{x})+p(y=0|\boldsymbol{x})=1$, we have

$$\begin{aligned} p(y=1|\boldsymbol{x}) &= \frac{e^{(\boldsymbol{w}^\mathsf{T}\boldsymbol{x}+b)}}{1+e^{(\boldsymbol{w}^\mathsf{T}\boldsymbol{x}+b)}}, \\ p(y=0|\boldsymbol{x}) &= \frac{1}{1+e^{(\boldsymbol{w}^\mathsf{T}\boldsymbol{x}+b)}}. \end{aligned} \tag{2.7}$$

Therefore we can use the maximum likelihood method [2] to estimate $\boldsymbol{w}$ and b for given data set $\mathcal{D}$. The log-likelihood function can be expressed as

$$l(\boldsymbol{w}, b) = \sum_{n=1}^{N} \ln p(y_n|\boldsymbol{x}_n; \boldsymbol{w}, b), \tag{2.8}$$

where $p(y_n|\boldsymbol{x}_n; \boldsymbol{w}, b) = y_n p(y_n = 1|\boldsymbol{x}_n; \boldsymbol{w}, b) + (1 - y_n)(p(y_n = 0|\boldsymbol{x}_n; \boldsymbol{w}, b))$. By substituting (2.7) into (2.8) for maximizing the log-likelihood function, the optimal parameters $\boldsymbol{w}^*$ and b^* can be obtained by solving the following optimization problem:

$$(\boldsymbol{w}^*, b^*) = \arg\min_{\boldsymbol{w}, b} \sum_{n=1}^{N} \left(-y_i(\boldsymbol{w}^\mathsf{T}\boldsymbol{x}_n + b) + \ln\left(1 + \exp^{\boldsymbol{w}^\mathsf{T}\boldsymbol{x}_n + b}\right)\right), \tag{2.9}$$

where the objective function is a differentiable continuous convex function. Thus the problem can be solved by using the general convex optimization theory [7] such as the gradient descent method and Newton's method, which will be introduced in Chapter 3. Moreover, the multiclass categorization problems can also be solved by degenerating them to multiple binary classification problems [8].

2.1.1.2 Support vector machine

Essentially, *support vector machine* (SVM) is a powerful tool for solving classification problems and regression problems. Given a training dataset $\mathcal{D} = \{(\boldsymbol{x}_1, y_1), (\boldsymbol{x}_2, y_2), \ldots, (\boldsymbol{x}_n, y_n)\}$ where $y_i \in \{-1, +1\}$, $i = 1, 2, \ldots, n$. SVM will exploit the most robust hyperplane to split the sample space of different classes, as shown in Fig. 2.3. In the situation of linearly separable dataset, parallel hyperplanes $\boldsymbol{w}^\mathsf{T}\boldsymbol{x} + b = -1$ and $\boldsymbol{w}^\mathsf{T}\boldsymbol{x} + b = 1$ can be chosen to separate the dataset through the *support vectors*, and the separating hyperplane $\boldsymbol{w}^\mathsf{T}\boldsymbol{x} + b = 0$ separates the two classes. The goal is maximizing the distance between the support vector and the hyperplane by optimizing the parameters $\boldsymbol{w}$ and b.

The distance between a sample point $\boldsymbol{x}_n$ and hyperplane $\boldsymbol{w}^\mathsf{T}\boldsymbol{x} + b = 0$ is denoted as $d_n = \frac{\boldsymbol{w}^\mathsf{T}\boldsymbol{x}_n}{\|\boldsymbol{w}\|} + \frac{b}{\|\boldsymbol{w}\|}$. Denoting by γ the distance between the

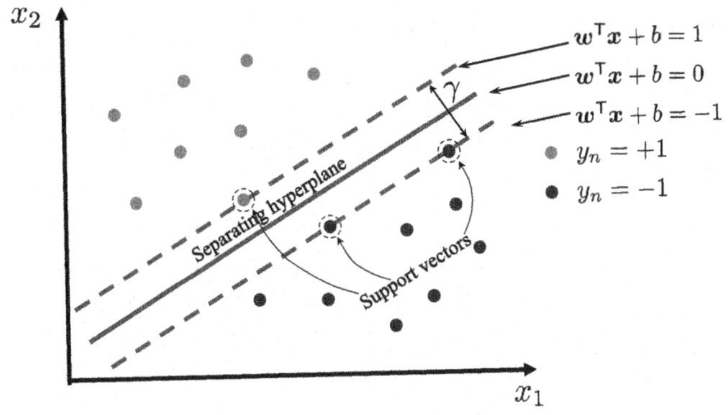

Figure 2.3 Illustration of hyperplane and support vector of SVM.

support vector and hyperplane, the optimization problem of SVM can be formulated as

$$\begin{aligned} &\underset{\boldsymbol{w},b}{\text{maximize}} && \gamma \\ &\text{subject to} && y_n\left(\frac{\boldsymbol{w}^{\mathsf{T}}\boldsymbol{x}_n}{\|\boldsymbol{w}\|}+\frac{b}{\|\boldsymbol{w}\|}\right)\geq\frac{\gamma}{2},\ n=1,2,\ldots,N, \end{aligned} \tag{2.10}$$

where $\left(\frac{\boldsymbol{w}^{\mathsf{T}}\boldsymbol{x}_i}{\|\boldsymbol{w}\|}+\frac{b}{\|\boldsymbol{w}\|}\right)$ can be positive for $y_n=+1$ or negative for $y_n=-1$. Therefore $y_n\left(\frac{\boldsymbol{w}^{\mathsf{T}}\boldsymbol{x}_n}{\|\boldsymbol{w}\|}+\frac{b}{\|\boldsymbol{w}\|}\right)$ must be positive and constrained to be greater than $\frac{\gamma}{2}$. To simplify the problem, we use the fact that $\gamma=\frac{2}{\|\boldsymbol{w}\|}$, which is the distance between $\boldsymbol{w}^{\mathsf{T}}\boldsymbol{x}+b=0$ and $\boldsymbol{w}^{\mathsf{T}}\boldsymbol{x}+b=1$. Thus problem (2.10) is equivalent to

$$\begin{aligned} &\underset{\boldsymbol{w},b}{\text{minimize}} && \tfrac{1}{2}\|\boldsymbol{w}\|^2 \\ &\text{subject to} && y_n\left(\boldsymbol{w}^{\mathsf{T}}\boldsymbol{x}_n+b\right)-1\geq 0,\ n=1,2,\ldots,N. \end{aligned} \tag{2.11}$$

Problem (2.11) is the basic formula of SVM, which can be solved by using the convex optimization software CVX [9]. To solve the problem more efficiently, the dual problem of (2.11) can be exploited. The Lagrangian function can be written as

$$L(\boldsymbol{w},b,\boldsymbol{\alpha})=\frac{1}{2}\|\boldsymbol{w}\|^2+\sum_{n=1}^{N}\alpha_n\left(1-y_n\left(\boldsymbol{w}^{\mathsf{T}}\boldsymbol{x}_n+b\right)\right). \tag{2.12}$$

By equating the partial derivatives $L(\boldsymbol{w}, b, \boldsymbol{\alpha})$ with respect to $\boldsymbol{w}$ and b to 0 we have

$$\boldsymbol{w} = \sum_{n=1}^{N} \alpha_n y_n \boldsymbol{x}_n, 0 = \sum_{n=1}^{N} \alpha_n y_n. \tag{2.13}$$

Therefore the dual problem of (2.11) can be expressed as

$$\begin{aligned} \underset{\boldsymbol{\alpha}}{\text{maximize}} \quad & \textstyle\sum_{n=1}^{N} \alpha_n - \frac{1}{2} \sum_{n_1=1}^{N} \sum_{n_2=1}^{N} \alpha_{n_1} \alpha_{n_2} y_{n_1} y_{n_2} \boldsymbol{x}_{n_1}^{\mathsf{T}} \boldsymbol{x}_{n_2} \\ \text{subject to} \quad & \textstyle\sum_{n=1}^{N} \alpha_n y_n = 0, \\ & \alpha_n \geq 0, \; n = 1, 2, \ldots, N, \end{aligned} \tag{2.14}$$

which is a quadratic programming problem and can be efficiently solved by several optimization algorithms like sequential minimal optimization [10]. Finally, the linear model of SVM is given by

$$g(\boldsymbol{x}) = \boldsymbol{w}^{\mathsf{T}} \boldsymbol{x} + b = \sum_{n=1}^{N} \alpha_n y_n \boldsymbol{x}_n^{\mathsf{T}} \boldsymbol{x} + b. \tag{2.15}$$

For the situation that the dataset is not linearly separable, the sample features can be mapped to a higher-dimensional space from the original space, that is, $\boldsymbol{x}' = \phi(\boldsymbol{x})$. The higher-dimensional $\boldsymbol{x}'$ may be linearly separable, which can be exploited to find the separating hyperplane. Similarly, the dual problem of the higher-dimensional dataset $\boldsymbol{x}' = \phi(\boldsymbol{x})$ can be expressed as

$$\begin{aligned} \underset{\boldsymbol{\alpha}}{\text{maximize}} \quad & \textstyle\sum_{n=1}^{N} \alpha_n - \frac{1}{2} \sum_{n_1=1}^{N} \sum_{n_2=1}^{N} \alpha_{n_1} \alpha_{n_2} y_{n_1} y_{n_2} \phi(\boldsymbol{x})_{n_1}^{\mathsf{T}} \phi(\boldsymbol{x}_{n_2}) \\ \text{subject to} \quad & \textstyle\sum_{n=1}^{N} \alpha_n y_n = 0, \\ & \alpha_n \geq 0, \; n = 1, 2, \ldots, N, \end{aligned} \tag{2.16}$$

and the linear model of higher-dimensional dataset is

$$g(\boldsymbol{x}) = \boldsymbol{w}^{\mathsf{T}} \boldsymbol{x} + b = \sum_{n=1}^{N} \alpha_n y_n \phi(\boldsymbol{x})_n^{\mathsf{T}} \phi(\boldsymbol{x}) + b. \tag{2.17}$$

Obviously, the key challenge is the calculation of $\phi(\boldsymbol{x})_{n_1}^{\mathsf{T}} \phi(\boldsymbol{x}_{n_2})$, which may be extremely higher-dimensional. To avoid this challenging problem, the kernel function is proposed as

$$\kappa(\boldsymbol{x}_{n_1}, \boldsymbol{x}_{n_2}) = \phi(\boldsymbol{x})_{n_1}^{\mathsf{T}} \phi(\boldsymbol{x}_{n_2}), \tag{2.18}$$

Table 2.1 Commonly adopted kernel functions.

Name	Formulation
Linear kernel	$\kappa(\boldsymbol{x}_{n_1}, \boldsymbol{x}_{n_2}) = \boldsymbol{x}_{n_1}^{\mathsf{T}} \boldsymbol{x}_{n_2}$
Polynomial kernel (homogeneous)	$\kappa(\boldsymbol{x}_{n_1}, \boldsymbol{x}_{n_2}) = (\boldsymbol{x}_{n_1}^{\mathsf{T}} \boldsymbol{x}_{n_2})^d,\ d \geq 1$
Polynomial kernel (inhomogeneous)	$\kappa(\boldsymbol{x}_{n_1}, \boldsymbol{x}_{n_2}) = (\boldsymbol{x}_{n_1}^{\mathsf{T}} \boldsymbol{x}_{n_2} + 1)^d,\ d \geq 1$
Gaussian kernel	$\kappa(\boldsymbol{x}_{n_1}, \boldsymbol{x}_{n_2}) = \exp\left(-\frac{\lVert \boldsymbol{x}_{n_1} - \boldsymbol{x}_{n_2} \rVert^2}{2\sigma^2}\right),\ \sigma > 0$
Laplace kernel	$\kappa(\boldsymbol{x}_{n_1}, \boldsymbol{x}_{n_2}) = \exp\left(-\frac{\lVert \boldsymbol{x}_{n_1} - \boldsymbol{x}_{n_2} \rVert}{\sigma}\right),\ \sigma > 0$
Sigmoid kernel	$\kappa(\boldsymbol{x}_{n_1}, \boldsymbol{x}_{n_2}) = \tanh\left(\beta \boldsymbol{x}_{n_1} \boldsymbol{x}_{n_2} + \theta\right),\ \beta > 0,\ \theta < 0$

which can be well designed to reduce the computational complexity. The commonly adopted kernel functions are listed in Table 2.1.

In addition to mapping the dataset to the high-dimensional space, the *soft margin* method can also enable the linearly separable property by tolerating errors on some samples. The hinge loss function is used to measure the dissatisfaction degree of the constraint (2.11), which is a *hard margin*. Therefore the optimization problem (2.11) can be relaxed as

$$\underset{\boldsymbol{w}, b}{\text{minimize}} \quad \frac{1}{2}\lVert \boldsymbol{w} \rVert^2 + \lambda \sum_{n=1}^{N} \max\left(0, 1 - y_n\left(\boldsymbol{w}^{\mathsf{T}} \boldsymbol{x}_n + b\right)\right), \tag{2.19}$$

which is convex and can be solved by using the gradient descent or other optimization algorithm [7].

2.1.1.3 Decision tree

Decision tree implements both classification and regression tasks by a tree structure, which is widely used for predicting. The decision tree consists of three parts, including internal nodes, leaf nodes, and branches. The internal nodes define a set of if–then decision rules of one feature, whereas the leaf nodes represent the labels (or a target value for a regression task). The branches determine conjunctions of features and the topology structure of the tree. Besides, a root node is the special internal node of the entry of decision tree. The structure of a typical decision tree is illustrated in Fig. 2.4.

Classification and Regression Tree (CART) is a recursive partitioning method to establish a classification or regression tree [11]. In the situation of classification task the partition criterion of CART is to minimize the *Gini* coefficient of the dataset. Specifically, given a training set $\mathcal{D}$ with N samples and K categories, we define the kth category has N_k samples, that

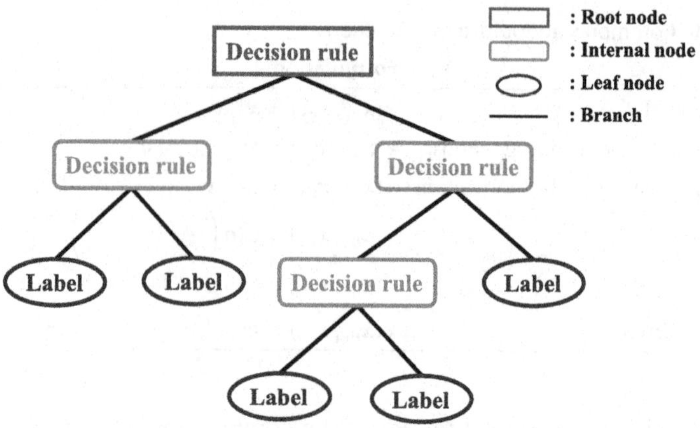

Figure 2.4 Decision tree structure.

is, $N = \sum_{k=1}^{K} N_k$. Therefore the Gini coefficient of $\mathcal{D}$ is defined as

$$\mathrm{Gini}(\mathcal{D}) = \sum_{k=1}^{K} \frac{N_k}{N}\left(1 - \frac{N_k}{N}\right) = 1 - \sum_{k=1}^{K}\left(\frac{N_k}{N}\right)^2, \tag{2.20}$$

which reflects the purity of dataset, that is, the probability of having different labels for two randomly chosen samples.

In the root node, CART will exploit a partition rule to separate the training dataset $\mathcal{D}$ into several partitions. We define the feature x_n as V possible discrete values, that is, $x_n \in \{x_n^1, x_n^2, \ldots, x_n^V\}$. Thus the dataset where the feature x_n of all samples is x_n^v is denoted by $\mathcal{D}^v$, and the number of samples is N^v. The Gini coefficient of feature x_n in $\mathcal{D}$ is presented as

$$\mathrm{Gini\_feature}(\mathcal{D}, x_n) = \sum_{v=1}^{V} \frac{N^v}{N} \mathrm{Gini}(\mathcal{D}^v). \tag{2.21}$$

Therefore the optimal partition feature in the root node is selected from

$$x^* = \arg\min_{x_n \in \mathbf{x}} \mathrm{Gini\_feature}(\mathcal{D}, x_n). \tag{2.22}$$

By repeating the above process to determine other internal nodes the leaf nodes are generated when the Gini coefficient of a subdataset is 0. Finally, the decision tree is confirmed.

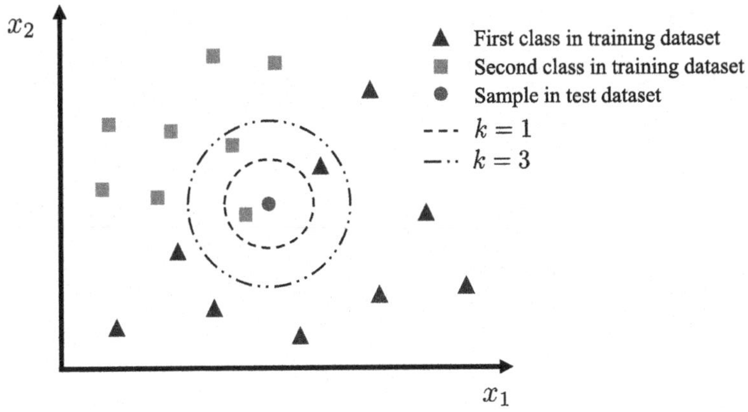

Figure 2.5 Illustration for k-NN when $k = 1$ and $k = 3$.

2.1.1.4 *k*-Nearest neighbors method

The k-nearest neighbors algorithm (k-NN) is a traditional nonparametric method used for classification and regression [12]. k-NN is a type of instance-based learning (a.k.a. lazy learning), which means that the training process only stores the samples and all the computation cost is induced in the test process to find the k nearest neighbors.

Given a training dataset $\mathcal{D} = \{(\boldsymbol{x}_n, y_n)\}_{n=1}^{N}$ and a test sample $\boldsymbol{x}_0$, the goal is to predict the category of $\boldsymbol{x}_0$. In the training process the dataset $\mathcal{D}$ is loaded and stored. After that, the test process searches k nearest neighbors from the training dataset, and k is the hyperparameter selected at the beginning. Generally, we can apply the voting method in the classification task, that is, choosing the most frequent label in the k nearest neighbors to be the label of $\boldsymbol{x}_0$ as shown in Fig. 2.5. Similarly, in the regression task the mean value of the labels of k nearest neighbors is set to be the label of $\boldsymbol{x}_0$.

Obviously, the key factor of k-NN is to choose the k nearest neighbors. Generally, the distance metric is denoted as the *Euclidean distance*

$$d(\boldsymbol{x}_0, \boldsymbol{x}_i) = \|\boldsymbol{x}_0 - \boldsymbol{x}_i\|_2. \tag{2.23}$$

Therefore, the k nearest neighbors can be selected based on the k minimal Euclidean distances from the training dataset $\mathcal{D}$. We denote the set of the k nearest neighbors by $\mathcal{D}^k \in \mathcal{D}$, that is, the number of $\mathcal{D}^k$ is k. Finally, we utilize the voting method or mean value to execute classification tasks or regression tasks.

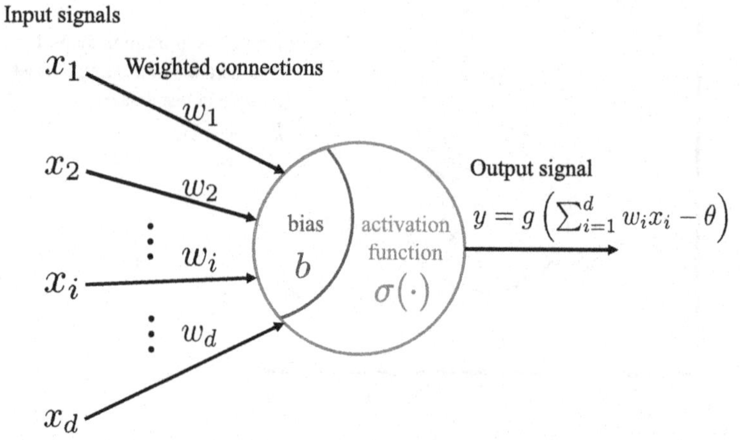

Figure 2.6 M-P neuron model.

To improve the performance of k-NN, large margin nearest neighbor or neighborhood components analysis can be adopted to enhance the accuracy [13]. The weighted nearest-neighbor classifier assigns weights to all neighbors to promote the performance [14] and condensed nearest neighbor reduces the dataset to decrease the amount of calculation [15].

2.1.1.5 Neural network

Neural network (NN) is a mathematical calculation framework inspired by the biological neural networks of animal brains. NN is also called an artificial neural network or connectionist model. In recent years, NN and its variants have achieved remarkable breakthrough among many emerging fields and are growing into the most compelling ML model, which generates a new field called deep learning (DL) [2]. In this section, we describe the most basic NN, whereas its variant model in DL is explained in Section 2.2.

The most basic component of NN is the neuron model. The McCulloch and Pitts (M-P) neuron model is widely used [16], as illustrated in Fig. 2.6. Particularly, the neuron receives the input signals $\{x_i\}_{i=1}^{d}$ from features or other neurons, which are transferred through weighted connection $\{w_i\}_{i=1}^{d}$. Then a bias b is added to the weighted input signal, and an *activation function* $\sigma(\cdot)$ is employed to generate the output signal. The M-P neuron

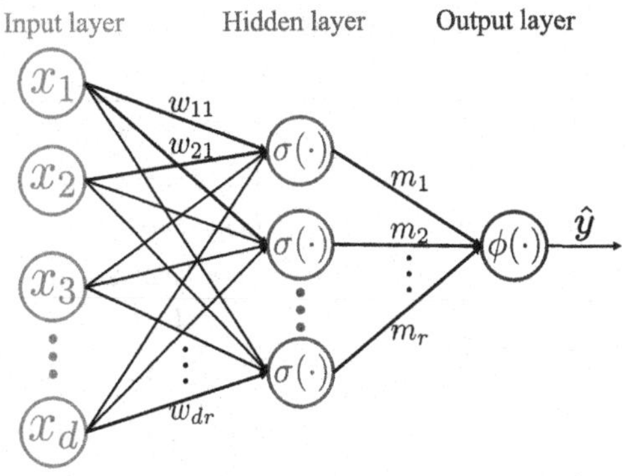

Figure 2.7 A multilayer perceptron with single hidden layer.

model can be described as a formula

$$y = g\left(\sum_{i=1}^{d} w_i x_i - \theta\right). \tag{2.24}$$

The NN connects numerous neurons with specified layer structures. The multilayer perceptron (MLP), which is a simple NN with a single hidden layer, is shown in Fig. 2.7. The *hidden layer* contains r neurons with an activation function to achieve a nonlinear mapping. Therefore the mathematical expression of MLP in Fig. 2.7 is

$$\hat{y} = \phi\left(\boldsymbol{m}^{\mathsf{T}}\sigma(\boldsymbol{W}^{\mathsf{T}}\boldsymbol{x} + \boldsymbol{b}_1) + b_2\right), \tag{2.25}$$

where $\boldsymbol{x} \in \mathbb{R}^d$ denotes the input vector that represents the sample features. $\boldsymbol{W} \in \mathbb{R}^{d\times r}$ and $\boldsymbol{b} \in \mathbb{R}^r$ are the weights and bias between input layer neurons and hidden layer neurons, respectively, and all hidden layer neurons have the same activation function $\sigma(\cdot)$. By using the weights $\boldsymbol{m} \in \mathbb{R}^r$ and bias b_2 the output value $\hat{y}$ is generated by applying the activation function $\phi(\cdot)$.

Without loss of generality, the common activation functions are listed in Table 2.2. In particular, the sigmoid function can return output in the range from 0 to 1, but its gradient can approximate 0, which will lead to the gradient vanishing problem, and its output is not zero-centered, which will result in that the inputs of the next neurons will be all positive. The tanh function solves the zero-centered problem but also has the gradient vanishing problem. The rectified linear unit (ReLU) is the most famous activation function, which has a very fast calculation speed and solves the

Table 2.2 Common activation functions.

Name	Formulation
Sigmoid	$\sigma(x)=\frac{1}{1+e^{-x}}$
Tanh	$\sigma(x)=\frac{e^x-e^{-x}}{e^x+e^{-x}}$
Rectified Linear Unit (ReLU)	$\sigma(x)=\max(0,x)$
Parametric ReLU	$\sigma(x)=\max(\alpha x,x)$
Exponential Linear Unit(ELU)	$\sigma(x)=\begin{cases} x & \text{if } x>0, \\ \alpha(e^x-1) & \text{otherwise} \end{cases}$
Softmax	$\sigma_i(\boldsymbol{x})=\frac{e^{x_i}}{\sum_{j=1}^{d} e^{x_j}}$ for $i=1,\ldots,d$
Maxout	$\sigma(\boldsymbol{x})=\max_i x_i$

Table 2.3 Widely used loss functions.

Name	Definition
Square loss	$\mathcal{L}(\boldsymbol{y},\hat{\boldsymbol{y}})=\sum_{n=1}^{N}(y_n-\hat{y}_n)^2$
Absolute error	$\mathcal{L}(\boldsymbol{y},\hat{\boldsymbol{y}})=\sum_{n=1}^{N}\lvert y_n-\hat{y}_n\rvert$
Hinge loss	$\mathcal{L}(\boldsymbol{y},\hat{\boldsymbol{y}})=\sum_{n=1}^{N}\max(0,1-y_n\hat{y}_n)$
Cross entropy loss	$\mathcal{L}(\boldsymbol{y},\hat{\boldsymbol{y}})=\sum_{n=1}^{N}-(y_n\log(\hat{y}_n)+(1-y_n)\log(1-\hat{y}_n))$

vanishing gradient problem when the input is greater than 0. However, its output is also not zero-centered and maybe never activated when the input is less than 0, that is, its gradient is 0. The parametric ReLU and exponential linear unit (ELU) are variations of ReLU but exhibit poorer performance than ReLU. On the other hand, some multiple input activation functions are widely used in NN such as softmax function and maxout function, which obtain structured output labels.

The MLP model executes various classification and regression tasks if the weights and bias are learned accurately. The learning process of NN is turned into an optimization problem, which minimizes the *loss function* by optimizing the weights and bias. Without loss of generality, we list the widely used loss functions in Table 2.3, where $\boldsymbol{y}$ is the label of training dataset, and $\hat{\boldsymbol{y}}$ is the corresponding score from (2.25). We take the square loss as an example. The corresponding loss function for dataset $\mathcal{D}=\{(\boldsymbol{x}_n,y_n)\}_{n=1}^{N}$ is defined as

$$\mathcal{L}(\boldsymbol{W},\boldsymbol{b}_1,\boldsymbol{m},b_2)=\sum_{n=1}^{N}\left(y_n-\phi\left(\boldsymbol{m}^{\top}\sigma(\boldsymbol{W}^{\top}\boldsymbol{x}_n+\boldsymbol{b}_1)+b_2\right)\right)^2. \tag{2.26}$$

Therefore the pivotal problem is finding the optimal weights and bias by solving the following optimization problem:

$$\underset{\boldsymbol{W},\boldsymbol{b}_1,\boldsymbol{m},b_2}{\text{minimize}} \quad \mathcal{L}(\boldsymbol{W}, \boldsymbol{b}_1, \boldsymbol{m}, b_2), \tag{2.27}$$

which can be solved efficiently by the gradient descent method.

The *learning* process of NN involves adjusting the weights and biases to improve the accuracy of the training and test samples, which can be accomplished by minimizing the observed errors, that is, the loss function. The gradient descent method requires an efficient and accurate calculation of gradients. The *back-propagation* (BP) algorithm can be adopted to calculate the gradients, which consist of weights and biases of all layers. The BP algorithm uses the chain rule of derivative calculation to compute the gradient of weights and biases layer by layer. Without loss of generality, we consider an L-layer NN. The formulation of the feed-forward network, that is, the sample score, is

$$\hat{y} = h^L(\boldsymbol{W}^L h^{L-1}(\boldsymbol{W}^{L-1} \cdots h^1(\boldsymbol{W}^1 \boldsymbol{x}))), \tag{2.28}$$

where $\boldsymbol{W}^l$ includes the weights and biases in the lth layer. Besides, we denote by $y^l = h^l(\boldsymbol{W}^l h^{l-1}(\boldsymbol{W}^{l-1} \cdots h^1(\boldsymbol{W}^1 \boldsymbol{x})))$ the output of the lth layer, that is, $\hat{y} = y^L$. Thus, for the loss function $\mathcal{L}(y - \hat{y})$, the gradient of $\boldsymbol{W}^l$ is calculated by

$$\frac{\partial \mathcal{L}(y-\hat{y})}{\partial \boldsymbol{W}^l} = \frac{\partial \mathcal{L}(y-\hat{y})}{\partial \hat{y}} \frac{\partial \hat{y}}{\partial y^{L-1}} \frac{\partial y^{L-1}}{\partial y^{L-2}} \cdots \frac{\partial y^{l+1}}{\partial y^l} \frac{\partial y^l}{\partial \boldsymbol{W}^l}. \tag{2.29}$$

Hence the gradients of all weights and biases in each layer can be calculated by the chain rule. The NN model will be learned from the gradient descent methods, that is,

$$\boldsymbol{W}^l = \boldsymbol{W}^l - \eta \frac{\partial \mathcal{L}(y-\hat{y})}{\partial \boldsymbol{W}^l}, \tag{2.30}$$

where η is the learning rate. Except for the classical gradient descent algorithm, the momentum and Nesterov methods can correct the gradient. Moreover, Adagrad and AdaDelta can adjust the learning rate. These methods speed up the convergence of the gradient descent algorithm. Especially, the adaptive moment estimation (Adam) has achieved an outstanding performance in the NN learning process, which utilizes the momentum method and AdaDelta method [17].

2.1.2 Unsupervised learning

The unsupervised learning algorithms extract natural patterns in a dataset without labels. Dimensionality reduction and cluster analysis are primary methods in unsupervised learning. The dimensionality reduction aims to learn a new feature space to capture the characteristics of the original dataset, aiming to reduce the cost of data storage and calculation. Besides, the cluster analysis devotes to a group or segment the unlabeled dataset according to the statistics of features. The unlabeled dataset is denoted as $\mathcal{D} = \{\boldsymbol{x}_1, \boldsymbol{x}_2, \ldots, \boldsymbol{x}_N\}$, where $\boldsymbol{x}_n \in \mathbb{R}^d$ for all n. In this section, we discuss the general unsupervised learning algorithms in detail.

2.1.2.1 *k*-Means algorithm

k-means algorithm is a simple unsupervised learning algorithm for cluster analysis, which is effortless to implement and address the desirable performance. We first present this algorithm and then discuss its variant to achieve better performance.

Given the training dataset $\mathcal{D} = \{\boldsymbol{x}_1, \boldsymbol{x}_2, \ldots, \boldsymbol{x}_N\}$, *k*-means algorithm partitions the samples to k clusters, denoted by $\{C_1, C_2, \ldots, C_k\}$. The metric of the *k*-means algorithm is to make the samples in the clusters as close as possible and the distance between the clusters as large as possible, which is illustrated in Fig. 2.8. Therefore the *k*-means algorithm aims to minimize the squared error:

$$\underset{\{C_1, C_2, \ldots, C_k\}}{\text{minimize}}\, E = \sum_{i=1}^{k} \sum_{\boldsymbol{x} \in C_i} \|\boldsymbol{x} - \boldsymbol{\mu}_i\|_2^2, \tag{2.31}$$

where $\boldsymbol{\mu}_i = \frac{1}{|C_i|} \sum_{\boldsymbol{x} \in C_i} \boldsymbol{x}$ denotes the centroid of each cluster, and $|C_i|$ is the sample number of cluster C_i. The cluster number k is specified before training.

The optimization problem (2.31) needs to inspect all cluster partitions of dataset $\mathcal{D}$, which is an NP hard problem [18]. Therefore a heuristic algorithm is proposed to return the approximate solution of (2.31) through iteration, which is presented in Algorithm 1.

In practical applications, the cluster number k should be appropriately chosen to achieve a good performance. Besides, the *k*-means++ algorithm optimizes the initialization of centroids to accelerate the convergence [19], Elkan's *k*-means algorithm reduces the distance calculation cost through the triangle inequality [20], and mini-batch *k*-means are used in big data, which reduces the calculation cost at the cost of slight accuracy [21].

Algorithm 1: k-Means algorithm.

Input: training dataset $\mathcal{D}$ and cluster number k.
Output: clusters $\{C_1, C_2, \ldots, C_k\}$.
repeat
  Randomly initialize centroids $\{\boldsymbol{\mu}_1, \boldsymbol{\mu}_2, \ldots, \boldsymbol{\mu}_k\}$ from $\mathcal{D}$.
  for $n = 1, \ldots N$ **do**
    Partition sample $\boldsymbol{x}_n$ by $\lambda_n = \arg\min_{i \in \{1,2,\ldots,k\}} \|\boldsymbol{x}_n - \boldsymbol{\mu}_i\|_2^2$ and append to corresponding cluster $C_{\lambda_n} = C_{\lambda_n} \cup \{\boldsymbol{x}_n\}$.
  end for
  for $i = 1, \ldots k$ **do**
    Update new centroids $\boldsymbol{\mu}_i = \frac{1}{|C_i|} \sum_{\boldsymbol{x} \in C_i} \boldsymbol{x}$, $i \in \{1, 2, \ldots, k\}$.
  end for
until no changes in all centroids

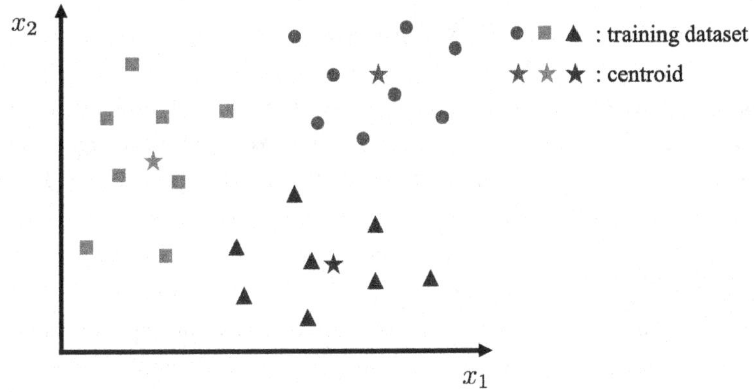

Figure 2.8 k-Means result with $k = 3$.

2.1.2.2 Principal component analysis

The principal component analysis (PCA) is commonly used in dimension reduction. The reduced dataset presents less features for each sample, that is, fewer computation and possibly better performance compared to other ML algorithms. We also use the training dataset notation as $\mathcal{D} = \{\boldsymbol{x}_1, \boldsymbol{x}_2, \ldots, \boldsymbol{x}_N\}$ and $\boldsymbol{x}_n \in \mathbb{R}^d$ for all n. Therefore the training dataset can be presented as a matrix $\boldsymbol{X} = [\boldsymbol{x}_1, \boldsymbol{x}_2, \ldots, \boldsymbol{x}_N] \in \mathbb{R}^{d \times N}$. The goal is finding a projection matrix $\boldsymbol{P} = [\boldsymbol{p}_1, \boldsymbol{p}_2, \ldots, \boldsymbol{p}_{d'}] \in \mathbb{R}^{d \times d'}$, where $\boldsymbol{p}_j$, $j \in \{1, 2, \ldots, d'\}$, form an orthonormal basis. Then we obtain the reduced dataset $\boldsymbol{X}' = \boldsymbol{P}^\top \boldsymbol{X} \in \mathbb{R}^{d' \times N}$.

The dataset $\boldsymbol{X}$ should be centralized with zero mean, that is,

$$\boldsymbol{x}_n = \boldsymbol{x}_n - \frac{1}{N}\sum_{i=1}^{N}\boldsymbol{x}_i, \quad n \in \{1, 2, \ldots, N\}. \tag{2.32}$$

It is expected that the low-dimensional samples are separated as much as possible, which makes the variance of the matrix $\boldsymbol{X}'$ as large as possible. The variance of $\boldsymbol{X}'$ is denoted $\mathrm{tr}(\boldsymbol{X}'^{\mathsf{T}}\boldsymbol{X}') = \mathrm{tr}(\boldsymbol{P}^{\mathsf{T}}\boldsymbol{X}\boldsymbol{X}^{\mathsf{T}}\boldsymbol{P})$, where $\mathrm{tr}(\cdot)$ is the trace of a matrix. Therefore the optimization problem can be expressed as

$$\begin{aligned} \underset{\boldsymbol{P}}{\text{minimize}} \quad & \mathrm{tr}(\boldsymbol{P}^{\mathsf{T}}\boldsymbol{X}\boldsymbol{X}^{\mathsf{T}}\boldsymbol{P}) \\ \text{subject to} \quad & \boldsymbol{P}^{\mathsf{T}}\boldsymbol{P} = \boldsymbol{I}. \end{aligned} \tag{2.33}$$

This problem can be solved by using the Lagrange multiplier method, which leads to the optimal solution as

$$\boldsymbol{X}\boldsymbol{X}^{\mathsf{T}}\boldsymbol{p}_j = \lambda_j \boldsymbol{p}_j. \tag{2.34}$$

Therefore we calculate the eigenvalue decomposition of $\boldsymbol{X}\boldsymbol{X}^{\mathsf{T}} \in \mathbb{R}^{d\times d}$ and sort the eigenvalues as $\lambda_1 \geq \lambda_2 \geq \cdots \geq \lambda_d$. Then we choose the eigenvectors corresponding to the first d' eigenvalues, that is, $\boldsymbol{P} = [\boldsymbol{p}_1, \boldsymbol{p}_2, \ldots, \boldsymbol{p}_{d'}]$. Finally, the reduced dataset is obtained by $\boldsymbol{X}' = \boldsymbol{P}^{\mathsf{T}}\boldsymbol{X}$.

2.1.2.3 Autoencoder

Autoencoder is a type of NN used to learn an encoding representation of one sample in an unsupervised way. The autoencoder comprises a *encoder* and decoder, where the encoder aims at encoding the original data sample into *code*, and decoder decodes the code into restored sample data. The purpose of autoencoder is encoding the original sample data to code without losing important information, that is, the sample data can be restored from code by decoder. The structure of autoencoder is illustrated in Fig. 2.9. The samples in input and output layers can be feature vectors, image matrices, and so on. The encoder and decoder are constituted by ordinary NN in Section 2.1.1.5, convolutional NN in Section 2.2.1, and so on. The code is presented as vectors or matrices.

The autoencoder can be described by mathematical expressions. We define the mapping function of encoder as $E : \mathcal{X} \rightarrow \mathcal{C}$, where $\mathcal{X}$ and $\mathcal{C}$ denote the input space and code space, respectively. Therefore the mapping function of the decoder is presented by $D : \mathcal{C} \rightarrow \mathcal{X}$. Given a training dataset

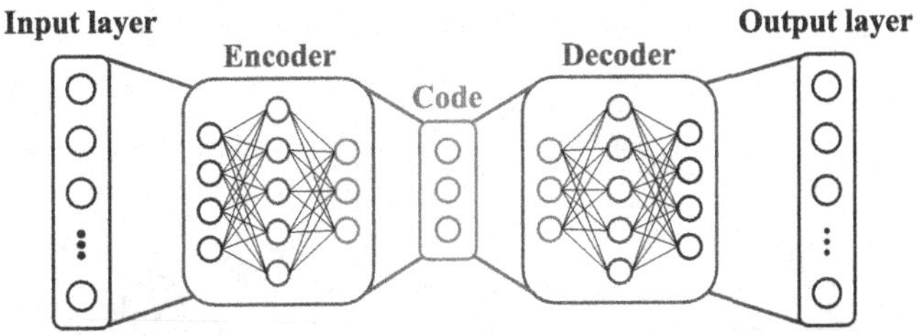

Figure 2.9 Illustration of autoencoder.

$\mathcal{D} = \{\boldsymbol{x}_1, \boldsymbol{x}_2, \ldots, \boldsymbol{x}_N\}$, the code of each sample is expressed as

$$\boldsymbol{c}_n = E(\boldsymbol{x}_n), \quad n \in \{1, 2, \ldots, N\}, \tag{2.35}$$

and the restored sample is given by

$$\hat{\boldsymbol{x}}_n = D(\boldsymbol{c}_n) = D(E(\boldsymbol{x}_n)), \quad n \in \{1, 2, \ldots, N\}. \tag{2.36}$$

The autoencoder aims to minimize the reconstruction error (such as squared error) between original samples and restored samples by optimizing encoder and decoder, that is,

$$\underset{E(\cdot),D(\cdot)}{\text{minimize}} \sum_{n=1}^{N} \|\boldsymbol{x}_n - D(E(\boldsymbol{x}_n))\|_2^2, \tag{2.37}$$

which presumes that the original samples are encoded to the low-dimensional code. Moreover, the code can be decoded to restored samples, which are similar to the original samples. Particularly, we present a simple example with one-layer encoder and decode. The encoder is $\boldsymbol{c} = E(\boldsymbol{x}) = \sigma^1(\boldsymbol{W}^1\boldsymbol{x} + \boldsymbol{b}_1)$, and the decoder is expressed as $\hat{\boldsymbol{x}} = D(\boldsymbol{c}) = \sigma^2(\boldsymbol{W}^2\boldsymbol{c} + \boldsymbol{b}_2) = \sigma^2(\boldsymbol{W}^2\sigma^1(\boldsymbol{W}^1\boldsymbol{x} + \boldsymbol{b}_1) + \boldsymbol{b}_2)$, where $\sigma^1(\cdot)$ and $\sigma^2(\cdot)$ are activation functions, and $\boldsymbol{W}^1$, $\boldsymbol{W}^2$, $\boldsymbol{b}_1$, and $\boldsymbol{b}_2$ are weights and biases. The corresponding optimization problem is given by

$$\underset{\boldsymbol{W}^1,\boldsymbol{W}^2,\boldsymbol{b}_1,\boldsymbol{b}_2}{\text{minimize}} \sum_{n=1}^{N} \|\boldsymbol{x}_n - \sigma^2(\boldsymbol{W}^2\sigma^1(\boldsymbol{W}^1\boldsymbol{x}_n + \boldsymbol{b}_1) + \boldsymbol{b}_2)\|_2^2. \tag{2.38}$$

As mentioned in Section 2.1.1.5, problem (2.38) can be solved by using the gradient descent algorithm, and the gradients are calculated by back-propagation.

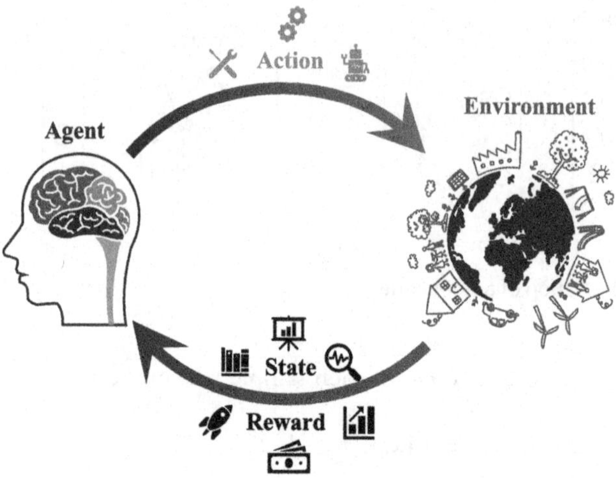

Figure 2.10 Typical framework of reinforcement learning.

2.1.3 Reinforcement learning

Reinforcement learning (RL) algorithms have achieved enormous success in fields such as robotic control, chess competition, and so on [22,23]. RL is another machine learning paradigm, which learns decision policy without the need of training dataset. The main idea of RL is that the agent takes an action based on the current state in a dynamic environment to maximize the long-term cumulative reward, which is illustrated in Fig. 2.10.

The mathematical model of RL is based on a Markov decision process. The *state* space of the environment and agent is denoted by $\mathcal{S}$, and the *action* space of the agent is $\mathcal{A}$. Therefore the *probability of transition* from state s to state s' under action a at time t is denoted as $P_a(s, s') = \Pr(s_{t+1} = s' \mid s_t = s, a_t = a)$, where $s, s' \in \mathcal{S}$, $a \in \mathcal{A}$. Then the immediate *reward* after transition from s to s' with action a is denoted by $R_a(s, s')$. Besides, the rule that determines whether what the agent observes can be full observability, that is, whether the agent can obtain all the state information of the current environment.

In the training phase of RL the agent interacts with the environment in discrete time steps, which consists of obtaining observed state information from environment and determining actions accordingly. At each time step t, the agent receives the current observable status information o_t from environment state s_t. Then the agent takes action a_t from the set of available action space $\mathcal{A}$ according to *policy* $\pi(a, s) = Pr(a_t = t|s_t = s)$. The environment transmits to a new state s_{t+1} according to the probability of transition $P_a(s_t, s_{t+1})$ and returns a feedback with reward $r_t = R_a(s_t, s_{t+1})$. Therefore the transition (s_t, a_t, r_t, s_{t+1}) is determined. Each agent aims to learn the best policy, which leads to the highest reward throughout the training process. Therefore we define the *value function* $V_\pi(s)$ by γ-discounted cumulative reward as

$$V_\pi(s) = \mathbb{E}[R] = \mathbb{E}\left[\sum_{t=0}^{\infty} \gamma^t r_t | s_0 = s\right], \tag{2.39}$$

which denotes the long-term reward with policy π and initial state s, where $\gamma \in (0, 1]$ is the discount factor, which indicates the importance of future rewards, and $\mathbb{E}$ is the expectation. The goal of RL is maximizing the total future rewards to find the optimal policy, that is,

$$\underset{\pi}{\text{maximize}}\ \mathbb{E}\left[\sum_{t=0}^{\infty} \gamma^t r_t | s_0 = s\right]. \tag{2.40}$$

The algorithm can be divided into value-based and policy-based algorithms based on the learning target. We will introduce the Q-learning algorithm (value-based) and policy gradient algorithm (policy-based) to seek the optimal policy.

2.1.3.1 Q-learning

Q-learning aims to find the optimal policy by maximizing the expected total reward from current state to all successive steps after [24]. The Q-value indicates the maximum expected total rewards for an action taken in a given state, which is called the action-value function:

$$Q(s, a) = \mathbb{E}\left[r_{t+1} + \gamma r_{t+1} + \cdots + \gamma^{T-t-1} r_T | s_t = s, a_t = a\right]. \tag{2.41}$$

The optimal action in state s_t is denoted by $a^* = \arg\max_a Q(s_t, a)$. Therefore the pivotal problem of Q-Learning is estimating Q-table $Q(s, a)$ for $s \in \mathcal{S}$ and $a \in \mathcal{A}$ accurately. The iterative estimation algorithm is summarized in Algorithm 2.

The ε-greedy method chooses the optimal action according to the maximum Q-value $a^* = \arg\max_a Q(s_t, a)$ with probability ε and randomly selects an action with probability $1 - \varepsilon$. The update formula of Q-value can be written as

$$Q(s_t, a_t) \leftarrow Q(s_t, a_t) + \eta\left[r_{t+1} + \gamma \max_a Q(s_{t+1}, a) - Q(s_t, a_t)\right], \tag{2.42}$$

Algorithm 2: Q-learning algorithm.

Initialize Q-table $Q(s, a), \forall s \in \mathcal{S}, a \in \mathcal{A}$ arbitrarily
for each episode **do**
  Initialize s_0, $t = 1$.
  repeat
    Choose a_t from s_t using policy derived from Q-table $Q(s, a)$ (e.g., ε-greedy).
    Take action a_t, observe r_{t+1}, s_{t+1}
    $Q(s_t, a_t) \leftarrow Q(s_t, a_t) + \eta\,[r_{t+1} + \gamma \max_a Q(s_{t+1}, a) - Q(s_t, a_t)]$.
    $t \leftarrow t + 1$.
  until State s_t is terminal.
end for

where η is learning rate. Particularly, $r_{t+1} + \gamma \max_a Q(s_{t+1}, a) = r_{t+1} + \gamma[r_{t+2} + \gamma \max_a Q(s_{t+2}, a)] = r_{t+1} + \gamma r_{t+2} + \gamma^2 r_{t+3} + \cdots$ is understood as the actual value of the estimated value $Q(s_t, a_t)$. The updated value $r_{t+1} + \gamma \max_a Q(s_{t+1}, a) - Q(s_t, a_t)$ represents the gap of the actual and estimated values. The Q-values will be accurately estimated after a large number of iterative updates. Finally, the estimated Q values can be used to determine the accurate decision by $a^* = \arg\max_a Q(s_t, a)$.

Furthermore, SARSA as a variant of Q-learning updates the Q-value after several steps [25]. The deep Q-network (DQN) utilizes DL models to estimate the Q-values of actions, which applies the state as input feature and the Q-value as output label [26].

2.1.3.2 Policy gradient

The policy gradient algorithm optimizes the probability of each action being selected. The likelihood ratio gradient estimation (a.k.a. the reinforce method) updates the policy $\pi_\theta(s, a)$ based on all transitions (s_t, a_t, r_t) for all t, where θ represents the parameters of NN, and $\pi_\theta(s, a)$ is the probability of action a in state s with parameters θ. The training method of $\pi_\theta(s, a)$ with respect to θ is summarized in Algorithm 3.

The policy update formula is written as

$$\theta \leftarrow \theta + \eta \nabla_\theta \log \pi_\theta(s_t, a_t) v_t, \tag{2.43}$$

which maximize the selected probability of executed actions and corresponding state by gradient ascent. The update step is denoted by

Algorithm 3: Policy gradient algorithm.

Initialize θ arbitrarily.
for each episode **do**
  Execute policy π_θ to get track $\{s_1, a_1, r_2, s_2, a_2, \ldots, s_{T-1}, a_{T-1}, r_T\}$.
  for $t = 1, 2, \ldots, T-1$ **do**
    $\theta \leftarrow \theta + \eta \nabla_\theta \log \pi_\theta(s_t, a_t) v_t$.
  end for
end for

$\nabla_\theta \log \pi_\theta(s_t, a_t)$, which is the gradient of $\pi_\theta(s_t, a_t)$ with respect to θ. The gradient can be calculated by back-propagation. Particularly, v_t is defined as

$$v_t = r_{t+1} + \gamma r_{t+2} + \cdots + \gamma^{T-t-1} r_T, \tag{2.44}$$

which is the state-value function as step t, that is, the γ-discounted cumulative reward in the future. If the γ-discounted cumulative reward v_t is small, then the update step will be small, and the probability of the action in this step will not be improved too much. Contrarily, if the γ-discounted cumulative reward v_t is large, then the parameter with respect to the action will be updated in a large step.

Moreover, the actor-critic algorithm combines the value-based algorithm (such as Q-learning) and policy-based algorithm (such as policy gradient) to achieve better performance. Actor is designed to choose appropriate action, and the critic estimated Q-value to judge pros and cons of the action [27].

2.2. Models of deep learning

2.2.1 Convolutional neural network

Convolutional neural network (CNN or ConvNet) is a variant of NN in Section 2.1.1.5, which is also constituted by learnable weights and biases. It has presented exemplary performance on computer vision. The most significant breakthrough is using the convolution and pooling operations to extract features from images or other tensor structured data. Therefore CNN usually has three typical layers: *convolutional layer*, *pooling layer*, and *fully connected layer*, which are arbitrarily stacked to establish a CNN architecture.

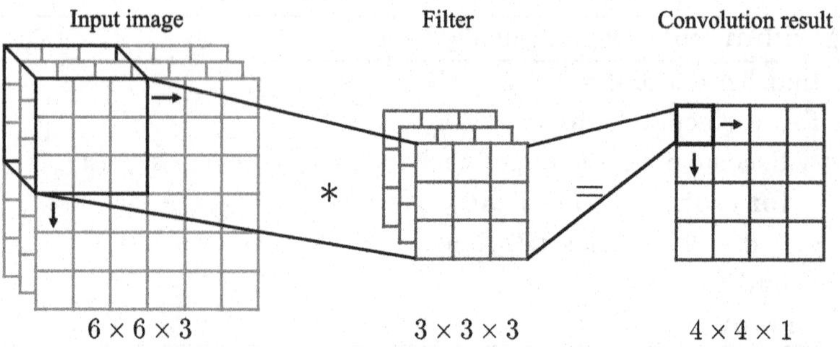

Figure 2.11 Illustration of convolution operation.

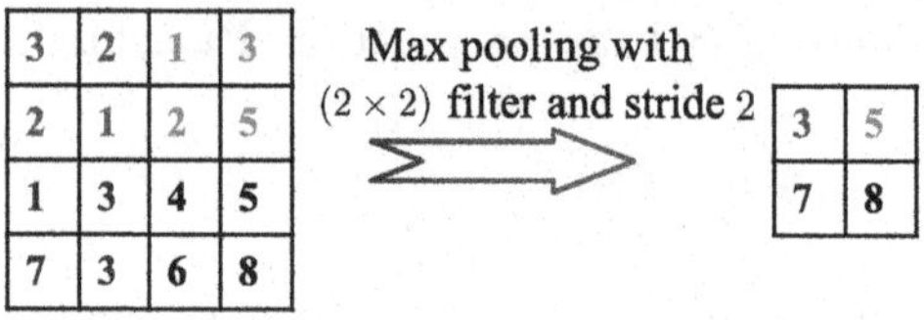

Figure 2.12 Illustration of pooling operation.

To understand the convolution and pooling operation, as shown in Fig. 2.11, we consider a (6 × 6 × 3) image tensor to illustrate the convolution operation, which has width 6, height 6, and 3 color channels. We define a [3 × 3 × 3] *filter*. Then we select a [3 × 3 × 3] region of image. We calculate the dot production of small region image and filter to obtain a value. The *stride* is the number of pixel shifts over the image tensor, and we define stride as 1 and move the filter along width or height to calculate the other values. Finally, we obtain a (4 × 4 × 1) matrix. If we define 12 different filters, then we can calculate a (4 × 4 × 12) dimension output tensor, which is called a *feature map*.

The pooling operation aims to reduce the number of parameters while retaining the important information and consists of max pooling, average pooling, and sum pooling. The max pooling operation is presented in Fig. 2.12 with (2 × 2) filter and stride 2 to take the largest element from the region selected by filter.

For better understanding CNN architecture, we explain a simple CNN to solve CIFAR-10 classification problem, which has 32 × 32 × 3 input images and a 10 × 1 classification score output. The details are illustrated in Fig. 2.13 and explained as follows.

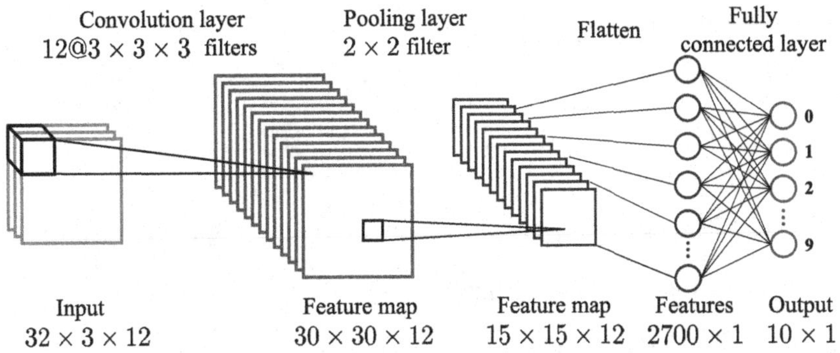

Figure 2.13 Illustration of convolutional neural network.

- Input layer: the original pixel values of input image (32 × 32 × 3) are input with width 32, height 32, and 3 color channels R,G,B.
- Convolutional layer: this layer computes the dot product between weights and a small region of input layer one by one. Then a (30 × 30 × 12) dimension layer is obtained by using 12 filters with (3 × 3 × 3) kernel. Generally, an elementwise Relu function or other activation function is used after dot product, which will not change the data dimension.
- Pooling layer: a downsampling operation with (2 × 2) filter is implemented among width and height, which results in a (15 × 15 × 12) dimension layer.
- Fully connected layer: the classification score is computed by using ordinary NN, where the input vector is the flattened vector (2700 × 1), and the 10 × 1 dimension output presents the score of 10 categories of CIFAR-10.

Some popular architectures like AlexNet, VGGNet, GoogLeNet, and ResNet are also structured based on CNN [28]. They have achieved excellent performance in image recognition, semantic segmentation, object detection, and so on.

2.2.2 Recurrent neural network

The traditional NNs split all the samples independently with each other, which ignores the influence of potential relationship between them. This will result in degraded performance when solving the sequential information tasks like text translation. Therefore the recurrent neural network

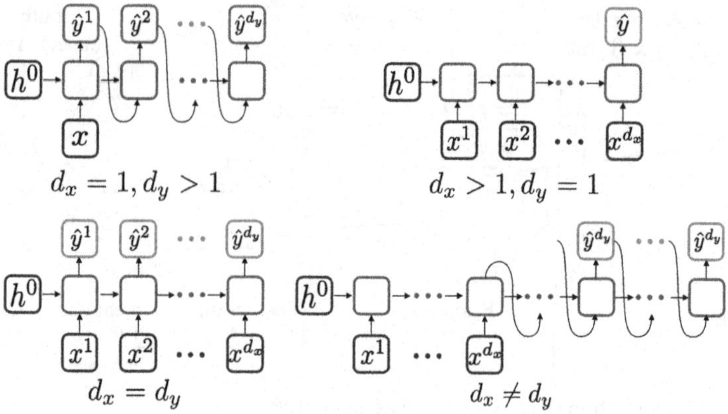

Figure 2.14 The framework of recurrent neural network in different situation.

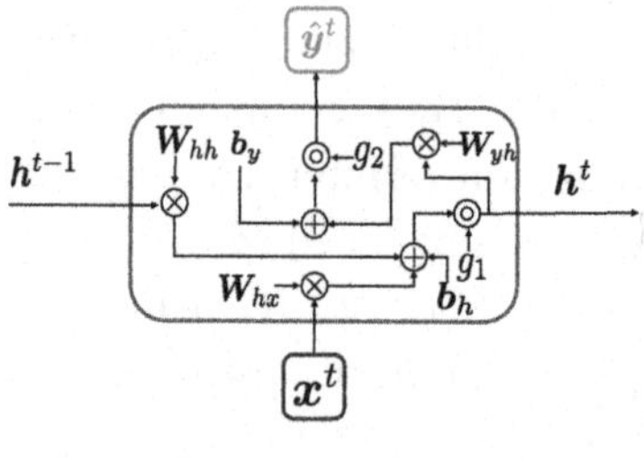

Figure 2.15 The repeated structure of RNN.

(RNN) is proposed to deal with the challenge by generating a "memory", which holds the calculated information of sequential samples.

The RNN frameworks in different situations are presented in Fig. 2.14, where d_x and d_y denote the numbers of input samples and output labels, respectively. Fig. 2.14 illustrates the situation of $d_x = 1$, $d_y > 1$, which indicates that there is one input sample, and the number of output samples is greater than 1. This framework can be used in music generation. The situation of $d_x > 1$, $d_y = 1$, $d_x = d_y$, and $d_x \neq d_y$ can be used in sentiment classification, name entity recognition, and machine translation, respectively.

Specifically, the repeated structure is shown in Fig. 2.15. The equation can be formulated as

$$\boldsymbol{h}^t = g_1(\boldsymbol{W}_{hh}\boldsymbol{h}^{t-1} + \boldsymbol{W}_{hx}\boldsymbol{x}^t + \boldsymbol{n}_h), \tag{2.45}$$

$$y^t = g_2(W_{yh}h^t + W_y), \tag{2.46}$$

where h^t is the hidden layer vector, x^t and y^t are the input and output vectors in t time step, that is, the tth sample. Especially, W_{hh}, W_{hx}, W_{yh}, b_h, b_y are the coefficients that are shared temporally, and g_1, g_2 are activation functions. Besides, the loss function can be represented as

$$\text{loss} = \sum_{t=1}^{d_y} \mathcal{L}(\hat{y}^t, y^t), \tag{2.47}$$

where $\mathcal{L}(\cdot)$ is the loss function similar to NN, which can also be minimized by the gradient descent and other algorithms.

However, the vanishing and exploding gradient problems are often happened in the backpropagation training process of RNN. It is mainly because of multiplicative gradient that can be exponentially decreasing/increasing with respect to the number of layers. Then, the gated recurrent unit (GRU) and long short-term memory units (LSTM) [29] are proposed to deal with the problems.

2.2.3 Graph neural network

To deal with the non-Euclidean data structure, that is, the shortest path between two points is not necessarily a straight line, the CNN and RNN architectures are proposed to process the image data and sequential data. However, there are lots of irregular data structures like social graph, 3D mesh, and molecular graph. Therefore the graph neural network (GNN) arises to solve this problem. The GNN models the relation between nodes and features in nodes, which emerges the breakthrough in the graph analysis research area [30,31].

The graph is a data structure consisting of nodes and edge components, as illustrated in Fig. 2.16. Without loss of generality, a graph $\mathcal{G}$ can be described by the set of nodes $\mathcal{V}$ and edges $\mathcal{E}$, which can be either directed or undirected. Therefore GNN is a type of NN that directly calculates on the graph structure. The typical applications of GNN include node classification, link prediction, and embedding node/substructure/graph structure to a vector.

In the node classification problem, each node n is characterized by its feature x_n and associated with label y_n. If a partially labeled graph $\mathcal{G}$ is given, then the goal of GNN is to utilize the labeled nodes to predict the labels of the unlabeled nodes. The GNN learns to represent each node by a d-dimensional vector h_n, which embeds the information of its neighborhood

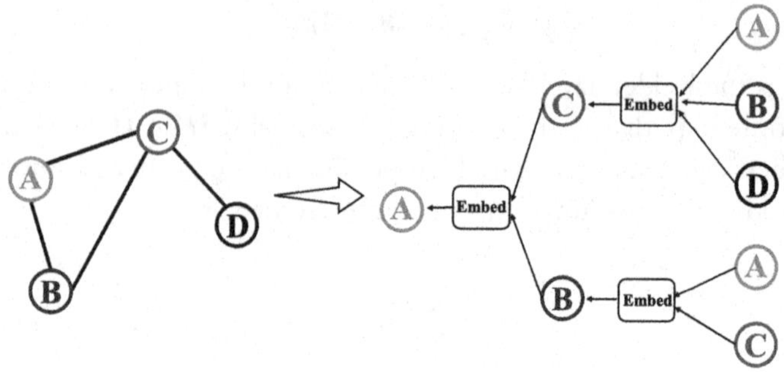

Figure 2.16 An overview of graph neural network.

as

$$\boldsymbol{h}_b = f(\boldsymbol{x}_n, \boldsymbol{x}_{\mathrm{ed}[n]}, \boldsymbol{h}_{\mathrm{ne}[n]}, \boldsymbol{x}_{\mathrm{ne}[n]}), \tag{2.48}$$

where $\boldsymbol{x}_{\mathrm{ed}[n]}$ denotes the features of the edges connecting with n, $\boldsymbol{h}_{\mathrm{ne}[n]}$ shows the embedded vectors of the neighbor nodes of n, and $\boldsymbol{x}_{\mathrm{ne}[n]}$ represents the features of the neighbor nodes of n. Besides, f is the mapping function that projects these inputs onto a d-dimensional space. The operation is often called message passing or neighborhood aggregation. Thus an additional goal is to seek a unique solution for $\boldsymbol{h}_v$, which can use the Banach fixed point theorem and rewrite the above equation as an iteratively update process as

$$\boldsymbol{H}^{t+1} = F(\boldsymbol{H}^t, \boldsymbol{X}), \tag{2.49}$$

where $\boldsymbol{H}$ and $\boldsymbol{X}$ denote the concatenations of all $\boldsymbol{h}$ and $\boldsymbol{x}$, respectively.

The output of the GNN is computed by combining the state $\boldsymbol{h}_n$ and the feature $\boldsymbol{x}_n$ to an output function g, that is,

$$\hat{y}_n = g(\boldsymbol{h}_n, \boldsymbol{x}_n). \tag{2.50}$$

The mapping functions f and g can be implement by NN, CNN, or others. Therefore the loss can be straightforwardly formulated as follows:

$$\mathrm{loss} = \sum_{t=1}^{d_y} N(\hat{y}_n, y_n), \tag{2.51}$$

which can be optimized via the gradient descent and other algorithms.

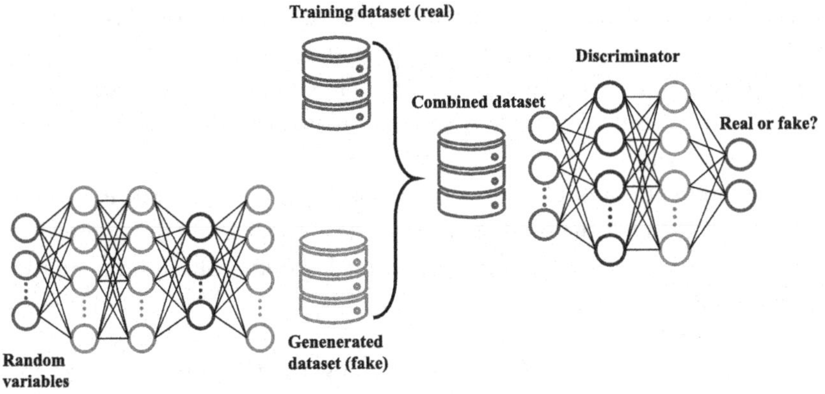

Figure 2.17 Architecture of generative adversarial network model.

2.2.4 Generative adversarial network

Generative adversarial network (GAN) is an unsupervised learning algorithm to create new data samples that resemble the training data [32]. GAN aims to train a generative model by framing the problem as two supervised learning submodels, which is shown in Fig. 2.17.

- Generator model: generate new plausible samples from the random input.
- Discriminator model: classify samples as real (from the training data) or fake (generated).

The generator model receives a random vector as input and generates a sample (e.g., image, text), which has the same dimension as the training sample. The goal of the generator model is generating a sample that is hard to be distinguished as fake. The input vector usually is randomly sampled from a Gaussian distribution. After training, the generator model forms a latent equivalent representation of the training data (real) distribution. The discriminator model treats the training samples (real) and generated samples (fake) as the input space and the class (real or fake) as the output space. The goal of discriminator model is classifying them as accurate as possible. Therefore the generator model generates plausible samples to confuse discriminator model, and the discriminator model distinguishes the real or fake samples as much as possible, which can be regarded as game theory. Therefore the mathematical expression of GAN can be represented by

$$\underset{\mathcal{G}}{\text{minimize}}\,\underset{\mathcal{D}}{\text{maximize}}\, V(\mathcal{G},\mathcal{D}) = \mathbb{E}_{\boldsymbol{x}\sim p_{\text{data}}(\boldsymbol{x})} \log \mathcal{D}(\boldsymbol{x}) + \mathbb{E}_{\boldsymbol{z}\sim p_g(\boldsymbol{z})} \log(1-\mathcal{D}(\mathcal{G}(\boldsymbol{z}))), \tag{2.52}$$

where $\mathcal{G}$ and $\mathcal{D}$ denote the generator and discriminator models, respectively, $\boldsymbol{x}$ is the training sample, and its distribution is $p_{\text{data}}(\boldsymbol{x})$, $\boldsymbol{z}$ is the random input vector, and its distribution is $p_g(\boldsymbol{z})$. Thus $\mathcal{G}(\boldsymbol{z})$ is the generated fake sample, and $\boldsymbol{x}$ is the real sample. $D(\boldsymbol{x})$ can be understood as the probability of the real sample.

As aforementioned, the min-max problem can be split into two optimization problems as the optimizing generator model $\mathcal{G}$ and the optimizing discriminator model $\mathcal{D}$. The generator model $\mathcal{G}$ optimization problem can be expressed as

$$\underset{\mathcal{G}}{\text{minimize}}\ V(\mathcal{G},\mathcal{D}) = \mathbb{E}_{\boldsymbol{z}\sim p_g(\boldsymbol{z})} \log(1 - \mathcal{D}(\mathcal{G}(\boldsymbol{z})). \tag{2.53}$$

When optimizing $\mathcal{G}$, we assume that $\mathcal{D}$ is fixed. Thus the problem can be equivalently understood as $\max\limits_{\mathcal{G}} \mathcal{D}(\mathcal{G}(\boldsymbol{z})$ to 1, that is, the generated fake samples $\mathcal{G}(\boldsymbol{z})$ are judged as real, where 1 represents real, and 0 represents fake.

Then the optimization problem of the discriminator model $\mathcal{D}$ is

$$\underset{\mathcal{D}}{\text{maximize}}\ V(\mathcal{G},\mathcal{D}) = \mathbb{E}_{\boldsymbol{x}\sim p_{\text{data}}(\boldsymbol{x})} \log \mathcal{D}(\boldsymbol{x}) + \mathbb{E}_{\boldsymbol{z}\sim p_g(\boldsymbol{z})} \log(1 - \mathcal{D}(\mathcal{G}(\boldsymbol{z})). \tag{2.54}$$

The first item of this formulation $\max\limits_{\mathcal{D}} \mathbb{E}_{\boldsymbol{x}\sim p_{\text{data}}(\boldsymbol{x})} \log \mathcal{D}(\boldsymbol{x})$ is adopted to judge the training data as real, that is, close to 1, whereas the second item can be equivalently understood as $\min\limits_{\mathcal{D}} \mathcal{D}(\mathcal{G}(\boldsymbol{z})$ to classify the generated fake samples $\mathcal{G}(\boldsymbol{z})$ as fake, that is, close to 0.

These two problems can be optimized by using the back-propagation algorithm. Therefore the two models train each other during the game process. In recent years, there have been many variants of GAN. For example, Wasserstein GAN (WGAN) [33] cancels the sigmoid function in the discriminator model, which maps the output value to the interval of $[0, 1]$, and changes the log function in loss function $V(\mathcal{G},\mathcal{D})$.

2.3. Summary

In this chapter, we summarized the general AI models, including ML and DL models. The models can be used in various applications according to different characteristics of data samples. The descriptions of these models can give clear understandability of AI model training and inference, which is helpful in the following chapters.

References

[1] Y.S. Abu-Mostafa, M. Magdon-Ismail, H.-T. Lin, Learning from Data, vol. 4, AML-Book New York, Mar. 2012.

[2] I. Goodfellow, Y. Bengio, A. Courville, Y. Bengio, Deep Learning, vol. 1, MIT Press, Oct. 2016.

[3] Y. Shi, K. Yang, T. Jiang, J. Zhang, K.B. Letaief, Communication-efficient edge AI: algorithms and systems, IEEE Commun. Surv. Tutor. 22 (Jul. 2020) 2167–2191.

[4] K.B. Letaief, W. Chen, Y. Shi, J. Zhang, Y.A. Zhang, The roadmap to 6G: AI empowered wireless networks, IEEE Commun. Mag. 57 (Aug. 2019) 84–90.

[5] M. Chen, U. Challita, W. Saad, C. Yin, M. Debbah, Artificial neural networks-based machine learning for wireless networks: a tutorial, IEEE Commun. Surv. Tutor. 21 (Jul. 2019) 3039–3071.

[6] E. Alpaydin, Introduction to Machine Learning, MIT Press, Mar. 2020.

[7] S. Boyd, S.P. Boyd, L. Vandenberghe, Convex Optimization, Camb. University Press, Mar. 2004.

[8] E.L. Allwein, R.E. Schapire, Y. Singer, Reducing multiclass to binary: a unifying approach for margin classifiers, J. Mach. Learn. Res. 1 (Dec. 2000) 113–141.

[9] M. Grant, S. Boyd, CVX: Matlab software for disciplined convex programming, version 2.1, http://cvxr.com/cvx, Mar. 2014.

[10] J. Platt, Sequential minimal optimization: a fast algorithm for training support vector machines, Tech. Rep. MSR-TR-98-14, Apr. 1998.

[11] L. Breiman, J. Friedman, C.J. Stone, R.A. Olshen, Classification and Regression Trees, CRC Press, Jan. 1984.

[12] N.S. Altman, An introduction to kernel and nearest-neighbor nonparametric regression, Am. Stat. 46 (Aug. 1992) 175–185.

[13] K.Q. Weinberger, L.K. Saul, Distance metric learning for large margin nearest neighbor classification, J. Mach. Learn. Res. 10 (Feb. 2009).

[14] R.J. Samworth, et al., Optimal weighted nearest neighbour classifiers, Ann. Stat. 40 (Aug. 2012) 2733–2763.

[15] P. Hart, The condensed nearest neighbor rule (corresp.), IEEE Trans. Inf. Theory 14 (May. 1968) 515–516.

[16] W.S. McCulloch, W. Pitts, A logical calculus of the ideas immanent in nervous activity, Bull. Math. Biophys. 5 (Dec. 1943) 115–133.

[17] D.P. Kingma, J. Ba, Adam: a method for stochastic optimization, preprint, arXiv:1412.6980, Dec. 2014.

[18] D. Aloise, A. Deshpande, P. Hansen, P. Popat, NP-hardness of Euclidean sum-of-squares clustering, Mach. Learn. 75 (May 2009) 245–248.

[19] D. Arthur, S. Vassilvitskii, k-means++: the advantages of careful seeding, Tech. Rep., Stanford, Jun. 2006.

[20] C. Elkan, Using the triangle inequality to accelerate k-means, in: Proc. Int. Conf. on Mach. Learn. (ICML), Dec. 2003, pp. 147–153.

[21] D. Sculley, Web-scale k-means clustering, in: Proc. Int. Conf. on World Wide Web, Apr. 2010, pp. 1177–1178.

[22] L.P. Kaelbling, M.L. Littman, A.W. Moore, Reinforcement learning: a survey, J. Artif. Intell. Res. 4 (May. 1996) 237–285.

[23] K. Arulkumaran, M.P. Deisenroth, M. Brundage, A.A. Bharath, Deep reinforcement learning: a brief survey, IEEE Signal Process. Mag. 34 (Nov. 2017) 26–38.

[24] C.J. Watkins, P. Dayan, Q-learning, Mach. Learn. 8 (May. 1992) 279–292.

[25] G.A. Rummery, M. Niranjan, On-Line Q-Learning Using Connectionist Systems, vol. 37, University of Cambridge, Sep. 1994.

[26] V. Mnih, K. Kavukcuoglu, D. Silver, A.A. Rusu, J. Veness, M.G. Bellemare, A. Graves, M. Riedmiller, A.K. Fidjeland, G. Ostrovski, et al., Human-level control through deep reinforcement learning, Nature 518 (Feb. 2015) 529–533.

[27] V. Mnih, A.P. Badia, M. Mirza, A. Graves, T. Lillicrap, T. Harley, D. Silver, K. Kavukcuoglu, Asynchronous methods for deep reinforcement learning, in: Proc. Int. Conf. on Mach. Learn. (ICML), Jun. 2016, pp. 1928–1937.
[28] A. Khan, A. Sohail, U. Zahoora, A.S. Qureshi, A survey of the recent architectures of deep convolutional neural networks, Artif. Intell. Rev. 53 (Dec. 2020) 5455–5516.
[29] S. Hochreiter, J. Schmidhuber, Long short-term memory, Neural Comput. 9 (Nov. 1997) 1735–1780.
[30] Z. Wu, S. Pan, F. Chen, G. Long, C. Zhang, P.S. Yu, A comprehensive survey on graph neural networks, IEEE Trans. Neural Netw. Learn. Syst. 32 (Mar. 2021) 4–24.
[31] X. Dong, D. Thanou, L. Toni, M. Bronstein, P. Frossard, Graph signal processing for machine learning: a review and new perspectives, IEEE Signal Process. Mag. 37 (Oct. 2020) 117–127.
[32] A. Creswell, T. White, V. Dumoulin, K. Arulkumaran, B. Sengupta, A.A. Bharath, Generative adversarial networks: an overview, IEEE Signal Process. Mag. 35 (Jan. 2018) 53–65.
[33] M. Arjovsky, S. Chintala, L. Bottou, Wasserstein generative adversarial networks, in: Proc. Int. Conf. on Mach. Learn. (ICML), Jul. 2017, pp. 214–223.

CHAPTER THREE

Convex optimization

3.1. First-order methods

In this section, we present several first-order methods for different optimization problems. First of all, we briefly introduce the concept of convex optimization problems, which have provable optimal solutions [1].

A *convex set* contains all the line segments through any two distinct points in the set C, that is,

$$\boldsymbol{x}_1, \boldsymbol{x}_2 \in C \Rightarrow \theta \boldsymbol{x}_1 + (1-\theta)\boldsymbol{x}_2 \in C, \tag{3.1}$$

where $0 \leq \theta \leq 1$. Similarly, a function $f : \mathbb{R}^n \to \mathbb{R}$ is said to be a *convex function* if the domain $\mathsf{dom} f$ is a convex set and

$$f(\theta \boldsymbol{x} + (1-\theta)\boldsymbol{y}) \leq \theta f(\boldsymbol{x}) + (1-\theta) f(\boldsymbol{y}) \tag{3.2}$$

for all $\boldsymbol{x}, \boldsymbol{y} \in \mathsf{dom} f$ and $0 \leq \theta \leq 1$.

In general, convex optimization problems can be expressed as

$$\begin{aligned} \underset{\boldsymbol{x}\in\mathbb{R}^n}{\text{minimize}} \quad & f_0(\boldsymbol{x}) \\ \text{subject to} \quad & f_i(\boldsymbol{x}) \leq 0, \quad i = 1, \ldots, m, \\ & h_i(\boldsymbol{x}) = 0, \quad i = 1, \ldots, p, \end{aligned} \tag{3.3}$$

where $\boldsymbol{x} = [x_1, \ldots, x_n]^\top$ is the *optimization variable*, and $f_0 : \mathbb{R}^n \to \mathbb{R}$ is the *objective function*. Besides, $f_i : \mathbb{R}^n \to \mathbb{R}$, $i = 1, \ldots, m$, and $h_i : \mathbb{R}^n \to \mathbb{R}$, $i = 1, \ldots, p$, denote the *inequality constraint functions* and *equality constraint functions*, respectively. It is worth noting that the constraints are convex sets.

We present several popular optimization algorithms for solving different convex optimization problems as follows.

3.1.1 Gradient method for unconstrained problems

A differentiable unconstrained minimization problem can be written as

$$\begin{aligned} \underset{\boldsymbol{x}}{\text{minimize}} \quad & f(\boldsymbol{x}) \\ \text{subject to} \quad & \boldsymbol{x} \in \mathbb{R}^n, \end{aligned} \tag{3.4}$$

Mobile Edge Artificial Intelligence
https://doi.org/10.1016/B978-0-12-823817-2.00012-7

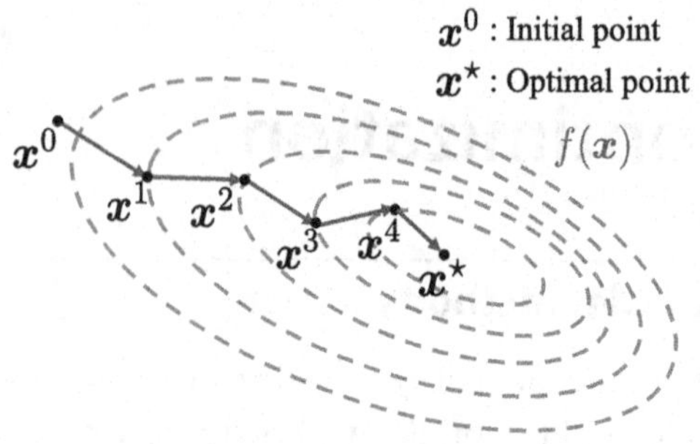

Figure 3.1 Illustration of gradient descent method for unconstrained problems.

where the objective function $f(\boldsymbol{x})$ is differentiable.

The iterative descent algorithm starts with an initial point $\boldsymbol{x}^0$ and constructs a sequence $\{\boldsymbol{x}^t\}$ that satisfies $f(\boldsymbol{x}^{t+1}) < f(\boldsymbol{x}^t)$, $t = 0, 1, \ldots$. We say that $\boldsymbol{d}$ is a *descent direction* at $\boldsymbol{x}$ if the directional derivative

$$f'(\boldsymbol{x}; \boldsymbol{d}) := \lim_{\tau \to 0} \frac{f(\boldsymbol{x} + \tau \boldsymbol{d}) - f(\boldsymbol{x})}{\tau} = \nabla f(\boldsymbol{x})^\top \boldsymbol{d} < 0. \tag{3.5}$$

In each iteration the algorithm searches in the descent direction $\boldsymbol{x}^{t+1} = \boldsymbol{x}^t + \eta_t \boldsymbol{d}^t$, where $\boldsymbol{d}^t$ is the descent direction at $\boldsymbol{x}^t$, and $\eta_t > 0$ is the step size. One of the most important examples is the *gradient descent*

$$\boldsymbol{x}^{t+1} = \boldsymbol{x}^t - \eta_t \nabla f(\boldsymbol{x}^t), \tag{3.6}$$

where the descent direction is $\boldsymbol{d}^t = -\nabla f(\boldsymbol{x}^t)$. The gradient descent is also known as the steepest descent since by (3.5) and the Cauchy–Schwarz inequality

$$\arg\min_{\boldsymbol{d}:\|\boldsymbol{d}\|_2 \le 1} f'(\boldsymbol{x}; \boldsymbol{d}) = \arg\min_{\boldsymbol{d}:\|\boldsymbol{d}\|_2 \le 1} \nabla f(\boldsymbol{x})^\top \boldsymbol{d} = -\frac{\nabla f(\boldsymbol{x})}{\|\nabla f(\boldsymbol{x})\|_2}, \tag{3.7}$$

which is the direction that the objective value improves most. An illustrating example of gradient descent is shown in Fig. 3.1.

The line search methods can be used to improve the convergence rate by searching appropriate step size. The strategy to find an appropriate step size η_t is the *exact line search* rule, which determines the step size as follows

$$\eta_t = \arg\min_{\eta \ge 0} f(\boldsymbol{x}^t - \eta \nabla f(\boldsymbol{x}^t)), \tag{3.8}$$

which is the maximum step size to minimize the objective function.

However, the optimization problem (3.8) may be hard to solve. Therefore a simple and effective scheme is the *backtracking line search*, which is described in Algorithm 4. The backtracking line search method is based on the Armijo condition $f(\boldsymbol{x}^t - \eta\nabla f(\boldsymbol{x}^t)) < f(\boldsymbol{x}^t) - \alpha\eta\|\nabla f(\boldsymbol{x}^t)\|_2^2$, which ensures a sufficient decrease of objective values.

Algorithm 4: Backtracking line search for gradient descent.

Initialize $\eta = 1$, $0 < \alpha \le 1/2$, $0 < \beta < 1$.
while $f(\boldsymbol{x}^t - \eta\nabla f(\boldsymbol{x}^t)) > f(\boldsymbol{x}^t) - \alpha\eta\|\nabla f(\boldsymbol{x}^t)\|_2^2$ **do**
  $\eta \leftarrow \beta\eta$.
end while

3.1.2 Gradient method for constrained problems

Constrained convex problems are considered by restricting the optimization variables in convex sets, that is,

$$\begin{aligned} \underset{\boldsymbol{x}}{\text{minimize}} \quad & f(\boldsymbol{x}) \\ \text{subject to} \quad & \boldsymbol{x} \in C, \end{aligned} \tag{3.9}$$

where f is a convex function, and $C \subset \mathbb{R}^n$ is a closed convex set.

To address the constrained optimization problems, the Frank–Wolfe algorithm (a.k.a. the conditional gradient algorithm) is proposed to satisfy the constrains and is shown in Algorithm 5. The Frank–Wolfe algorithm utilizes $\boldsymbol{y}^t := \arg\min_{\boldsymbol{x}\in C}\langle\nabla f(\boldsymbol{x}^t), \boldsymbol{x}\rangle$ to find the direction satisfying the constrains.. Then the optimization variables are updated by $\boldsymbol{x}^{t+1} = (1-\eta_t)\boldsymbol{x}^t + \eta_t\boldsymbol{y}^t$, where $\boldsymbol{x}^t, \boldsymbol{y}^t \in C$, and η_t is a constant selected by line search. Thus $\boldsymbol{x}^{t+1} \in C$ is satisfied because of the definition of a convex set.

Algorithm 5: Frank–Wolfe algorithm.

---

for each $t = 0, 1, \ldots$ **do**
  $\boldsymbol{y}^t := \underset{\boldsymbol{x}\in C}{\arg\min}\langle\nabla f(\boldsymbol{x}^t), \boldsymbol{x}\rangle$.
  $\boldsymbol{x}^{t+1} = (1-\eta_t)\boldsymbol{x}^t + \eta_t\boldsymbol{y}^t$.
end for

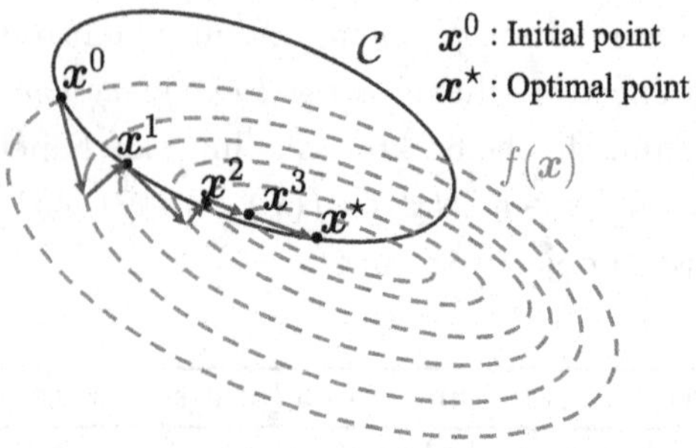

Figure 3.2 Illustration of projected gradient descent method for constrained problems.

Besides, the projected gradient method is also developed to solve constrained convex problems. The projection operation is represented as

$$\mathcal{P}_C(\boldsymbol{x}) := \arg\min_{\boldsymbol{z}\in C} \|\boldsymbol{x} - \boldsymbol{z}\|_2^2, \tag{3.10}$$

which is the Euclidean projection onto C. Therefore the update in each step can be written as

$$\boldsymbol{x}^{t+1} = \mathcal{P}_C(\boldsymbol{x}^t - \eta_t \nabla f(\boldsymbol{x}^t)), \tag{3.11}$$

which is illustrated in Fig. 3.2.

3.1.3 Subgradient descent method

Differentiability of the objective function f is critical for the validity of gradient methods to solve problems (3.4) and (3.9). However, there are plenty of nondifferentiable functions (e.g., ℓ_1 minimization and nuclear norm minimization). This will result in expensive computation cost to find the steepest descent direction. Besides, the gradient descent method may not converge to the optimal points for certain popular step size rules.

Practically, the *subgradient-based method* is a popular technique, which can deal with the nondifferentiability of objective functions:

$$\boldsymbol{x}^{t+1} = \mathcal{P}_C(\boldsymbol{x}^t - \eta_t \boldsymbol{g}^t), \tag{3.12}$$

where $\boldsymbol{g}^t$ is any subgradient of f at $\boldsymbol{x}^t$.

The definition of a subgradient $\boldsymbol{g}$ of f at the point $\boldsymbol{x}$ is

$$f(\boldsymbol{z}) \geq f(\boldsymbol{x}) + \boldsymbol{g}^\top(\boldsymbol{z} - \boldsymbol{x}), \ \forall \boldsymbol{z}, \tag{3.13}$$

and the subgradient of f at $\boldsymbol{x}$ is called the *subdifferential* of f at $\boldsymbol{x}$ [2]. The subdifferential is denoted by $\partial f(\boldsymbol{x})$, which is a set and not unique. There are some properties of subdifferential such as the scaling $\partial(\alpha f) = \alpha\partial f$ (for $\alpha > 0$), summation $\partial(f_1 + f_2) = \partial f_1 + \partial f_2$, and chain rule $\partial h(\boldsymbol{x}) = g'(f(\boldsymbol{x}))\partial f(\boldsymbol{x})$, where $h = g(f(\boldsymbol{x}))$.

3.1.4 Mirror descent method

A proximal viewpoint of the update formula of projected gradient descent in (3.11) is presented as

$$\boldsymbol{x}^{t+1} = \arg\min_{\boldsymbol{x}\in C}\left\{f(\boldsymbol{x}^t) + \left\langle\nabla f(\boldsymbol{x}^t), \boldsymbol{x} - \boldsymbol{x}^t\right\rangle + \frac{1}{2\eta_t}\|\boldsymbol{x} - \boldsymbol{x}^t\|_2^2\right\}. \tag{3.14}$$

The discrepancy between f and its first-order approximation is captured by the quadratic proximity term $\|\boldsymbol{x} - \boldsymbol{x}^t\|_2^2$. Generally, the discrepancy between f and its linear approximation is locally well approximated by the homogeneous penalty $\frac{1}{2\eta_t}\|\boldsymbol{x} - \boldsymbol{x}^t\|_2^2$. However, the issues arise when the local geometry sometimes is highly inhomogeneous or even non-Euclidean.

The mirror descent method adjusts the gradient updates to fit the problem geometry, which replaces the quadratic proximity $\|\boldsymbol{x} - \boldsymbol{x}^t\|_2^2$ with distance-like metric D_ϕ [3]:

$$\boldsymbol{x}^{t+1} = \arg\min_{\boldsymbol{x}\in C}\left\{f(\boldsymbol{x}^t) + \left\langle\nabla f(\boldsymbol{x}^t), \boldsymbol{x} - \boldsymbol{x}^t\right\rangle + \frac{1}{\eta_t}D_\phi(\boldsymbol{x}, \boldsymbol{x}^t)\right\}, \tag{3.15}$$

where $D_\phi(\boldsymbol{x}, \boldsymbol{z}) := \phi(\boldsymbol{x}) - \phi(\boldsymbol{z}) - \langle\nabla\phi(\boldsymbol{z}), \boldsymbol{x} - \boldsymbol{z}\rangle$ is the Bregman divergence for convex and differentiable ϕ. Particularly, the update formula (3.15) can be explained by Fig. 3.3. More generally, the update formula (3.15) can be written as

$$\boldsymbol{x}^{t+1} = \arg\min_{\boldsymbol{x}\in C}\left\{f(\boldsymbol{x}^t) + \left\langle\boldsymbol{g}^t, \boldsymbol{x} - \boldsymbol{x}^t\right\rangle + \frac{1}{\eta_t}D_\phi(\boldsymbol{x}, \boldsymbol{x}^t)\right\}, \tag{3.16}$$

where $\boldsymbol{g}^t \in \partial f(\boldsymbol{x}^t)$ for nondifferentiable objective functions.

Therefore the local geometry via appropriate Bregman divergence metrics is a generalization of the squared Euclidean distance, for example, the squared Mahalanobis distance, Kullback–Leibler (KL) divergence, and so on. The selected Bregman divergence should fit the local curvature of f and the geometry of the constraint set C.

The squared Mahalanobis distance is defined as $D_\phi(\boldsymbol{x}, \boldsymbol{z}) = \frac{1}{2}(\boldsymbol{x} - \boldsymbol{z})^\mathsf{T}\mathbf{Q}(\boldsymbol{x} - \boldsymbol{z})$, which is generated by $\phi(\boldsymbol{x}) = \frac{1}{2}\boldsymbol{x}^T\mathbf{Q}\boldsymbol{x}$. The KL diver-

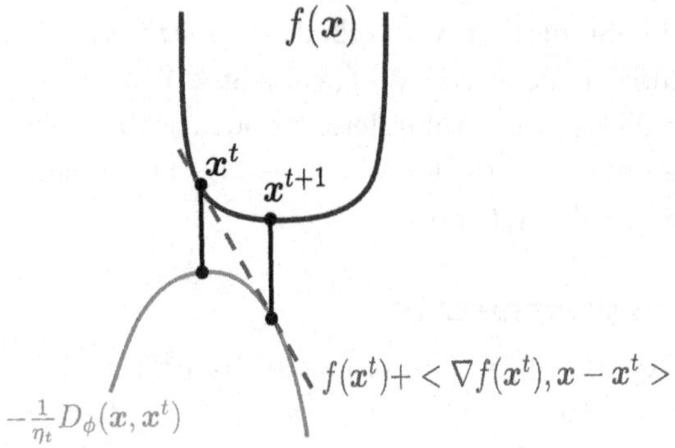

Figure 3.3 Illustration of mirror gradient descent method.

gence is $D_\phi(\boldsymbol{x}, \boldsymbol{z}) = D_{KL}(\boldsymbol{x}\|\boldsymbol{z}) := \sum_i x_i \log \frac{x_i}{z_i}$, which is generated by $\phi(\boldsymbol{x}) = \sum_i x_i \log \frac{x_i}{z_i}$ if $C := \{\boldsymbol{x} \in \mathbb{R}^n_+ | \sum_i x_i = 1\}$ is the probability simplex.

Then the Bregman projection is defined as

$$\mathcal{P}_{C,\phi}(\boldsymbol{x}) := \arg\min_{\boldsymbol{z}\in C} D_\phi(\boldsymbol{z}, \boldsymbol{x}), \tag{3.17}$$

given a point $\boldsymbol{x}$ and constraint set C. Using the Bregman divergence, the mirror descent is described as

$$\nabla\phi(\boldsymbol{y}^{t+1}) = \nabla\phi(\boldsymbol{x}^t) - \eta_t \boldsymbol{g}^t, \tag{3.18}$$

where $\boldsymbol{g}^t \in \partial f(\boldsymbol{x}^t)$, and

$$\boldsymbol{x}^{t+1} \in \mathcal{P}_{C,\phi}(\boldsymbol{y}^{t+1}) = \arg\min_{\boldsymbol{z}\in C} D_\phi(\boldsymbol{z}, \boldsymbol{y}^{t+1}), \tag{3.19}$$

which performs gradient descent in certain dual space.

3.1.5 Proximal gradient method

The proximal gradient method is designed to efficiently deal with the composite objective functions:

$$\begin{aligned} \underset{\boldsymbol{x}}{\text{minimize}} \quad & F(\boldsymbol{x}) := f(\boldsymbol{x}) + h(\boldsymbol{x}) \\ \text{subject to} \quad & \boldsymbol{x} \in \mathbb{R}^n, \end{aligned} \tag{3.20}$$

where f is convex and smooth, and h is convex but may be nondifferentiable. To describe the proximal gradient method, we first revisit the gradient descent

$$\begin{aligned} & \boldsymbol{x}^{t+1} = \boldsymbol{x}^t - \eta_t \nabla f(\boldsymbol{x}^t) \\ \Leftrightarrow \quad & \boldsymbol{x}^{t+1} = \arg\min_{\boldsymbol{x} \in C} \left\{ f(\boldsymbol{x}^t) + \left\langle \nabla f(\boldsymbol{x}^t), \boldsymbol{x} - \boldsymbol{x}^t \right\rangle + \tfrac{1}{2\eta_t} \|\boldsymbol{x} - \boldsymbol{x}^t\|_2^2 \right\}. \end{aligned} \tag{3.21}$$

Then the proximal operator is defined as

$$\mathsf{prox}_{\eta_t h}(\boldsymbol{x}) := \arg\min_{\boldsymbol{z}} \left\{ \frac{1}{2\eta_t} \|\boldsymbol{z} - \boldsymbol{x}\|_x^2 + h(\boldsymbol{z}) \right\} \tag{3.22}$$

for any convex function h. Therefore the update formula of the proximal gradient method can be expressed as

$$\boldsymbol{x}^{t+1} = \mathsf{prox}_{\eta_t h}(\boldsymbol{x}^t - \eta_t \nabla f(\boldsymbol{x}^t)), \tag{3.23}$$

which alternates between gradient updates on f and proximal minimization on h. If prox_h is inexpensive, then the proximal gradient method will be efficient.

The proximal operator $\mathsf{prox}_{\eta_t h}(\boldsymbol{x}) := \arg\min_{\boldsymbol{z}} \left\{ \frac{1}{2\eta_t} \|\boldsymbol{z} - \boldsymbol{x}\|_x^2 + h(\boldsymbol{z}) \right\}$ is efficient for many widely used functions (in particular, regularizers) and covers many well-known optimization algorithms. There are plenty of properties to further simplify the calculation of the proximal operator, which are in detail explained in [1].

3.1.6 Accelerated gradient method

Gradient descent focuses on improving the cost per iteration, which might sometimes be too "short-sighted". Therefore we can exploit history information (i.e., past iterations) and add buffers (like momentum) to yield a smooth trajectory.

We consider the following simple optimization problem:

$$\underset{\boldsymbol{x} \in \mathbb{R}^n}{\text{minimize}} \quad f(\boldsymbol{x}), \tag{3.24}$$

where $f(\boldsymbol{x})$ is differentiable.

The heavy-ball method update can be presented as

$$\boldsymbol{x}^{t+1} = \boldsymbol{x}^t - \eta_t \nabla f(\boldsymbol{x}^t) + \theta^t (\boldsymbol{x}^t - \boldsymbol{x}^{t-1}), \tag{3.25}$$

where $\theta^t(\boldsymbol{x}^t - \boldsymbol{x}^{t-1})$ is the momentum term, which adds inertia to the "ball" (i.e., includes a momentum term) to mitigate zigzagging.

Moreover, Nesterov's idea alternates between gradient updates and proper extrapolation, where each iteration takes nearly the same cost as the gradient descent [4]. It is worth mentioning that it is not a descent method (i.e., $f(\boldsymbol{x}^{t+1}) \leq f(\boldsymbol{x}^t)$ may not hold) and the update formula can be expressed as

$$\boldsymbol{x}^{t+1} = \boldsymbol{y}^t - \eta_t \nabla f(\boldsymbol{y}^t), \tag{3.26}$$

$$\boldsymbol{y}^{t+1} = \boldsymbol{x}^{t+1} + \frac{t}{t+3}(\boldsymbol{x}^{t+1} - \boldsymbol{x}^t). \tag{3.27}$$

It is worth noting that Nesterov's momentum coefficient $\frac{t}{t+3} = 1 - \frac{1}{t}$ is specified to achieve excellent performance.

Besides, for composite models as problem (3.20), the fast iterative shrinkage-thresholding (FISTA) algorithm is developed as

$$\boldsymbol{x}^{t+1} = \mathrm{prox}_{\eta_t h}(\boldsymbol{y}^t - \eta_t \nabla f(\boldsymbol{y}^t)), \tag{3.28}$$

$$\boldsymbol{y}^{t+1} = \boldsymbol{x}^{t+1} + \frac{\theta_t - 1}{\theta_{t+1}}(\boldsymbol{x}^{t+1} - \boldsymbol{x}^t), \tag{3.29}$$

where $\boldsymbol{y}^0 = \boldsymbol{x}^0$, $\theta_0 = 1$, and $\theta_{t+1} = \frac{1+\sqrt{1+4\theta_t^2}}{2}$ [5]. The FISTA algorithm adopts the momentum coefficients originally proposed by Nesterov.

3.1.7 Smoothing for nonsmooth optimization

For the simple optimization problem (3.24), if f is convex but not necessarily differentiable, then the subgradient methods yield ε-accuracy in $O\left(\frac{1}{\varepsilon^2}\right)$ iterations, where ε-accuracy is defined by $\|\nabla f(\boldsymbol{x})\|_2 \leq \varepsilon$. In contrast, if f is smooth, that is, differentiable in the domain, then accelerated GD yields ε-accuracy in $O\left(\frac{1}{\varepsilon}\right)$ iterations, significantly outperforming the nonsmooth case.

If the first-order oracle exists, which is a black box model taken as inputs a point $\boldsymbol{x}$ and outputs a subgradient of f at $\boldsymbol{x}$), then we cannot improve upon $O\left(\frac{1}{\varepsilon^2}\right)$ in general [1]. Practically, we rarely obtain pure black box models. However, one possible strategy is to approximate the nonsmooth objective by a smooth function and then to optimize the smooth approximation instead.

A convex function f is said to be L-smooth if $f(\boldsymbol{y}) \leq f(\boldsymbol{x}) + \nabla f(\boldsymbol{x})^\mathsf{T}(\boldsymbol{y} - \boldsymbol{x}) + \frac{L}{2}\|\boldsymbol{x} - \boldsymbol{y}\|_2^2$ for all $\boldsymbol{x}$, $\boldsymbol{y}$, that is, $\|\nabla^2 f(\boldsymbol{x})\|_2 \leq L$ for all $\boldsymbol{x}$. Therefore a convex function f is called (α, β)-smoothable if there exists a convex function f_μ satisfying the approximation accuracy $f_\mu(\boldsymbol{x}) \leq f(\boldsymbol{x}) \leq f_\mu(\boldsymbol{x}) + \beta\mu$

and smoothness $\|\nabla^2 f(\boldsymbol{x})\|_2 \leq \frac{\alpha}{\mu}$ for any $\mu > 0$. Particularly, f_μ is called a $\frac{1}{\mu}$-smooth approximation of f with parameters (α, β). Note that μ can be adjusted to balance the tradeoff between approximation accuracy and smoothness.

The Moreau envelope (or Moreau–Yosida regularization) of a convex function f with parameter $\mu > 0$ is defined as

$$M_{\mu f}(\boldsymbol{x}) := \inf_{\boldsymbol{z}} \left\{ f(\boldsymbol{z}) + \frac{1}{2\mu} \|\boldsymbol{x} - \boldsymbol{z}\|_2^2 \right\}, \tag{3.30}$$

where $M_{\mu f}$ is a smoothed or regularized form of f, and it is equivalent to minimizing f and minimizing $M_{\mu f}$ [6].

It is worth noting the connection between the Moreau envelope and proximal operator. The proximal operator $\mathsf{prox}_f(\boldsymbol{x})$ is the unique point that achieves the infimum that defines M_f, that is,

$$M_{\mu f}(\boldsymbol{x}) = f(\mathsf{prox}_{\mu f}(\boldsymbol{x})) + \frac{1}{2} \|\boldsymbol{x} - \mathsf{prox}_{\mu f}(\boldsymbol{x})\|_2^2, \tag{3.31}$$

and M_f is continuously differentiable with gradients, that is, $\nabla M_{\mu f}(\boldsymbol{x}) = \frac{1}{\mu}(\boldsymbol{x} - \mathsf{prox}_{\mu f}(\boldsymbol{x}))$. Therefore we have

$$\mathsf{prox}_{\mu f}(\boldsymbol{x}) = \boldsymbol{x} - \mu \nabla M_{\mu f}(\boldsymbol{x}), \tag{3.32}$$

which means that $\mathsf{prox}_{\mu f}(\boldsymbol{x})$ is the gradient step for minimizing $M_{\mu f}(\boldsymbol{x})$.

Besides, the conjugation method can also smooth the function. The conjugation function of the function f is defined as

$$f^*(\boldsymbol{y}) = \sup_{\boldsymbol{x} \in \mathsf{dom} f} \left(\boldsymbol{y}^{sfT} \boldsymbol{x} - f(\boldsymbol{x}) \right), \tag{3.33}$$

where $\sup S$ is the supremum of a set S.

Suppose $f = g^*$, that is, $f(\boldsymbol{x}) = \sup_{\boldsymbol{z}}\{< \boldsymbol{z}, \boldsymbol{x} > -g(\boldsymbol{z})\}$. A smooth approximation of f is established by adding a strongly convex component to its dual, namely,

$$f_\mu(\boldsymbol{x}) = \sup_{\boldsymbol{z}}\{< \boldsymbol{z}, \boldsymbol{x} > -g(\boldsymbol{z}) - \mu d(\boldsymbol{z})\} = (g + \mu d)^* \tag{3.34}$$

for some 1-strongly convex and continuous function $d(\boldsymbol{z}) \geq 0$, which is called a proximity function. Therefore $g + \mu d$ is μ-strongly convex, and f_μ is $\frac{1}{\mu}$-smooth. Moreover, we have $f_\mu(\boldsymbol{x}) \leq f(\boldsymbol{x}) \leq f_\mu(\boldsymbol{x}) + \mu D$ with

$D := \sup_x d(\boldsymbol{x})$, which means that f_μ is a $\frac{1}{\mu}$-smooth approximation of f with parameters $(1, D)$ [1].

Finally, we consider the composite optimization problem

$$\underset{\boldsymbol{x}}{\text{minimize}} \quad F(\boldsymbol{x}) = f(\boldsymbol{x}) + h(\boldsymbol{x}), \tag{3.35}$$

where f is convex and (α, β)-smoothable, and h is convex but may be non-differentiable. Therefore we can construct the $\frac{1}{\mu}$-smooth approximation f_μ of f with parameters (α, β). The update formula to solve problem (3.35) is given by

$$\boldsymbol{x}^{t+1} = \mathsf{prox}_{\eta_t h}(\boldsymbol{y}^t - \eta_t \nabla f_\mu(\boldsymbol{y}^t)), \tag{3.36}$$

$$\boldsymbol{y}^{t+1} = \boldsymbol{x}^{t+1} + \frac{\theta^t - 1}{\theta^{t+1}}(\boldsymbol{x}^{t+1} - \boldsymbol{x}^t), \tag{3.37}$$

where $\boldsymbol{y}^0 = \boldsymbol{x}^0$, $\theta^0 = 1$, and $\theta^{t+1} = \frac{1+\sqrt{1+4\theta_t^2}}{2}$. In the update formula, FISTA is used to accelerate convergence, and the proximal gradient method disposes the composite function.

3.1.8 Dual and primal-dual methods

Then constrained convex optimization problem is written as

$$\begin{aligned} &\underset{\boldsymbol{x}}{\text{minimize}} \quad f(\boldsymbol{x}) \\ &\text{subject to} \quad \boldsymbol{A}\boldsymbol{x} + \boldsymbol{b} \in C, \end{aligned} \tag{3.38}$$

where f is convex, and C is a convex set. The projection onto such a feasible set may sometimes be highly nontrivial even when projection onto C is easy.

More generally, we consider the problem

$$\underset{\boldsymbol{x}}{\text{minimize}} \quad f(\boldsymbol{x}) + h(\boldsymbol{A}\boldsymbol{x}), \tag{3.39}$$

where f and h are convex. Computing the cost of proximal operator with respect to $\tilde{h}(\boldsymbol{x}) := h(\boldsymbol{A}\boldsymbol{x})$ could be difficult even when the calculation of prox_h is inexpensive [1]. If we add the auxiliary variable $\boldsymbol{z} = \boldsymbol{A}\boldsymbol{x}$, then problem (3.39) is equivalent to

$$\begin{aligned} &\underset{\boldsymbol{x}}{\text{minimize}} \quad f(\boldsymbol{x}) + h(\boldsymbol{z}) \\ &\text{subject to} \quad \boldsymbol{A}\boldsymbol{x} = \boldsymbol{z}, \end{aligned} \tag{3.40}$$

and the Lagrangian dual formulation is described as

$$\underset{\lambda}{\text{maximize}} \quad \min_{x,z} f(x) + h(z) + < \lambda, Ax - z >, \tag{3.41}$$

$$\Leftrightarrow \quad \underset{\lambda}{\text{maximize}} \quad \min_{x} \left\{ < A^{\mathsf{T}}\lambda, x > + f(x) \right\} + \min_{z} \left\{ hf(z) - < \lambda, z > \right\}, \tag{3.42}$$

$$\Leftrightarrow \quad \underset{\lambda}{\text{maximize}} \quad -f^*(-A^{\mathsf{T}}\lambda) - h^*(\lambda), \tag{3.43}$$

where f^* and h^* are the Fenchel conjugates of f and h, respectively. The dual formulation is useful if the proximal operator with respect to h can be easily obtained and f^* is smooth. Then we can use the Moreau decomposition $\mathsf{prox}_{h^*}(x) = x - \mathsf{prox}_h(x)$.

The proximal gradient methods will be utilized to the dual problem as

$$\lambda^{t+1} = \mathsf{prox}_{\eta_t h^*}\left(\lambda^t + \eta_t A \nabla f^*(-A^{\mathsf{T}}\lambda^t)\right). \tag{3.44}$$

Moreover, the primal representation of dual proximal gradient methods are explicitly shown in Algorithm 6, where x^t is a primal sequence, which is not always feasible.

Algorithm 6: Primal representation of dual proximal gradient methods.

for $t = 0, 1, \cdots$ **do**

$x^t = \arg\min_{x}\{f(x) + < A^{\mathsf{T}}\lambda^t, x >)\}.$

$\lambda^{t+1} = \lambda^t + \eta_t A x^t - \eta_t \mathsf{prox}_{\eta_t^{-1} h}(\eta_t^{-1}\lambda^t + Ax^t).$

end for

By the definition of x^t we have $-A^{\mathsf{T}}\lambda^t \in \partial f(x^t)$. Combining the conjugate subgradient theorem and the smoothness of f^* yields

$$x^t = \nabla f^*(-A^{\mathsf{T}}\lambda^t). \tag{3.45}$$

Therefore the dual proximal gradient update rule in Algorithm (3.44) can be rewritten as

$$\lambda^{t+1} = \mathsf{prox}_{\eta_t h^*}\left(\lambda^t + \eta_t A x^t\right). \tag{3.46}$$

Moreover, from the extended Moreau decomposition $\mathsf{prox}_{h^*}(x) = x - \mathsf{prox}_h(x)$ we know that $\mathsf{prox}_{\eta_t h^*}\left(\lambda^t + \eta_t A x^t\right) = \lambda^t + \eta_t A x^t - \eta_t \mathsf{prox}_{\eta_t^{-1} h}(\eta_t^{-1}\lambda^t$

$+\boldsymbol{A}\boldsymbol{x}^t)$. Therefore the dual proximal gradient update rule can also be expressed as

$$\boldsymbol{\lambda}^{t+1} = \boldsymbol{\lambda}^t + \eta_t \boldsymbol{A}\boldsymbol{x}^t - \eta_t \text{prox}_{\eta_t^{-1}h}\left(\eta_t^{-1}\boldsymbol{\lambda}^t + \boldsymbol{A}\boldsymbol{x}^t\right). \tag{3.47}$$

3.1.9 Alternating direction method of multipliers

In this section, we consider the two-block problem

$$\begin{aligned} \underset{\boldsymbol{x},\boldsymbol{z}}{\text{minimize}} \quad & F(\boldsymbol{x},\boldsymbol{z}) := f_1(\boldsymbol{x}) + f_2(\boldsymbol{z}) \\ \text{subject to} \quad & \boldsymbol{A}\boldsymbol{x} + \boldsymbol{B}\boldsymbol{z} = \boldsymbol{b}, \end{aligned} \tag{3.48}$$

where f_1 and f_2 are both convex but may be nonsmooth. Although this problem can be solved via the Douglas–Rachford splitting, we will introduce another paradigm for solving this problem.

We can obtain the Lagrangian dual problem as

$$\begin{aligned} & \underset{\boldsymbol{\lambda}}{\text{maximize}} \quad \min_{\boldsymbol{x},\boldsymbol{z}} f_1(\boldsymbol{x}) + f_2(\boldsymbol{z}) + < \boldsymbol{\lambda}, \boldsymbol{A}\boldsymbol{x} + \boldsymbol{B}\boldsymbol{z} - \boldsymbol{b} >, \\ \Leftrightarrow \ & \underset{\boldsymbol{\lambda}}{\text{maximize}} \quad -f_1^*(-\boldsymbol{A}^\mathsf{T}\boldsymbol{\lambda}) - f_2^*(-\boldsymbol{B}^\mathsf{T}\boldsymbol{\lambda})) - < \boldsymbol{\lambda}, \boldsymbol{b} >, \\ \Leftrightarrow \ & \underset{\boldsymbol{\lambda}}{\text{minimize}} \quad f_1^*(-\boldsymbol{A}^\mathsf{T}\boldsymbol{\lambda}) + f_2^*(-\boldsymbol{B}^\mathsf{T}\boldsymbol{\lambda})) + < \boldsymbol{\lambda}, \boldsymbol{b} > . \end{aligned} \tag{3.49}$$

The proximal point method for solving this dual problem is given by

$$\boldsymbol{\lambda}^{t+1} = \arg\min_{\boldsymbol{\lambda}} \left\{ f_1^*(-\boldsymbol{A}^\mathsf{T}\boldsymbol{\lambda}) + f_2^*(-\boldsymbol{B}^\mathsf{T}\boldsymbol{\lambda})) + < \boldsymbol{\lambda}, \boldsymbol{b} > + \frac{1}{2\rho}\|\boldsymbol{\lambda} - \boldsymbol{\lambda}^t\|_2^2 \right\}. \tag{3.50}$$

This is equivalent to the augmented Lagrangian method (or the method of multipliers)

$$\begin{aligned} (\boldsymbol{x}^{t+1}, \boldsymbol{z}^{t+1}) &= \arg\min_{\boldsymbol{x},\boldsymbol{z}} \left\{ f_1(\boldsymbol{x}) + f_2(\boldsymbol{z}) + \frac{\rho}{2}\left\| \boldsymbol{A}\boldsymbol{x} + \boldsymbol{B}\boldsymbol{z} - \boldsymbol{b} + \frac{1}{\rho}\boldsymbol{\lambda}^t \right\| \right\}, \\ \boldsymbol{\lambda}^{t+1} &= \boldsymbol{\lambda}^t + \rho(\boldsymbol{A}\boldsymbol{x}^{t+1} + \boldsymbol{B}\boldsymbol{z}^{t+1} - \boldsymbol{b}), \end{aligned} \tag{3.51}$$

where $\rho > 0$ is the penalty parameter. However, the primal update step is often as expensive as solving the original problem, and minimization of $\boldsymbol{z}$ cannot be carried out separately.

Rather than computing an exact primal estimate for the augmented Lagrangian method, we can minimize $\boldsymbol{x}$ and $\boldsymbol{z}$ sequentially via alternating minimization:

$$\begin{aligned} \boldsymbol{x}^{t+1} &= \arg\min_{\boldsymbol{x}} \left\{ f_1(\boldsymbol{x}) + \frac{\rho}{2} \left\| \boldsymbol{A}\boldsymbol{x} + \boldsymbol{B}\boldsymbol{z}^t - \boldsymbol{b} + \frac{1}{\rho}\boldsymbol{\lambda}^t \right\| \right\}, \\ \boldsymbol{z}^{t+1} &= \arg\min_{\boldsymbol{z}} \left\{ f_2(\boldsymbol{z}) + \frac{\rho}{2} \left\| \boldsymbol{A}\boldsymbol{x}^{t+1} + \boldsymbol{B}\boldsymbol{z} - \boldsymbol{b} + \frac{1}{\rho}\boldsymbol{\lambda}^t \right\| \right\}, \\ \boldsymbol{\lambda}^{t+1} &= \boldsymbol{\lambda}^t + \rho(\boldsymbol{A}\boldsymbol{x}^{t+1} + \boldsymbol{B}\boldsymbol{z}^{t+1} - \boldsymbol{b}), \end{aligned} \tag{3.52}$$

which is called the alternating direction method of multipliers (ADMM) [7]. The ρ controls relative priority between primal and dual convergence. The ADMM method is useful if updating $\boldsymbol{x}^t$ and updating $\boldsymbol{z}^t$ are both inexpensive and blends the benefits of dual decomposition and the augmented Lagrangian method. The roles of $\boldsymbol{x}$ and $\boldsymbol{z}$ are almost symmetric. ADMM is slow to converge to high accuracy and often converges to modest accuracy within a few tens of iterations, which is sufficient for many large-scale applications.

3.1.10 Stochastic gradient method

The stochastic programming problem can generally be written as

$$\underset{\boldsymbol{x}}{\text{minimize}} \quad F(\boldsymbol{x}) = \mathbb{E}[f(\boldsymbol{x}; \boldsymbol{\xi})], \tag{3.53}$$

where $\boldsymbol{\xi}$ is random, and $\mathbb{E}[\cdot]$ is expectation. We suppose that $f(\cdot; \boldsymbol{\xi})$ is convex for every $\boldsymbol{\xi}$. Hence F is convex and can present the expected risk or population risk. Particularly, the empirical risk minimization is one significant stochastic programming problem, which is an essential mathematical problem for the AI algorithm in Chapter 2. The empirical risk minimization problem is presented as

$$\underset{\boldsymbol{x}}{\text{minimize}} \quad F(\boldsymbol{x}) := \tfrac{1}{N} \textstyle\sum_{n=1}^{N} f(\boldsymbol{x}; \{\boldsymbol{a}_n, y_n\}), \tag{3.54}$$

where $\{\boldsymbol{a}_n, y_n\}_{n=1}^N$ are N random samples, and $f(\boldsymbol{x}; \boldsymbol{a}_n, y_n)$ is known as the objective function, for example, the quadratic loss $f(\boldsymbol{x}; \boldsymbol{a}_n, y_n) = (\boldsymbol{a}_n^\mathsf{T}\boldsymbol{x} - y_n)^2$. If we choose index $j \sim \mathsf{Unif}(1, 2, \ldots, N)$ uniformly at random, then we have $F(\boldsymbol{x}) = \mathbb{E}_j[f(\boldsymbol{x}; \{\boldsymbol{a}_j, y_j\})]$.

Generally, the gradient descent method can be employed in problem (3.53), and the update formula is

$$\boldsymbol{x}^{t+1} = \boldsymbol{x}^t - \eta_t \mathbb{E}[\nabla_{\boldsymbol{x}} f(\boldsymbol{x}; \boldsymbol{\xi})]. \tag{3.55}$$

However, the distribution of $\boldsymbol{\xi}$ may be unknown, and the evaluation of high-dimensional expectation is often expensive even if the distribution is known. Therefore the stochastic gradient descent (SGD) is proposed to obtain the stochastic approximation of gradients. The update formula is

$$\boldsymbol{x}^{t+1} = \boldsymbol{x}^t - \eta_t \boldsymbol{g}(\boldsymbol{x}^t; \boldsymbol{\xi}^t), \tag{3.56}$$

where $\boldsymbol{g}(\boldsymbol{x}^t; \boldsymbol{\xi}^t)$ is a unbiased estimate of $\nabla F(\boldsymbol{x}^t)$, that is,

$$\mathbb{E}[\boldsymbol{g}(\boldsymbol{x}^t; \boldsymbol{\xi})] = \nabla F(\boldsymbol{x}^t). \tag{3.57}$$

Thus SGD is a stochastic algorithm for finding a critical point $\boldsymbol{x}$ obeying $\nabla F(\boldsymbol{x}) = \mathbb{E}[\boldsymbol{g}(\boldsymbol{x}; \boldsymbol{\xi})] = \boldsymbol{0}$.

Particularly, we consider the solution of empirical risk minimization (3.54) through SGD. In each iteration, we choose index j uniformly at random and execute the update formula

$$\boldsymbol{x}^{t+1} = \boldsymbol{x}^t - \eta_t \nabla_{\boldsymbol{x}} f(\boldsymbol{x}^t; \{\boldsymbol{a}_j, y_j\}), \tag{3.58}$$

which is efficient and cheap to exploits information [8]. It is worth noting that the step size (a.k.a. the learning rate) can be constant or selected by line search methods in Section 3.1.1, and the convergence can be accelerated by the heavy-ball method or Nesterov's method in Section 3.1.6.

3.2. Second-order methods

The first-order gradient methods just rely on the function value and the first-order derivative. In this section, we summarize the second-order methods to constitute the descent direction according to first- and second-order derivatives, such as Newton's method. Generally, it is expensive to calculate the second-order derivative of the objective function. Therefore several methods are proposed to approximate the second-order derivative with cheap calculation costs, such as the quasi-Newton method, Gauss–Newton method, and natural gradient method. These methods are presented as follows.

3.2.1 Newton's method

For the unconstrained optimization problem

$$\underset{\boldsymbol{x}}{\text{minimize}} \quad f(\boldsymbol{x}), \tag{3.59}$$

Newton's method utilizes the first- and second-order derivatives to approximate the objective function. The second-order Taylor expansion of the objective function $f(\boldsymbol{x})$ at point $\boldsymbol{x}^t$ is

$$f(\boldsymbol{x}) \approx f(\boldsymbol{x}^t) + \nabla f(\boldsymbol{x}^t)(\boldsymbol{x} - \boldsymbol{x}^t) + \frac{1}{2}(\boldsymbol{x} - \boldsymbol{x}^t)^{\mathsf{T}} \nabla^2 f(\boldsymbol{x}^t)(\boldsymbol{x} - \boldsymbol{x}^t), \tag{3.60}$$

where $\nabla^2 f(\boldsymbol{x})$ is called the Hessian matrix of $f(\boldsymbol{x}^t)$, that is, $\nabla^2 f(\boldsymbol{x})_{ij} = \frac{\partial^2 f(\boldsymbol{x})}{\partial x_i \partial x_j}$. The essential condition for the extremum point of $f(\boldsymbol{x})$ is $\nabla f(\boldsymbol{x}) = 0$. Thus the first-order derivative of second-order approximation (3.60) is

$$\nabla f(\boldsymbol{x}) = \nabla f(\boldsymbol{x}^t) + \nabla^2 f(\boldsymbol{x}^t)(\boldsymbol{x} - \boldsymbol{x}^t) = 0. \tag{3.61}$$

The update rule of Newton's method is obtained by solving equation (3.61), which can be presented as

$$\boldsymbol{x}^{t+1} = \boldsymbol{x}^t - (\nabla^2 f(\boldsymbol{x}^t))^{-1} \nabla f(\boldsymbol{x}^t). \tag{3.62}$$

Newton's method can achieve quadratic convergence.

3.2.2 Quasi-Newton method

Generally, Newton's method requires storing and inverting Hessian matrix $\nabla^2 f(\boldsymbol{x}^t)$, which may lead to enormous computation cost and prohibitive storage requirement. Therefore the quasi-Newton method is proposed to approximate the inverted Hessian matrix $(\nabla^2 f(\boldsymbol{x}^t))^{-1}$.

We denote the update formula as

$$\boldsymbol{x}^{t+1} = \boldsymbol{x}^t - \eta_t \boldsymbol{H}_t \nabla f(\boldsymbol{x}^t), \tag{3.63}$$

where $\boldsymbol{H}_t$ is the surrogate of $(\nabla^2 f(\boldsymbol{x}^t))^{-1}$. It is challenging to find an approximation of $(\nabla^2 f(\boldsymbol{x}^t))^{-1}$ by using only the gradient information and limited memory to achieve superlinear convergence.

From Taylor's formula for $f(\boldsymbol{x})$ at point $\boldsymbol{x}^{t+1}$ and its derivative, we obtain the secant equation as

$$\boldsymbol{H}_{t+1} \left(\nabla f(\boldsymbol{x}^{t+1}) - \nabla f(\boldsymbol{x}^t) \right) = (\boldsymbol{x}^{t+1} - \boldsymbol{x}^t). \tag{3.64}$$

The Broyden–Fletcher–Goldfarb–Shanno (BFGS) method is proposed to generate $\boldsymbol{H}_{t+1}$ in addition to the secant equation, which is illustrated in Algorithm 7. The BFGS method does not need to solve linear systems, invert matrices, and specify initialization, which can approximate the inverse Hessian at $\boldsymbol{x}^0$.

Algorithm 7: BFGS method for quasi-Newton method.

for $t = 0, 1, \ldots$ **do**
  $\boldsymbol{x}^{t+1} = \boldsymbol{x}^t - \eta_t \boldsymbol{H}_t \nabla f(\boldsymbol{x}^t)$.
  $\boldsymbol{s}_t = \boldsymbol{x}^{t+1} - \boldsymbol{x}^t$, $\boldsymbol{y}_t = \nabla f(\boldsymbol{x}^{t+1}) - \nabla f(\boldsymbol{x}^t)$, $\rho_t = \frac{1}{\boldsymbol{y}_t^\top \boldsymbol{s}_t}$.
  $\boldsymbol{H}_{t+1} = (\boldsymbol{I} - \rho_t \boldsymbol{s}_t \boldsymbol{y}_t^\top)\boldsymbol{H}_t(\boldsymbol{I} - \rho_t \boldsymbol{s}_t \boldsymbol{y}_t^\top) + \rho_t \boldsymbol{s}_t \boldsymbol{s}_t^\top$.
end for

3.2.3 Gauss–Newton method

The Gauss–Newton method is a particular case of Newton's method, which is used to solve nonlinear least squares problems.

We denote the data points as $\{(\boldsymbol{a}_1, y_1), (\boldsymbol{a}_2, y_2), \ldots, (\boldsymbol{a}_N, y_N)\}$, where $\boldsymbol{a} \in \mathbb{R}^d$. A nonlinear function $f(\boldsymbol{x}; \boldsymbol{a})$ needs to be estimated to fit the N data points. Therefore the least squares problem can be written as

$$\underset{\boldsymbol{a}}{\text{minimize}} \quad l(\boldsymbol{x}) = \textstyle\sum_{n=1}^N \|f(\boldsymbol{x}; \boldsymbol{a}_n) - y_n\|_2^2. \tag{3.65}$$

Then we can calculate the derivative of x_j as follows:

$$\frac{\partial l(\boldsymbol{x})}{\partial x_j} = \sum_{n=1}^N 2(f(\boldsymbol{x}; \boldsymbol{a}_n) - y_n)\frac{\partial f(\boldsymbol{x}; \boldsymbol{a}_n)}{\partial x_j}. \tag{3.66}$$

We denote the Jacobi matrix as $\boldsymbol{J}(\boldsymbol{x})$, where $J_{ij} = \frac{\partial f(\boldsymbol{x}; \boldsymbol{a}_i)}{x_j}$. Besides, we define the vector $\boldsymbol{r}(\boldsymbol{x})$, where $\boldsymbol{r}_i = f(\boldsymbol{x}; \boldsymbol{a}_i) - y_i$. Obviously, (3.66) can be rewritten as

$$\nabla l(\boldsymbol{x}) = 2\boldsymbol{J}(\boldsymbol{x})^\top \boldsymbol{r}(\boldsymbol{x}). \tag{3.67}$$

Moreover, the Hessian matrix of $l(\boldsymbol{x})$ is given by

$$\frac{\partial^2 l(\boldsymbol{x})}{\partial x_j \partial x_j} = 2\sum_{n=1}^N \left(\frac{\partial f(\boldsymbol{x}; \boldsymbol{a}_n)}{\partial x_i}\frac{\partial f(\boldsymbol{x}; \boldsymbol{a}_n)}{\partial x_j} + (f(\boldsymbol{x}; \boldsymbol{a}_n) - y_n)\frac{\partial^2 f(\boldsymbol{x}; \boldsymbol{a}_n)}{\partial x_j \partial x_j} \right). \tag{3.68}$$

We have

$$\nabla^2 l(\boldsymbol{x}) = 2\left(\boldsymbol{J}(\boldsymbol{x})^\top \boldsymbol{J}(\boldsymbol{x}) + \boldsymbol{S}(\boldsymbol{x})\right), \tag{3.69}$$

where $\boldsymbol{S}(\boldsymbol{x})_{ij} = \sum_{n=1}^N (f(\boldsymbol{x}; \boldsymbol{a}_n) - y_n)\frac{\partial^2 f(\boldsymbol{x}; \boldsymbol{a}_n)}{\partial x_j \partial x_j}$. Finally, substituting the first-order derivative (3.67) and second-order derivative to update the rule of

Newton's method (3.62), we have

$$x^{t+1} = x^t - (\nabla^2 f(x^t))^{-1}\nabla f(x^t) = x^t - \left(J(x^t)^\top J(x^t) + S(x^t)\right)^{-1} J(x^t)^\top r(x^t). \tag{3.70}$$

Generally, the calculation of $S(x)$, which contains the second-order derivative of $f(x; a)$, is ignored. Finally, the update rule of the Gauss–Newton method is obtained as

$$x^{t+1} = x^t - \left(J(x^t)^\top J(x^t))\right)^{-1} \cdot J(x^t)^\top r(x^t), \tag{3.71}$$

which is efficient to solve nonlinear least squares problems.

3.2.4 Natural gradient method

According to the fundamental gradient descent method (3.6), the descent direction is denoted as $d^t = -\nabla f(x^t)$, which is based on the fact that the variation of objective function and optimization variables are measured in the Euclidean space, that is, $\|x\|_2^2 = \sum_{i=1}^d x_i^2$. However, the metric that measures the variation of probability attributes caused by changes in parameters is improper in the Euclidean space, that is, the variations of $p(x; w)$ and $p(x; w + \Delta w)$, where $p(x; w)$ is the probability distribution with respect to parameters w. Therefore the distance of probability distributions can be measured by the KL divergence as

$$D_{\text{KL}}(p(x; w)||p(x; w + \Delta w)) = \mathbb{E}_{p(x;w)}\left[\frac{p(x; w)}{p(x; w + \Delta w)}\right]. \tag{3.72}$$

The gradient descent is called the natural gradient method when the distance is measured by the KL divergence [9].

To understand the natural gradient method, the Riemannian metric is introduced to measure the distance between w and $w + \Delta w$, that is,

$$|\Delta w|^2 = \sum_{i,j} g_{ij}\Delta w_i \Delta w_j = \Delta w^\top \mathbf{G} \Delta w, \tag{3.73}$$

where Δw_i is the ith entry of Δw, and $\mathbf{G}$ is a specified matrix. If $\mathbf{G} = I$, then the Riemannian metric degenerates to the Euclidean distance. Therefore the Riemannian space can be regarded as the generalization of Euclidean space.

The natural gradient method is not simply optimizing parameters by learning rate, but using the optimization effect. Therefore, in each step, we will solve the following subproblem:

$$\begin{aligned} \underset{\Delta w}{\text{minimize}} \quad & l(\boldsymbol{w}+\Delta \boldsymbol{w}) \\ \text{subject to} \quad & |\Delta \boldsymbol{w}| \leq \varepsilon. \end{aligned} \tag{3.74}$$

By substituting (3.73) and the first-order Taylor expansion $l(\boldsymbol{w}+\Delta\boldsymbol{w}) = l(\boldsymbol{w}) + \nabla l(\boldsymbol{w})\Delta\boldsymbol{w}$ the Lagrangian dual problem of (3.74) is presented as

$$\underset{\Delta w}{\text{minimize}} \quad l(\boldsymbol{w}) + \nabla l(\boldsymbol{w})\Delta\boldsymbol{w} + \lambda(\tfrac{1}{2}\Delta\boldsymbol{w}^{\mathsf{T}}\mathbf{G}(\boldsymbol{w})\Delta\boldsymbol{w} - \varepsilon), \tag{3.75}$$

where λ is a Lagrange multiplier. Calculating the first-order derivative of the objective function in (3.75) and obtaining the zero point, we have

$$\Delta\boldsymbol{w} = -\frac{1}{\lambda}\mathbf{G}^{-1}(\boldsymbol{w})\nabla l(\boldsymbol{w}), \tag{3.76}$$

where $\frac{1}{\lambda}$ can be seen as the step size. Therefore the update formula of the natural gradient method can be written as

$$\boldsymbol{w}^{t+1} = \boldsymbol{w}^{t} - \frac{1}{\lambda}\mathbf{G}^{-1}(\boldsymbol{w}^{t})\nabla l(\boldsymbol{w}^{t}). \tag{3.77}$$

For instance, we aim to find an optimal $\boldsymbol{w}^*$, which approximates the unknown natural probability distribution $q(\boldsymbol{x})$ by the estimated probability distribution $p(\boldsymbol{x};\boldsymbol{w})$. This is a basic AI problem. The commonly used loss function is the negative cross entropy

$$l(\boldsymbol{w}) = -\mathbb{E}_{q(\boldsymbol{x})}\left[\log p(\boldsymbol{x};\boldsymbol{w})\right] = D_{\mathrm{KL}}(q(\boldsymbol{x})||p(\boldsymbol{x};\boldsymbol{w})) - \mathbb{E}_{q(\boldsymbol{x})}\left[\log q(\boldsymbol{x})\right], \tag{3.78}$$

where $-\mathbb{E}_{q(\boldsymbol{x})}\left[\log q(\boldsymbol{x})\right]$ is a constant.

Therefore the second-order derivative of objective function is

$$\nabla^2 l(\boldsymbol{w}) = -\mathbb{E}_{q(\boldsymbol{x})}\left[\frac{\partial^2 \log p(\boldsymbol{x};\boldsymbol{w})}{\partial^2 \boldsymbol{w}}\right], \tag{3.79}$$

which is impossible to calculate because of the unknown natural probability distribution $q(\boldsymbol{x})$.

The Fisher information matrix is proposed to approximate the second-order derivative as

$$\begin{aligned} \mathbf{G}(\boldsymbol{w}) &= -\mathbb{E}_{p(\boldsymbol{x};\boldsymbol{w})}\left[\frac{\partial^2 \log p(\boldsymbol{x};\boldsymbol{w})}{\partial^2 \boldsymbol{w}}\right] \\ &= -\mathbb{E}_{p(\boldsymbol{x};\boldsymbol{w})}\left[\left(\frac{\partial \log p(\boldsymbol{x};\boldsymbol{w})}{\partial \boldsymbol{w}}\right)\left(\frac{\partial \log p(\boldsymbol{x};\boldsymbol{w})}{\partial \boldsymbol{w}}\right)^{\mathsf{T}}\right], \end{aligned} \tag{3.80}$$

which is equivalent to (3.79) when the parametric distributing $p(\boldsymbol{x}; \boldsymbol{w})$ ideally approaches the true distribution $q(\boldsymbol{x})$.

3.3. Summary

In this chapter, we summarized various optimization algorithms to solve different optimization problems. The algorithms are classified as first- and second-order algorithms according to the use of different derivative information. In the following chapters, we design optimization algorithms based on the algorithms in this chapter, which are expected to achieve excellent performance and convergence.

References

[1] S. Boyd, S.P. Boyd, L. Vandenberghe, Convex Optimization, Camb. University Press, Mar. 2004.
[2] A. Beck, First-Order Methods in Optimization, SIAM, Oct. 2017.
[3] S. Bubeck, et al., Convex optimization: algorithms and complexity, Found. Trends Mach. Learn. 8 (May 2015) 231–357.
[4] W. Su, S.P. Boyd, E.J. Candes, A differential equation for modeling Nesterov's accelerated gradient method: theory and insights, in: Proc. Neural Inf. Process. Syst. (NIPS), vol. 14, Dec. 2014, pp. 2510–2518.
[5] A. Beck, M. Teboulle, A fast iterative shrinkage-thresholding algorithm for linear inverse problems, SIAM J. Imaging Sci. 2 (Mar. 2009) 183–202.
[6] A. Beck, M. Teboulle, Smoothing and first order methods: a unified framework, SIAM J. Optim. 22 (Jun. 2012) 557–580.
[7] S.P. Boyd, N. Parikh, E. Chu, B. Peleato, J. Eckstein, Distributed optimization and statistical learning via the alternating direction method of multipliers, Found. Trends Mach. Learn. 3 (May. 2011) 1–122.
[8] L. Bottou, F.E. Curtis, J. Nocedal, Optimization methods for large-scale machine learning, SIAM Rev. 60 (May 2018) 223–311.
[9] S.-I. Amari, Natural gradient works efficiently in learning, Neural Comput. 10 (Feb. 1998) 251–276.

Summary

References

CHAPTER FOUR

Mobile edge AI

4.1. Overview

One of the fundamental differences between cloud AI and mobile edge AI is the limited resources available at edge nodes. Therefore a number of frameworks have been proposed to support efficient mobile edge AI. One of the most straightforward approaches to perform edge AI inference tasks is deploying AI models on the devices of end users, which does not incur any communication costs during inference. It is called *on-device inference* whose design principles are summarized in Chapter 4.2.1. When the local resources are insufficient for on-device inference, computation offloading is a promising technique that offloads the inference tasks in part or as a whole from end devices to proximate edge servers. The design principle of *edge inference via computation offloading* is summarized in Chapter 4.2.2. Training an AI model is much more resource intensive and often requires pooling the resources of distributed edge nodes connected with bandwidth-limited communication links. The methodologies for model training at mobile network edges vary according to the distributed structure of data and model parameters. Thus it can be categorized as *data partition-based edge training* framework and *model partition-based edge training* framework, which will be summarized in Chapter 4.3. Edge AI systems are also characterized by coded computing paradigms, which are included in Chapter 4.4.

4.2. Edge inference

4.2.1 On-device inference

Collecting data from end devices to be processed by the intelligent engine at the remote cloud center is usually not able to support the ubiquitous intelligent services with low-latency and privacy requirements. On-device inference makes it possible to timely respond to the environment and privacy-sensitive behaviors irrespective of cloud connectivity. The main difficulty of achieving on-device intelligence is due to the limited resources of a single device, for example, computing power and storage size, whereas task inference is usually resource intensive [1]. The hardwares of end devices are usually limited and fixed, whereas the hardwares of cloud servers

Mobile Edge Artificial Intelligence
https://doi.org/10.1016/B978-0-12-823817-2.00013-9

can be easily upgraded to have more memory, powerful CPU cores, and GPU cards. A closely related concept is called *TinyML* [2], whose goal is to push machine learning inference to ultralow-power devices.

To unleash the full potential of on-device inference, design of both hardware and software is required. On one hand, the AI models will be tailored to fit the stringent constraints of end devices. The model size and computational complexity should be much smaller than that in cloud AI. Therefore lightweight models will be designed while guaranteeing the performance. A number of researches focus on the design of resource-efficient machine learning algorithms [3] and compressing a large AI model into a smaller one [4], which can be deployed on end devices with limited storage size and computing power. Efforts in hardware design to facilitate inference include the designs on the next generation of general purpose MCUs (microcontroller units) [5] and on hardwares for low-power inference and specific tasks [6]. We will provide a representative example of pruning a neural network to a much smaller one in Chapter 5.

4.2.2 Edge inference via computation offloading

For resource-constrained mobile devices, an intuitive approach for edge inference is to push computational tasks to proximal edge servers to achieve low-latency inference [7]. This is called *server-based edge inference*, which has attracted extensive research attentions [8,9]. Server-based edge inference is often adopted by Internet-of-Things (IoT) devices, which are incapable of performing local computations. Another approach is to offload partial computational task to the edge server and perform a part of computations locally, which is called *device-edge joint inference*. It is achieved by splitting the AI model into two parts, which are performed at and distributed to deploy mobile device and edge server, respectively, for privacy and latency concerns.

4.2.2.1 Server-based edge inference

An illustrative structure of server-based edge inference is presented in Fig. 4.1. For this approach, the entire AI model is deployed on the edge server, and each mobile device simply uploads the raw input data to the proximal edge server. The edge server performs inference tasks based on the trained model and transmits the results back to mobile devices. It is particularly suitable for IoT devices that have limited resources. To achieve efficient inference, it is critical to improve the communication efficiency of uplink input data transmission and delivery of downlink results.

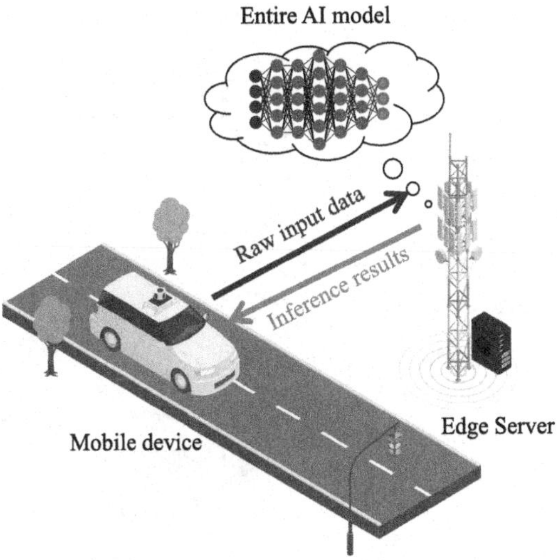

Figure 4.1 A representative structure of server-based computation offloading edge inference system.

For uplink input data transmission, an effective approach is reducing the required communication bandwidth. For example, Chen et al. [10] proposed to send only key frames for object detection. Liu et al. [11] proposed to optimize the image compression method from the perspective of image recognition task instead of human visual system (e.g., JPEG compression). Furthermore, some works considered the joint data encoding and transmission for inference tasks, such as Chinchali et al. [12] for vision tasks and Kurka et al. [13] for image retrieval. For downlink transmission, a number of works have been proposed to study cooperative transmission strategies to improve communication efficiency. We will present a typical approach in Chapter 7, which offloads each inference task to multiple servers that transmit inference results via cooperative downlink transmission [8]. Hua et al. [9] proposed to apply reconfigurable intelligent surface (RIS) [14], which is a cost-effective approach to adjust wireless signal propagation environments, to improve the communication efficiency of edge inference systems.

4.2.2.2 Device-edge joint inference

Another important strategy of computation offloading-based edge inference considers the hierarchical structure of computational tasks. In particular, by splitting the tasks and offloading a portion of tasks to edge servers the inference results could be obtained by the partial model parameters and

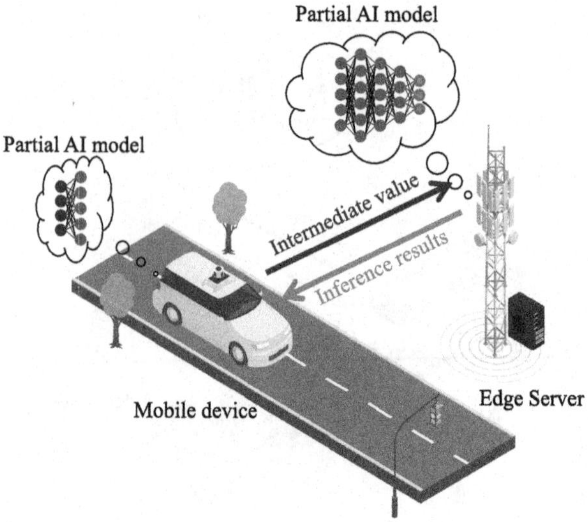

Figure 4.2 A representative structure of device-edge joint inference system.

the input intermediate values from mobile devices. This is called device-edge joint inference. The motivation of device-edge joint inference is to simultaneously take advantages of the low latency of local computations on device and powerful computational resources of edge servers. A representative structure of device-edge joint inference is splitting a deep learning model into two parts and deploy the first few layers on end devices, as illustrated in Fig. 4.2. A class of methods [15,16] have focused on determining the split point of a trained deep neural network (DNN), taking into account transmission latency, energy consumption, storage, computation time, and so on. In addition, it was found that the first few layers of neural networks may produce inference results with satisfactory performance [17]. Thus there is another class of methods adopting the early exit technique to achieve low-latency inference [18,19]. There are also works [20,21] considering encoded transmission and data pruning methods to reduce the required communication bandwidth of uploading intermediate values computed by the local devices.

4.3. Edge training

In addition to directly train the model on a single edge device or a single edge server, distributed edge training systems are recently proposed to pool the distributed resources across a fleet of edge nodes. We categorize distributed edge training systems into two kinds, *data partition-based edge training* and *model partition-based edge training*, which are introduced in the following.

4.3.1 Data partition-based edge training

We call a distributed training system a data partition-based edge training system when each participating node holds only a subset of the training data and all model parameters locally. In such systems the AI model is usually trained by on-device local computations and periodical local updates exchange. This framework is compatible with many popular model architectures and scales up for large number of participating nodes and massive data. However, it requires a large-sized memory to store all model parameters (e.g., all weights of a DNN). Due to the existence of a center node, there are distributed and decentralized system modes for data partition-based edge training systems, as illustrated in Fig. 4.3.

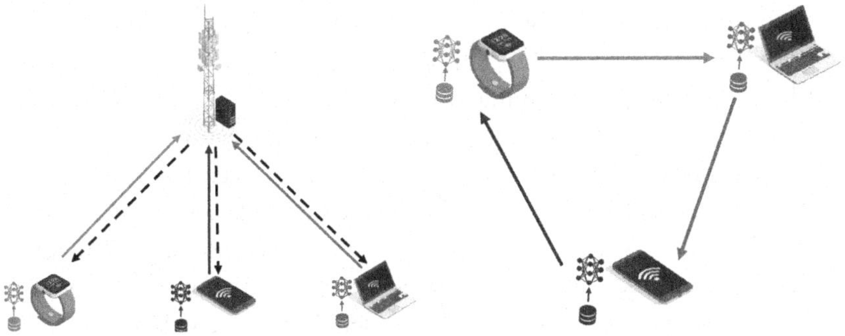

(a) Distributed mode **(b)** Decentralized mode

Figure 4.3 Two different system modes of edge training systems.

4.3.1.1 Distributed mode

In distributed mode the center node behaves as a coordinating center and periodically aggregates local updates from all edge devices as illustrated in Fig. 4.3a. Researchers from Google defined it as *federated learning* [22,23], that is, coordinating a fleet of nodes, each with a subset of data instances to train a global AI model. We summarize the main directions of existing researches as follows.

- **Fast model aggregation:** To improve the communication efficiency of aggregation, a number of over-the-air computation-based approaches for fast model aggregation have recently been proposed [24–26]. Over-the-air computation [27] can efficiently aggregate distributed updates by exploiting the signal superposition property of a wireless multiple access channel. We will provide a detailed procedure of over-the-air computation-based fast model aggregation approach in Chapter 8. The aggregation frequency should be carefully designed [28,29] to achieve efficient training in consideration of the computation capability of each device and the communication bandwidth for data aggregation.
- **Resource allocation:** Optimizing the allocation strategy of wireless resources can also improve the performance of edge training. For example, Abad et al. [30] considered the hierarchical federated learning scheme to reduce the aggregation frequency from devices to the aggregation center. Yang et al. [31] designed the resource allocation strategy to weigh the trade-off between delay and energy consumption.
- **Data reshuffling:** Data shuffling is an effective way to improve the statistical performance of distributed machine learning. When the data across devices are non-IID, it brings considerable statistical gains to randomly reshuffling the training data every few iterations on devices [32]. However, it also brings overwhelming communication overhead. To address this issue, coded shuffling schemes have been proposed for efficient data exchange. Given a prespecified data placement rule, Lee et al. [33] proposed an index coding scheme for data shuffling. The works of [34,35] further studied the coding schemes with relaxed data placement strategies; Song et al. [34] considered that a new data instance is required by multiple devices (no more than a given number $c > 0$), and Jiang et al. [35] further considered that it is acceptable to update the data at only a part of devices instead of all.
- **Straggler mitigation:** Straggler mitigation is a critical problem since the training procedure may be severely slowed down by some stragglers. There are a line of works studying the coded computation approaches against stragglers. For example, Tandon et al. [36] proposed to encode the computed gradients according to the number of stragglers to mitigate stragglers. Maity et al. [37] proposed to encode the second moment with low-density parity-check (LDPC) code for robust gradient descent to mitigate stragglers.

4.3.1.2 Decentralized mode

Decentralized mode features with a number of edge devices directly exchanging information with each other. To our best knowledge, gossip communication [38] is a well-known protocol for supporting decentralized information exchange by evoking a random node as a local center node. After collecting updates from its neighbors, the local center node will broadcast the aggregated model to all its neighbor nodes. Different network topologies are studied and designed in many works [39,40].

4.3.2 Model partition-based edge training

In addition to data partition-based systems, there is another line of works studying model partition-based edge training systems, where an AI model is partitioned and distributedly deployed across multiple nodes. Each node only holds a subset of model parameters, and the entire model is collaboratively optimized. We summarize model partition-based edge training systems as the following two main types.

- **Model partition across device and edge server:** Users may be reluctant to expose their private data to edge servers, which are usually owned by service providers. In these cases, deploying a few layers on devices could protect the privacy of users' data and only exchange intermediate values with the edge server [41]. Wang et al. [42] proposed ARDEN, which is a partition approach in consideration of privacy and performance with fixed parameters on device and differential privacy technique.
- **Vertical federated learning across data providers:** For many industrial applications, data silos across different companies become one of the main bottleneck for providing elaborate intelligent services [43]. Service providers with vertically partitioned data (i.e., each provider holds different data attributes for the same users) usually have strong motivations to cooperate with each other to improve the performance of their intelligent services without revealing data to others. To address the data isolation issues, a line of works have studied popular AI model training procedure and proposed vertical federated learning frameworks for algorithms including *k*-means [44], linear regression [45], support vector machine (SVM) [46], decision tree [47], logistic regression [48,49], and XGBoost [50].

4.4. Coded computing

In addition to the AI systems mentioned above, there are also some other system architectures from a different point of view. There are edge AI systems benefiting from coded computing techniques, for example, MapReduce [51]. MapReduce is able to speed up computations of machine learning model training [52] and inference [53] procedures. Accomplishing a task with MapReduce-like framework usually consists of three phases: map phase, shuffle phase, and reduce phase, as shown in Fig. 6.1. In the map phase, each node computes intermediate values by simultaneously functioning on local data. In the shuffle phase, all nodes exchange intermediate values with each other. In the reduce phase, each node computes the output based on its collected intermediate values.

Coding techniques [54] are recently rediscovered to be beneficial for improving the efficiency of MapReduce-like distributed computing systems. Communication efficiency is one of the main bottlenecks for efficient distributed computing, for which a number of researches have studied the coded techniques for fast data shuffling. As far as we know, coded shuffling was first considered in the work of [55], which studied the wireline system. Li et al. [56] considered the distributed computing system with a wireless access point served as the coordinating center for K distributed devices. Yang et al. [53] further studied the achievable data rates of linear coding schemes for wireless MapReduce by taking the channel state information into consideration. Li et al. [57] proposed to reduce the communication overhead of the wireless MapReduce system without a coordinating center.

It is also found that coding techniques can be used to mitigate the effect of stragglers for the distributed computing system. The basic idea is to exploit the redundant computing to guarantee that the computing result could be reconstructed from most nodes. The authors in [58] proposed to utilize coding theory to address the straggler problem in a wireline distributed computing system. Coding techniques for wireless systems were then studied in [59,60]. Despite the fact that most of these works focused on linear computations, the work of [61] proposed a coding scheme to address the straggler problem of distributed nonlinear computation problems.

We will present a representative example of coding for wireless MapReduce system in Chapter 6, which provides a low-rank optimization approach to improve achieved data rates in the data shuffle phase by modeling the interference alignment condition.

4.5. Summary

In this chapter, we summarized the mobile edge AI frameworks from different perspectives. We hope the discussions in this chapter can help the readers quickly dive into mobile edge AI, which is an important and active research area. It can be found that data availability and the AI task structure have strong impact on the design of edge AI systems. Numerous efforts have been made to tackle the constraints of storage, computation, communication, privacy, and so on for different system architectures. Therefore, in Parts 2 and 3 of this book, we elaborate some representative designs of mobile edge AI, including edge inference and edge training systems.

References

[1] S. Dhar, J. Guo, J. Liu, S. Tripathi, U. Kurup, M. Shah, On-device machine learning: an algorithms and learning theory perspective, preprint, arXiv:1911.00623, 2019.
[2] C.R. Banbury, V.J. Reddi, M. Lam, W. Fu, A. Fazel, J. Holleman, X. Huang, R. Hurtado, D. Kanter, A. Lokhmotov, et al., Benchmarking TinyML systems: challenges and direction, preprint, arXiv:2003.04821, 2020.
[3] A. Kumar, S. Goyal, M. Varma, Resource-efficient machine learning in 2 KB RAM for the internet of things, in: International Conference on Machine Learning, 2017, pp. 1935–1944.
[4] S. Han, H. Mao, W.J. Dally, Deep compression: compressing deep neural networks with pruning, trained quantization and Huffman coding, in: Proc. Int. Conf. Learn. Representations (ICLR), 2016.
[5] E. Flamand, D. Rossi, F. Conti, I. Loi, A. Pullini, F. Rotenberg, L. Benini, Gap-8: a risc-v soc for ai at the edge of the iot, in: 2018 IEEE 29th International Conference on Application-Specific Systems, Architectures and Processors (ASAP), IEEE, 2018, pp. 1–4.
[6] B. Moons, D. Bankman, L. Yang, B. Murmann, M. Verhelst, Binareye: an always-on energy-accuracy-scalable binary CNN processor with all memory on chip in 28nm CMOS, in: 2018 IEEE Custom Integrated Circuits Conference (CICC), IEEE, 2018, pp. 1–4.
[7] Y. Mao, C. You, J. Zhang, K. Huang, K.B. Letaief, A survey on mobile edge computing: the communication perspective, IEEE Commun. Surv. Tutor. 19 (2017) 2322–2358.
[8] K. Yang, Y. Shi, W. Yu, Z. Ding, Energy-efficient processing and robust wireless cooperative transmission for edge inference, IEEE Int. Things J. 7 (10) (2020) 9456–9470.
[9] S. Hua, Y. Zhou, K. Yang, Y. Shi, Reconfigurable intelligent surface for green edge inference, preprint, arXiv:1912.00820, 2019.
[10] T.Y.-H. Chen, L. Ravindranath, S. Deng, P. Bahl, H. Balakrishnan, Glimpse: continuous, real-time object recognition on mobile devices, in: Proc. ACM Conf. Embedded Netw. Sensor Syst., ACM, 2015, pp. 155–168.
[11] Z. Liu, T. Liu, W. Wen, L. Jiang, J. Xu, Y. Wang, G. Quan, DeepN-JPEG: a deep neural network favorable JPEG-based image compression framework, in: Proc. Annu. Design Autom. Conf., ACM, 2018, p. 18.
[12] S.P. Chinchali, E. Cidon, E. Pergament, T. Chu, S. Katti, Neural networks meet physical networks: distributed inference between edge devices and the cloud, in: Proc. ACM Workshop on Hot Topics in Networks, ACM, 2018, pp. 50–56.

[13] D.B. Kurka, D. Gündüz, Deep joint source-channel coding of images with feedback, in: Proc. IEEE Int. Conf. Acoustics Speech Signal Process. (ICASSP), IEEE, 2020, pp. 5235–5239.
[14] X. Yuan, Y.-J. Zhang, Y. Shi, W. Yan, H. Liu, Reconfigurable-intelligent-surface empowered 6G wireless communications: challenges and opportunities, preprint, arXiv:2001.00364, 2020.
[15] J. Hauswald, T. Manville, Q. Zheng, R. Dreslinski, C. Chakrabarti, T. Mudge, A hybrid approach to offloading mobile image classification, in: Proc. IEEE Int. Conf. Acoustics Speech Signal Process. (ICASSP), 2014, pp. 8375–8379.
[16] K. Bhardwaj, C. Lin, A. Sartor, R. Marculescu, Memory-and communication-aware model compression for distributed deep learning inference on iot, preprint, arXiv: 1907.11804, 2019.
[17] S. Teerapittayanon, B. McDanel, H.-T. Kung, BranchyNet: fast inference via early exiting from deep neural networks, in: Proc. Int. Conf. Pattern Recognition (ICPR), 2016, pp. 2464–2469.
[18] S. Teerapittayanon, B. McDanel, H.-T. Kung, Distributed deep neural networks over the cloud, the edge and end devices, in: Proc. IEEE Int. Conf. Dist. Comput. Syst. (ICDCS), 2017, pp. 328–339.
[19] E. Li, L. Zeng, Z. Zhou, X. Chen, Edge AI: on-demand accelerating deep neural network inference via edge computing, IEEE Trans. Wirel. Commun. 19 (1) (Jan. 2020) 447–457.
[20] J.H. Ko, T. Na, M.F. Amir, S. Mukhopadhyay, Edge-host partitioning of deep neural networks with feature space encoding for resource-constrained internet-of-things platforms, in: Proc. IEEE Int. Conf. Advanced Video Signal Based Surveillance (AVSS), 2018, pp. 1–6.
[21] J. Shao, J. Zhang, BottleNet++: an end-to-end approach for feature compression in device-edge co-inference systems, in: Proc. IEEE Int. Conf. Commun. (ICC) Workshop on Edge Machine Learning for 5G Mobile Networks and Beyond, Dublin, Ireland, Jun. 2019.
[22] J. Konečný, H.B. McMahan, D. Ramage, Federated optimization: distributed optimization beyond the datacenter, NIPS Optim. Mach. Learn. Workshop (2015).
[23] B. McMahan, E. Moore, D. Ramage, S. Hampson, B.A. y Arcas, Communication-efficient learning of deep networks from decentralized data, in: Proc. Int. Conf. Artif. Intell. Stat. (AISTATS), 2017, pp. 1273–1282.
[24] K. Yang, T. Jiang, Y. Shi, Z. Ding, Federated learning via over-the-air computation, IEEE Trans. Wirel. Commun. 19 (Jan. 2020) 2022–2035.
[25] G. Zhu, Y. Wang, K. Huang, Broadband analog aggregation for low-latency federated edge learning, IEEE Trans. Wirel. Commun. 19 (Jan. 2020) 491–506.
[26] M.M. Amiri, D. Gunduz, Machine learning at the wireless edge: distributed stochastic gradient descent over-the-air, IEEE Trans. Signal Process. 68 (2020) 2155–2169.
[27] B. Nazer, M. Gastpar, Computation over multiple-access channels, IEEE Trans. Inf. Theory 53 (Oct. 2007) 3498–3516.
[28] S. Wang, T. Tuor, T. Salonidis, K.K. Leung, C. Makaya, T. He, K. Chan, Adaptive federated learning in resource constrained edge computing systems, IEEE J. Sel. Areas Commun. 37 (Jun. 2019) 1205–1221.
[29] J. Wang, G. Joshi, Adaptive communication strategies to achieve the best error-runtime trade-off in local-update SGD, preprint, arXiv:1810.08313, 2018.
[30] M.S.H. Abad, E. Ozfatura, D. Gunduz, O. Ercetin, Hierarchical federated learning across heterogeneous cellular networks, in: Proc. IEEE Int. Conf. Acoust. Speech Signal Process. (ICASSP), 2020, pp. 8866–8870.
[31] Z. Yang, M. Chen, W. Saad, C.S. Hong, M. Shikh-Bahaei, Energy efficient federated learning over wireless communication networks, preprint, arXiv:1911.02417, 2019.

[32] M.A. Attia, R. Tandon, Near optimal coded data shuffling for distributed learning, IEEE Trans. Inf. Theory 65 (11) (2019) 7325–7349.

[33] K. Lee, M. Lam, R. Pedarsani, D. Papailiopoulos, K. Ramchandran, Speeding up distributed machine learning using codes, IEEE Trans. Inf. Theory 64 (Mar. 2018) 1514–1529.

[34] L. Song, C. Fragouli, T. Zhao, A pliable index coding approach to data shuffling, in: Proc. IEEE Int. Symp. Inf. Theory (ISIT), Jun. 2017, pp. 2558–2562.

[35] T. Jiang, K. Yang, Y. Shi, Pliable data shuffling for on-device distributed learning, in: Proc. IEEE Int. Conf. Acoustics Speech Signal Process. (ICASSP), May 2019, pp. 7460–7464.

[36] R. Tandon, Q. Lei, A.G. Dimakis, N. Karampatziakis, Gradient coding: avoiding stragglers in distributed learning, in: Proc. Int. Conf. Mach. Learn. (ICML), vol. 70, 2017, pp. 3368–3376.

[37] R.K. Maity, A.S. Rawat, A. Mazumdar, Robust gradient descent via moment encoding and LDPC codes, in: Proc. IEEE Int. Symp. Inform. Theory (ISIT), Jul. 2019.

[38] S. Boyd, A. Ghosh, B. Prabhakar, D. Shah, Randomized gossip algorithms, IEEE/ACM Trans. Netw. 14 (SI) (2006) 2508–2530.

[39] G. Neglia, G. Calbi, D. Towsley, G. Vardoyan, The role of network topology for distributed machine learning, in: Proc. INFOCOM, 2019, pp. 2350–2358.

[40] A. Reisizadeh, S. Prakash, R. Pedarsani, A.S. Avestimehr, Codedreduce: a fast and robust framework for gradient aggregation in distributed learning, preprint, arXiv: 1902.01981, 2019.

[41] Y. Mao, S. Yi, Q. Li, J. Feng, F. Xu, S. Zhong, A privacy-preserving deep learning approach for face recognition with edge computing, in: USENIX Workshop on Hot Topics in Edge Computing (HotEdge), 2018.

[42] J. Wang, J. Zhang, W. Bao, X. Zhu, B. Cao, P.S. Yu, Not just privacy: improving performance of private deep learning in mobile cloud, in: Proc. ACM SIGKDD Int. Conf. Knowl. Discovery Data Mining (KDD), ACM, 2018, pp. 2407–2416.

[43] Q. Yang, Y. Liu, T. Chen, Y. Tong, Federated machine learning: concept and applications, ACM Trans. Intell. Syst. Technol. 10 (2) (2019) 12.

[44] J. Vaidya, C. Clifton, Privacy-preserving k-means clustering over vertically partitioned data, in: Proc. ACM SIGKDD Int. Conf. Knowl. Discovery Data Mining (KDD), ACM, 2003, pp. 206–215.

[45] A. Gascón, P. Schoppmann, B. Balle, M. Raykova, J. Doerner, S. Zahur, D. Evans, Secure linear regression on vertically partitioned datasets, IACR Cryptol. ePrint Arch. 2016 (2016) 892.

[46] H. Yu, J. Vaidya, X. Jiang, Privacy-preserving SVM classification on vertically partitioned data, in: Pacific-Asia Conf. Knowl. Discovery Data Mining, Springer, 2006, pp. 647–656.

[47] J. Vaidya, C. Clifton, Privacy-preserving decision trees over vertically partitioned data, in: IFIP Annu. Conf. Data Appl. Security Privacy, Springer, 2005, pp. 139–152.

[48] S. Hardy, W. Henecka, H. Ivey-Law, R. Nock, G. Patrini, G. Smith, B. Thorne, Private federated learning on vertically partitioned data via entity resolution and additively homomorphic encryption, preprint, arXiv:1711.10677, 2017.

[49] K. Yang, T. Fan, T. Chen, Y. Shi, Q. Yang, A quasi-Newton method based vertical federated learning framework for logistic regression, in: NeurIPS Workshops on Federated Learning for Data Privacy and Confidentiality, 2019.

[50] K. Cheng, T. Fan, Y. Jin, Y. Liu, T. Chen, Q. Yang, Secureboost: a lossless federated learning framework, preprint, arXiv:1901.08755, 2019.

[51] C.-T. Chu, S.K. Kim, Y.-A. Lin, Y. Yu, G. Bradski, K. Olukotun, A.Y. Ng, Map-reduce for machine learning on multicore, in: Proc. Neural Inf. Process. Syst. (NeurIPS), 2007, pp. 281–288.

[52] N. Basit, Y. Zhang, H. Wu, H. Liu, J. Bin, Y. He, A.M. Hendawi, MapReduce-based deep learning with handwritten digit recognition case study, in: Proc. IEEE Int. Conf. Big Data (Big Data), 2016, pp. 1690–1699.
[53] K. Yang, Y. Shi, Z. Ding, Data shuffling in wireless distributed computing via low-rank optimization, IEEE Trans. Signal Process. 67 (Jun. 2019) 3087–3099.
[54] J. Shyuan Ng, W.Y.B. Lim, N. Cong Luong, Z. Xiong, A. Asheralieva, D. Niyato, C. Leung, C. Miao, A survey of coded distributed computing, e-prints, arXiv:2008.09048, 2020.
[55] S. Li, M.A. Maddah-Ali, Q. Yu, A.S. Avestimehr, A fundamental tradeoff between computation and communication in distributed computing, IEEE Trans. Inf. Theory 64 (Jan. 2018) 109–128.
[56] S. Li, Q. Yu, M.A. Maddah-Ali, A.S. Avestimehr, A scalable framework for wireless distributed computing, IEEE/ACM Trans. Netw. 25 (Oct. 2017) 2643–2654.
[57] F. Li, J. Chen, Z. Wang, Wireless MapReduce distributed computing, in: Proc. IEEE Int. Symp. Inform. Theory (ISIT), 2018, pp. 1286–1290.
[58] E. Parrinello, E. Lampiris, P. Elia, Coded distributed computing with node cooperation substantially increases speedup factors, in: Proc. IEEE Int. Symp. Inform. Theory (ISIT), 2018, pp. 1291–1295.
[59] A. Reisizadeh, R. Pedarsani, Latency analysis of coded computation schemes over wireless networks, in: Proc. 55th Annu. Allerton Conf. Commun. Control Comput. (Allerton), 2017, pp. 1256–1263.
[60] S. Zhao, A node-selection-based sub-task assignment method for coded edge computing, IEEE Commun. Lett. 23 (5) (2019) 797–801.
[61] J. Kosaian, K. Rashmi, S. Venkataraman, Learning a code: machine learning for approximate non-linear coded computation, preprint, arXiv:1806.01259, 2018.

PART TWO

Edge inference

CHAPTER FIVE

Model compression for on-device inference

5.1. Background on model compression

As one of the flagship AI techniques, deep learning [1] has been widely used for image and speech processing and also plays a critical role in providing intelligent services for end users such as Internet-of-Things (IoT) devices [2]. It is usually infeasible to meet low-latency and privacy constraints of intelligent applications for end users with a traditional cloud-based AI engine. Although deploying AI models on mobile devices does not introduce additional communication load and information sharing with other nodes, intensive computation load with large AI models (especially, deep learning models) becomes one of the main bottlenecks for on-device inference. To achieve this goal, many model compression approaches for deep learning models have been proposed in the literature [3]:

- **Pruning:** The basic idea of pruning a DNN network is removing a number of connections between neurons to reduce the model complexity given a trained DNN. Network pruning has caught much attention due to its good performance and wide applicability. Early works of [4] and [5] used second-order derivative information to balance the tradeoff between model complexity and performance. The works [6,7] in recent years mainly focused on pruning unimportant weights of pretrained DNNs and training the pruned networks to improve the network performance. Heuristic Bayesian methods were proposed in [8,9] without convergence guarantee. The work of [10] proposed a layerwise convex pruning approach, where the performance drop is bounded by the sum error of all layers.
- **Quantization:** Quantization methods compress an AI model by using fewer bits to represent model parameters. Since the direct quantization on the trained model parameters could bring significant performance loss, the basic idea of quantization is quantizing the network weights during model training. For example, the work [11] adopted stochastic rounding during the model training procedure and used only 16-bit numbers to represent model parameters. There were also works [12]

Mobile Edge Artificial Intelligence
https://doi.org/10.1016/B978-0-12-823817-2.00015-2

considering the extreme case, where each neural network weight is represented by one bit.

- **Sketching:** As a powerful dimension reduction technique, randomized sketching [13,14] can also be used for model compression. Using a hash function, HashedNet [15] proposed to map the network weights of DNNs to a number of hash buckets. The network links mapped to the same hash bucket share the same weight value. It is further extended to convolutional neural networks (CNNs) by converting filter weights to frequency domain followed by hashing operations [16].
- **Matrix factorization:** The basic principle of matrix factorization for model compression is compression of the weights of DNNs into a lower dimension, which could be represented by the product of square matrices. The matrix factorization of a rank-r matrix $\boldsymbol{X} \in \mathbb{R}^{m\times n}$ is given by $\boldsymbol{X} = \boldsymbol{U}\boldsymbol{V}$, where $\boldsymbol{U} \in \mathbb{R}^{m\times r}$ and $\boldsymbol{V} \in \mathbb{R}^{r\times n}$. By exploiting this property the number of parameters can be compressed from mn to $(m+n)r$. Thus the computation complexity and storage size of DNNs [17] and CNNs [18] can be significantly reduced.
- **Sparse regularization:** Instead of pruning the pretrained network, there are a number of works proposing to add regularizers during training to induce sparsity of weights. The work of [19] used the $\ell_{2,1}$-norm regularization to induce the group sparsity of convolutional kernels for CNNs. The work [20] provided a structure sparsity learning method to regularize trivial filters, channels, filter shapes, and layer depths of DNNs.

In the following, we present a layerwise network pruning framework as a representative approach of model compression.

5.2. Layerwise network pruning

In this section, we describe the problem formulation for layerwise network pruning as a sequence of sparse optimization problems with nonconvex constraints. Then we present the convex relaxation method to address the nonconvex objective function and constraints.

5.2.1 Problem statement

Suppose that the training dataset consists of n training samples, each with d features, that is $\boldsymbol{X} = [\boldsymbol{x}_1, \ldots, \boldsymbol{x}_n] \in \mathbb{R}^{d\times n}$. An L-layer feedforward fully connected neural network model is trained based on the dataset $\boldsymbol{X}$ in advance. The pretrained weights for the lth layer are denoted as $\boldsymbol{W}_l \in \mathbb{R}^{d_{\ell-1}\times d_\ell}$. This chapter assumes the activation function as rectified linear units (ReLU) function. The output of the ℓth layer can thus be mathematically expressed as

$$\mathbf{X}_\ell = \max(\boldsymbol{W}_\ell^\top \mathbf{X}_{\ell-1}, 0), \ \ell = 1, \dots, L, \tag{5.1}$$

where $\mathbf{X}_0 = \boldsymbol{X}$ and $d_0 = d$. The ReLU activation function is given by elementwise version of $\max(\cdot, 0)$.

A layerwise pruning method Net-Trim was proposed in [10], which compresses neural networks with sparse optimization. As illustrated in Fig. 5.1, sparsified connections are designed to approach the performance of unpruned network with much fewer weights connections. The sparsity

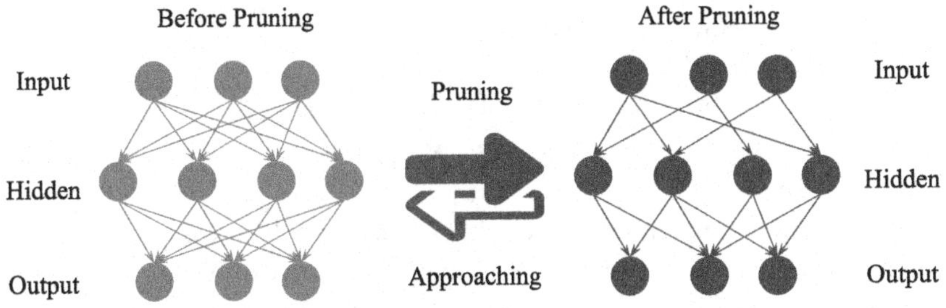

Figure 5.1 Illustration of network weights pruning.

of $\boldsymbol{W}_\ell$ represents the number of nonzero weights in the ℓth layer. The basic idea of layerwise pruning is finding the most sparse weights $\boldsymbol{W}$ while approximately preserving the output of the ℓth layer of the pruned network, that is,

$$\begin{aligned} \mathscr{P}_{5.1} : \underset{\boldsymbol{W} \in \mathbb{R}^{d_{\ell-1} \times d_\ell}}{\text{minimize}} \quad & \|\boldsymbol{W}\|_0 \\ \text{subject to} \quad & \|\max(\boldsymbol{W}^\top \mathbf{X}_{\ell-1}, 0) - \mathbf{X}_\ell\|_F \leq \epsilon, \end{aligned} \tag{5.2}$$

where $\|\boldsymbol{W}\|_0$ denotes the number of nonzero elements of a matrix $\boldsymbol{W}$, $\|\cdot\|_F$ denotes the Frobenius norm, and $\epsilon > 0$ controls the tolerance level of approximation error.

Sparse optimization has garnered much attention from signal processing [21], machine learning [22], wireless communication [23], and many other areas. Since the ℓ_0-norm is a nonconvex nonsmooth function, it is computationally difficult to solve sparse optimization problems. Note that the constraints of problem $\mathscr{P}_{5.1}$ are also nonconvex due to the existence of ReLU activation functions.

5.2.2 Convex approach for sparse objective and constraints

The work of [10] proposed a convex optimization approach to address nonconvex objective functions and nonconvex constraints. In particular, the sparse objective can be addressed by the ℓ_1-norm minimization. The ℓ_1-norm is a well-recognized convex surrogate for the ℓ_0-norm as its convex envelope [24]. Convex approximation for a nonconvex constraint is obtained according to the nonnegativity of each element of $\boldsymbol{X}_\ell$. That is, impose the (i,j)th entry of $\boldsymbol{W}^\top \boldsymbol{X}_{\ell-1}$ to be negative if the (i,j)th entry of $\boldsymbol{X}_\ell$ is zero and to be close to the (i,j)th entry of $\boldsymbol{X}_\ell$ otherwise. For the ℓth layer ($\ell > 1$), the convex optimization approach for network pruning can thus be expressed as

$$\begin{aligned} \underset{\boldsymbol{W}\in\mathbb{R}^{d_{\ell-1}\times d_\ell}}{\text{minimize}} \quad & \|\boldsymbol{W}\|_1 \\ \text{subject to} \quad & \left\|\text{Proj}_\Omega(\boldsymbol{W}^\top \boldsymbol{X}_{\ell-1} - \boldsymbol{X}_\ell)\right\|_F \le \epsilon \\ & \text{Proj}_{\Omega^c}(\boldsymbol{W}^\top \boldsymbol{X}_{\ell-1}) \le 0, \end{aligned} \tag{5.3}$$

where Ω^c is the complementary set of $\Omega \subseteq \{(i,j) : i = 1, \ldots, d_\ell, j = 1, \ldots, n\}$. The index set Ω consists of (i,j) where the (i,j)th entry of $\boldsymbol{X}_\ell$ is strictly positive. The orthogonal projection operator $\text{Proj}_\Omega(\cdot) : \mathbb{R}^{d_\ell \times n} \mapsto \mathbb{R}^{d_\ell \times n}$ preserves the elements in the index set Ω and sets the elements in the complementary set Ω^c as zeros:

$$\text{the } (i,j)\text{th entry of } \text{Proj}_\Omega(\boldsymbol{X}) := \begin{cases} X_{i,j}, & (i,j) \in \Omega, \\ 0, & (i,j) \in \Omega^c. \end{cases} \tag{5.4}$$

Note that the target of network pruning formulation $\mathscr{P}_{5.1}$ is finding the best compression ratio given a certain tolerance level of distortions for the outputs. Therefore we can also relax the stringent nonpositive constraint (5.3) to allow a certain level of constraint violation, which yields the following reformulation:

$$\begin{aligned} \mathscr{P}_{5.1.\text{convex}} : \underset{\boldsymbol{W}\in\mathbb{R}^{d_{\ell-1}\times d_\ell}}{\text{minimize}} \quad & \|\boldsymbol{W}\|_1 \\ \text{subject to} \quad & \left\|\text{Proj}_\Omega(\boldsymbol{W}^\top \boldsymbol{X}_{\ell-1} - \boldsymbol{X}_\ell)\right\|_F \le \epsilon \\ & \text{Proj}_{\Omega^c}(\boldsymbol{W}^\top \boldsymbol{X}_{\ell-1} - \epsilon_1 \boldsymbol{I}) \le 0. \end{aligned} \tag{5.5}$$

The parameter $\epsilon_1 \ge 0$ controls the distortion between the output of the pruned network and original trained network, and $\boldsymbol{I}$ denotes the identity matrix.

5.3. Nonconvex network pruning method with log-sum approximation

In addition to convex approaches, there are many efforts on finding tractable nonconvex surrogates for the ℓ_0-norm. In this section, we present a log-sum approximation [25] for sparse function to promote sparser solutions and yield a greater compression ratio for the neural network model, based on which we adopt an iteratively reweighted approach to solve the resulting nonconvex optimization problem.

5.3.1 Log-sum approximation for sparse optimization

A nonconvex surrogate for the ℓ_0-norm is the log-sum function proposed in [26] to induce sparse solutions given by

$$\|\boldsymbol{W}\|_0 \approx \sum_{i,j} \log(1 + s|w_{ij}|) \triangleq f_s(\boldsymbol{W}) \quad \text{with} \quad s > 0. \tag{5.6}$$

It is motivated by the fact that $f_s(\boldsymbol{W})$ approaches $\|\boldsymbol{W}\|_0$ as s goes to infinity. By placing larger penalties on the parameters close to *zero*, it has the capability of enhancing sparsity compared to the ℓ_1-norm relaxation. Then the resulting problem for pruning the ℓth layer is given by

$$\begin{aligned} \mathscr{P}_{5.1.\text{log-sum}}: \underset{\boldsymbol{W}\in\mathbb{R}^{d_{\ell-1}\times d_\ell}}{\text{minimize}} \quad & f_s(\boldsymbol{W}) \\ \text{subject to} \quad & \left\|\text{Proj}_{\Omega}(\boldsymbol{W}^\top \boldsymbol{X}_{\ell-1} - \boldsymbol{X}_\ell)\right\|_F \le \epsilon, \\ & \text{Proj}_{\Omega^c}(\boldsymbol{W}^\top \boldsymbol{X}_{\ell-1} - \epsilon_1 \boldsymbol{I}) \le 0. \end{aligned} \tag{5.7}$$

5.3.2 Iteratively reweighed minimization for log-sum approximation

This subsection provides an iteratively reweighted approach to address the nonconvexity of the objective function in problem $\mathscr{P}_{5.1.\text{log-sum}}$. Specifically, the $(k+1)$th iterate $\boldsymbol{W}^{[k+1]}$ is computed by minimizing the sum of weighed linear term $\sum_{i,j} a_{ij}^{[k]}|w_{ij}|$ and the proximal term $\frac{\beta}{2}\|\boldsymbol{W} - \boldsymbol{W}^{[k]}\|_F^2$. The linear term is derived from linearizing the objective function f_s with respect to the absolute values of $|w_{ij}|$, that is, $\boldsymbol{W}^{[k+1]}$ is given by the solution to the following convex optimization problem:

$$\mathscr{P}_{5.1.\text{log-sum}[k]}: \underset{\boldsymbol{W}\in\mathbb{R}^{d_{\ell-1}\times d_\ell}}{\text{minimize}} \quad p(\boldsymbol{W}; \boldsymbol{W}^{[k]}) = \sum_{i,j} a_{ij}^{[k]}|w_{ij}| + \frac{\beta}{2}\|\boldsymbol{W} - \boldsymbol{W}^{[k]}\|_F^2$$

$$\text{subject to} \quad \left\|\operatorname{Proj}_{\Omega}(\boldsymbol{W}^{\top}\boldsymbol{X}_{\ell-1} - \boldsymbol{X}_{\ell})\right\|_F \leq \epsilon,$$
$$\operatorname{Proj}_{\Omega^c}(\boldsymbol{W}^{\top}\boldsymbol{X}_{\ell-1}) \leq \operatorname{Proj}_{\Omega^c}(\epsilon_1 \boldsymbol{I}).$$

The proximal parameter β is strictly positive and controls the distance between two consecutive iterations. Each entry of the weight matrix $\boldsymbol{A}^{[k]}$ is given by

$$a_{ij}^{[k]} = \frac{\partial f_s}{\partial |w_{ij}^{[k]}|} = \frac{s}{1 + s|w_{ij}^{[k]}|}. \tag{5.8}$$

We can see that a small absolute value of w_{ij} leads to a larger weight in the next iteration, which enhances the sparsity of model parameters. The introduction of proximal term increases the stability of iterations and yields monotonic decrease of the objective value $f_s(\boldsymbol{W}^{[k]})$ [27]. The monotonic decrease property can be derived from the concavity of log-sum function:

$$p(\boldsymbol{W}^{[k+1]}; \boldsymbol{W}^{[k]}) = \min_{\boldsymbol{W}} p(\boldsymbol{W}; \boldsymbol{W}^{[k]}) \leq p(\boldsymbol{W}^{[k]}; \boldsymbol{W}^{[k]}) \tag{5.9}$$

$$\begin{aligned} f_s(\boldsymbol{W}^{[k+1]}) \leq & f_s(\boldsymbol{W}^{[k]}) + \sum_{i,j} a_{ij}^{[k]}(|w_{ij}^{[k+1]}| - |w_{ij}^{[k]}|) + \frac{\beta}{2}\|\boldsymbol{W} - \boldsymbol{W}^{[k]}\|_F^2 \\ = & f_s(\boldsymbol{W}^{[k]}) + p(\boldsymbol{W}^{[k+1]}; \boldsymbol{W}^{[k]}) - p(\boldsymbol{W}^{[k]}; \boldsymbol{W}^{[k]}) \\ \leq & f_s(\boldsymbol{W}^{[k]}). \end{aligned} \tag{5.10}$$

The overall procedure of the iteratively reweighted minimization algorithm for log-sum-based network pruning is concluded in Algorithm 8. As analyzed in [27], the iteratively reweighted algorithm guarantees the global convergence from arbitrarily feasible initial points. Each cluster point satisfies a first-order necessary optimality condition of problem $\mathscr{P}_{5.1.\text{log-sum}}$. To further improve the computational efficiency, the authors of [27] also designed an ADMM algorithm for each convex subproblem $\mathscr{P}_{5.1.\text{log-sum}[k]}$ and a novel criterion to terminate the iterations for each subproblem early before obtaining an exact solution.

5.4. Simulation results

In this section, we evaluate the performance of convex and nonconvex methods through extensive numerical experiments:

- **"Net-Trim"**: The work [10] proposed a convex approach termed **"Net-Trim"**, which adopted ℓ_1-norm relaxation to address the sparse objective function and convex reformulation to address the nonconvex

Algorithm 8: Iteratively reweighed minimization for log-sum-based network pruning.

Input: $\boldsymbol{X}_1, \ldots, \boldsymbol{X}_L$.

for $\ell = 2, \ldots K$ **do**
  $k \longleftarrow 0$
  while *not converges* **do**
    Compute $\boldsymbol{W}^{[k+1]}$ as the solution to problem $\mathscr{P}_{5.1.\text{log-sum}[k]}$.
    Update weights $a_{ij}^{[k]} = s/\left(1 + s|w_{ij}^{[k]}|\right)$.
    $k \longleftarrow k + 1$.
  end
  $\tilde{\boldsymbol{W}}_\ell \longleftarrow \boldsymbol{W}^{[k]}$
end

Output: Pruned neural network model parameters $\tilde{\boldsymbol{W}}_\ell, \ell = 2, \ldots, L$.

constraints, as presented in Chapter 5.2.2. The implementation details can be found in its released code provided in https://github.com/DNNToolBox/Net-Trim.

- **"Log-Sum":** The nonconvex method presented in Chapter 5.3 adopts the log-sum approximation to improve the compression ratio of **"Net-Trim"** method. We refer to it as **"Log-Sum"**.

We use the open-source Tensorflow tool, NVIDIA GeForce GTX 1080, and TITAN Xp GPUs to facilitate the DNN model training and network pruning procedures. In all simulations, we leave alone convolutional layers although the network pruning methods for fully connected layers can be readily extended to convolutional layers [28].

5.4.1 Handwritten digits classification

Consider the handwritten digits classification task on the MNIST dataset [29], which consists of $60,000$ data instances for training and $10,000$ data instances for test. We use a 4-layer fully connected network whose size is given by $784 \times 300 \times 1000 \times 300 \times 10$, that is, $\boldsymbol{W}_1 \in \mathbb{R}^{784\times300}$, $\boldsymbol{W}_2 \in \mathbb{R}^{300\times1000}$, $\boldsymbol{W}_3 \in \mathbb{R}^{1000\times300}$, $\boldsymbol{W}_4 \in \mathbb{R}^{300\times10}$. We evaluate the **"Net-Trim"** method and **"Log-Sum"** method for pruning the trained fully connected network. The test accuracy of unpruned fully connected network is 96.49%. During network pruning, the constraint violation parameter ϵ_1 is set proportional to ϵ and $1/\sqrt{N}$, that is, $\epsilon_1 = \epsilon/\sqrt{N}$ if not zero, where N is the size of $\mathbf{X}_{d_\ell}$. The performances of two methods for different values of ϵ, ϵ_1 are demonstrated in Table 5.1. The simulation results indicate that the nonconvex network pruning method **"Log-Sum"** considerably increases the compression ratio compared with the convex method **"Net-Trim"**. We also observe that allowing additional violation for nonpositive constraint (5.3) could improve the compression ratio without sacrificing the test accuracy.

Table 5.1 Network pruning performances for fully connected networks in terms of compression ratio (CR, %) and accuracy (ACC, %).

	Net-Trim				Log-Sum			
	$\epsilon_1 = 0$		$\epsilon_1 = \epsilon/\sqrt{N}$		$\epsilon_1 = 0$		$\epsilon_1 = \epsilon/\sqrt{N}$	
	CR	*ACC*	*CR*	*ACC*	*CR*	*ACC*	*CR*	*ACC*
$\epsilon = 0.01$	74.73	97.43	**74.73**	97.44	81.33	97.40	**81.39**	97.40
$\epsilon = 0.02$	79.60	97.33	**79.76**	97.31	85.86	97.38	**85.90**	97.35
$\epsilon = 0.04$	84.11	97.23	**84.62**	97.23	90.91	97.18	**91.06**	97.21
$\epsilon = 0.06$	86.29	97.09	**86.93**	97.03	93.37	97.10	**93.61**	96.97
$\epsilon = 0.08$	87.64	96.97	**88.38**	96.85	94.79	96.99	**95.09**	96.97
$\epsilon = 0.10$	88.64	96.73	**89.41**	96.66	95.68	96.79	**96.02**	96.82
$\epsilon = 0.20$	91.03	96.12	**92.24**	95.85	97.37	96.36	**97.78**	95.85
$\epsilon = 0.30$	92.36	95.14	**93.73**	94.41	98.04	94.87	**98.47**	94.53

5.4.2 Image classification

Consider the image classification task on the CIFAR-10 dataset [30], which consists of 60,000 images in 10 classes. There are 50,000 images for training and 10,000 images for test. We use a 5-layer convolutional neural network (CNN) model. The first two layers are convolutional layers that use 64 filters of size $5 \times 5 \times 3$ and $5 \times 5 \times 64$. Each convolutional layer is followed by a 3×3 max pooling layer with stride 2×2. In the following, there are three fully connected layers of size $2034 \times 384 \times 192 \times 10$. The test accuracy of pretrained CNN model is 79.09%. The performances of pruning the pretrained CNN model with **"Net-Trim"** and **"Log-Sum"** methods are shown in Table 5.2. It also indicates the advantage of the nonconvex **"Log-Sum"** method over **"Net-Trim"**, allowing certain level of violations for constraint (5.3). For example, the network compression ratio can be improved from 76.33% to 91.55% by adopting **"Log-Sum"** method given $\epsilon = 0.30$ and $\epsilon_1 = 0$, and can be further improved to 92.82% by setting nonzero ϵ_1.

Table 5.2 Network pruning performances for CNN in terms of compression ratio (CR, %) and accuracy (ACC, %).

	Net-Trim				Log-Sum			
	$\epsilon_1 = 0$		$\epsilon_1 = \epsilon/\sqrt{N}$		$\epsilon_1 = 0$		$\epsilon_1 = \epsilon/\sqrt{N}$	
	CR	*ACC*	*CR*	*ACC*	*CR*	*ACC*	*CR*	*ACC*
$\epsilon = 0.01$	24.51	78.31	**24.53**	78.25	43.25	78.34	**43.25**	78.60
$\epsilon = 0.02$	29.79	78.60	**29.81**	78.17	48.76	78.21	**49.11**	78.08
$\epsilon = 0.04$	39.53	78.40	**39.56**	77.71	58.79	78.65	**59.29**	78.18
$\epsilon = 0.06$	46.25	78.42	**46.58**	78.03	66.04	78.13	**66.44**	78.36
$\epsilon = 0.08$	51.54	78.25	**52.23**	78.43	71.52	77.87	**71.77**	78.14
$\epsilon = 0.10$	56.06	78.06	**56.74**	78.22	75.96	78.31	**76.20**	77.91
$\epsilon = 0.20$	69.53	78.11	**71.27**	77.68	87.14	76.60	**88.02**	76.51
$\epsilon = 0.30$	76.33	77.09	**78.93**	77.09	91.55	78.49	**92.82**	74.37

5.4.3 Keyword spotting inference

In this subsection, we conduct numerical experiments to verify the advantages of network pruning in reducing memory size and computational complexity. Consider the keyword spotting task on the Google speech commands dataset [31] using the DNN models provided in [32], which are presented in Table 5.3. Fully connected models are referred to as FC followed by the number of neurons in parentheses. We refer to the convolutional layer as Conv, followed by its hyperparameters including the number of feature maps, kernel sizes, and strides in parentheses. For example, Conv(28,10,4,1,1) denotes the convolutional layer with 28 filters, filter size in time and frequency $(10, 4)$, and stride in time and frequency $(1, 1)$. L represents the low-rank linear layer. We compare the performances of

Table 5.3 Network model description for keyword spotting.

	FC model	CNN model
Small size	FC(144)-FC(144)-FC(144)	Conv(28,10,4,1,1)-Conv(30,10,4,2,1)-L(16)-FC(128)
Middle size	FC(256)-FC(256)-FC(256)	Conv(64,10,4,1,1)-Conv(48,10,4,2,1)-L(16)-FC(128)
Large size	FC(436)-FC(436)-FC(436)	Conv(60,10,4,1,1)-Conv(76,10,4,2,1)-L(58)-FC(128)

pretrained fully connected network models and CNN models with performances of the pruned networks in terms of test accuracy, memory, and the number of operations including multiplications and additions. The **"Log-Sum"** method is adopted to prune all network models. The simulation results in Table 5.4 demonstrate that the memory sizes and number of operations are considerably reduced with **"Log-Sum"**-based network pruning

Table 5.4 Performance comparisons between the original model and the pruned models.

Neural network model	Original model			Pruned model		
	Test acc.	Memory	Ops	Test acc.	Memory	Ops
FC model (small)	83.03	76.3 KB	155.35 K	83.31	**48.6 KB**	**99.43 K**
FC model (middle)	85.56	184.1 KB	376.92 K	85.28	**109.8 KB**	**224.87 K**
FC model (large)	86.50	420.6 KB	861.38 K	86.77	**195.2 KB**	**399.77 K**
CNN model (small)	91.35	67.5 KB	4.99 M	90.55	**51.8 KB**	**4.96 M**
CNN model (middle)	91.88	174.0 KB	17.25 M	91.27	**152.9 KB**	**17.21 M**
CNN model (large)	92.07	464.4 KB	25.26 M	91.39	**221.2 KB**	**24.76 M**

method. The compression ratio for a large model can be much higher than for small models due to the large number of redundant connections.

5.5. Summary

In this chapter, we overviewed the network compression methods to achieve on-device inference. We presented the details of layerwise network pruning as a representative framework. Nonconvex log-sum method was provided to improve the performance of convex method using ℓ_1-norm relaxation. Then we developed an iteratively reweighted minimization approach to address the resulting nonconvex log-sum objective function. Simulation results demonstrated the advantages of using network pruning on reducing memory size and computational complexity. The nonconvex log-sum method was demonstrated to have a higher compression ratio than the ℓ_1-norm relaxation method.

References

[1] Y. LeCun, Y. Bengio, G. Hinton, Deep learning, Nature 521 (7553) (2015) 436–444.
[2] M. Mohammadi, A. Al-Fuqaha, S. Sorour, M. Guizani, Deep learning for IoT big data and streaming analytics: a survey, IEEE Commun. Surv. Tutor. 20 (4) (Fourthquarter 2018) 2923–2960.
[3] L. Deng, G. Li, S. Han, L. Shi, Y. Xie, Model compression and hardware acceleration for neural networks: a comprehensive survey, Proc. IEEE 108 (Apr. 2020) 485–532.
[4] Y. LeCun, J.S. Denker, S.A. Solla, Optimal brain damage, in: Adv. Neural Inf. Process. Syst. (NeurIPS), 1990, pp. 598–605.
[5] B. Hassibi, D.G. Stork, Second order derivatives for network pruning: optimal brain surgeon, in: Adv. Neural Inf. Process. Syst. (NeurIPS), 1993, pp. 164–171.
[6] S. Han, J. Pool, J. Tran, W. Dally, Learning both weights and connections for efficient neural network, in: Adv. Neural Inf. Process. Syst. (NeurIPS), 2015, pp. 1135–1143.
[7] S. Han, H. Mao, W.J. Dally, Deep compression: compressing deep neural networks with pruning, trained quantization and Huffman coding, in: Proc. Int. Conf. Learn. Representations (ICLR), 2016.
[8] K. Ullrich, E. Meeds, M. Welling, Soft weight-sharing for neural network compression, in: Proc. Int. Conf. Learn. Representations (ICLR), 2017.

[9] C. Louizos, K. Ullrich, M. Welling, Bayesian compression for deep learning, in: Pro. Adv. Neural. Inf. Process. Syst. (NIPS), 2017, pp. 3288–3298.
[10] A. Aghasi, A. Abdi, N. Nguyen, J. Romberg, Net-Trim: convex pruning of deep neural networks with performance guarantee, in: Pro. Adv. Neural. Inf. Process. Syst. (NIPS), 2017, pp. 3180–3189.
[11] S. Gupta, A. Agrawal, K. Gopalakrishnan, P. Narayanan, Deep learning with limited numerical precision, in: Proc. Int. Conf. Mach. Learn. (ICML), 2015, pp. 1737–1746.
[12] M. Courbariaux, Y. Bengio, J.-P. David, BinaryConnect: training deep neural networks with binary weights during propagations, in: Proc. Neural Inf. Process. Syst. (NeurIPS), 2015, pp. 3123–3131.
[13] M. Pilanci, M.J. Wainwright, Iterative Hessian sketch: fast and accurate solution approximation for constrained least-squares, J. Mach. Learn. Res. 17 (1) (2016) 1842–1879.
[14] H. Choi, T. Jiang, Y. Shi, Large-scale beamforming for massive MIMO via randomized sketching, preprint, arXiv:1903.05904, 2019.
[15] W. Chen, J. Wilson, S. Tyree, K. Weinberger, Y. Chen, Compressing neural networks with the hashing trick, in: Proc. Int. Conf. Mach. Learn. (ICML), 2015, pp. 2285–2294.
[16] W. Chen, J. Wilson, S. Tyree, K.Q. Weinberger, Y. Chen, Compressing convolutional neural networks in the frequency domain, in: Proc. ACM SIGKDD Int. Conf. Knowl. Discovery Data Mining (KDD), ACM, 2016, pp. 1475–1484.
[17] T.N. Sainath, B. Kingsbury, V. Sindhwani, E. Arisoy, B. Ramabhadran, Low-rank matrix factorization for deep neural network training with high-dimensional output targets, in: Proc. IEEE Int. Conf. Acoustics Speech Signal Process. (ICASSP), 2013, pp. 6655–6659.
[18] E.L. Denton, W. Zaremba, J. Bruna, Y. LeCun, R. Fergus, Exploiting linear structure within convolutional networks for efficient evaluation, in: Proc. Neural Inf. Process. Syst. (NeurIPS), 2014, pp. 1269–1277.
[19] V. Lebedev, V. Lempitsky, Fast ConvNets using group-wise brain damage, in: Proc. IEEE Conf. Comput. Vision Pattern Recognition (CVPR), 2016, pp. 2554–2564.
[20] W. Wen, C. Wu, Y. Wang, Y. Chen, H. Li, Learning structured sparsity in deep neural networks, in: Pro. Adv. Neural. Inf. Process. Syst. (NIPS), 2016, pp. 2074–2082.
[21] D. Malioutov, M. Cetin, A.S. Willsky, A sparse signal reconstruction perspective for source localization with sensor arrays, IEEE Trans. Signal Process. 53 (Aug. 2005) 3010–3022.
[22] H. Lee, A. Battle, R. Raina, A.Y. Ng, Efficient sparse coding algorithms, in: Adv. Neural Inf. Process. Syst. (NeurIPS), 2007, pp. 801–808.
[23] Y. Shi, J. Zhang, K.B. Letaief, Group sparse beamforming for green cloud-RAN, IEEE Trans. Wirel. Commun. 13 (May 2014) 2809–2823.
[24] J.A. Tropp, S.J. Wright, Computational methods for sparse solution of linear inverse problems, Proc. IEEE 98 (Jun. 2010) 948–958.
[25] T. Jiang, X. Yang, Y. Shi, H. Wang, Layer-wise deep neural network pruning via iteratively reweighted optimization, in: Proc. IEEE Int. Conf. Acoustics Speech Signal Process. (ICASSP), May 2019, pp. 5606–5610.
[26] M.S. Lobo, M. Fazel, S. Boyd, Portfolio optimization with linear and fixed transaction costs, Ann. Oper. Res. 152 (Jul. 2007) 341–365.
[27] H. Wang, X. Yang, T. Jiang, Y. Shi, J. Lin, A proximal iteratively reweighted approach for efficient network sparsification, IEEE Trans. Comput. (2020).
[28] A. Aghasi, A. Abdi, J. Romberg, Fast convex pruning of deep neural networks, SIAM J. Math. Data Sci. 2 (1) (2020) 158–188.
[29] Y. LeCun, L. Bottou, Y. Bengio, P. Haffner, Gradient-based learning applied to document recognition, Proc. IEEE 86 (Nov. 1998) 2278–2324.

[30] A. Krizhevsky, G. Hinton, et al., Learning multiple layers of features from tiny images, 2009.
[31] P. Warden, Speech commands: a public dataset for single-word speech recognition, Dataset available from http://download.tensorflow.org/data/speech_commands_v0, 2017, vol. 1.
[32] Y. Zhang, N. Suda, L. Lai, V. Chandra, Hello edge: keyword spotting on microcontrollers, preprint, arXiv:1711.07128, 2017.

CHAPTER SIX

Coded computing for on-device cooperative inference

6.1. Background on MapReduce

Due to the limited computation, storage, and power resources at edge devices [1], it is often infeasible to fit a large-size and computation-intensive AI model on a single mobile device. MapReduce [2] is a well-recognized framework to efficiently accomplish data-intensive tasks with distributed computing nodes. In recent years, researchers leverage the MapReduce distributed computing structure to pool the distributed computation and storage resources of mobile devices to efficiently accomplish machine learning tasks such as image recognition. In this chapter, we investigate the on-device cooperative inference system based on coded distributed computing.

The computation tasks to be accomplished in MapReduce framework rely on the entire dataset consisting of the prepositioned local data on distributed nodes. The computation task admits the structure of MapReduce, that is, it can be decomposed as the Reduce function of the intermediate values obtained by performing Map operations on the local data on each node. In mobile edge AI, each mobile device requires the output of its own computation task. Since the intermediate values required by the computation task for each device are available across a fleet of distributed nodes, all participating devices exchange intermediate values before computing the Reduce functions. Therefore the typical procedure of a MapReduce framework generally consists of three phases: *Map*, *Shuffle*, and *Reduce*. Intermediate values are computed based on local data on each node in the Map phase, exchanged in the Shuffle phase, and reduced to the computational result for each node in the Reduce phase.

To present the overall computation procedure of a MapReduce-based distributed computing system, we consider a typical distributed computing system consisting of K mobile devices. Assume that the whole dataset is evenly split to a set of F-bit files $f_1, \ldots, f_N$ and each device k has only access to a subset of files denoted by $\mathcal{F}_k \subseteq \{f_1, \ldots, f_N\}$. The computation task of device k is denoted as $\phi_k(d_k; f_1, \ldots, f_N)$, where d_k is the input. As

Mobile Edge Artificial Intelligence
https://doi.org/10.1016/B978-0-12-823817-2.00016-4

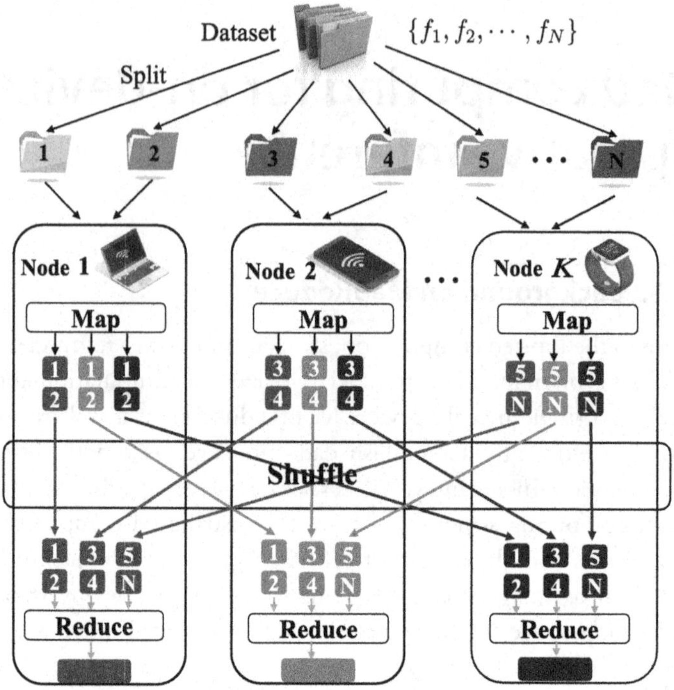

Figure 6.1 Distributed computing model.

a representative example, the dataset for object recognition is a library of the feature vectors of various objects. Given an input feature vector of an image, each mobile device requires the inference result of classification. Due to the limited storage size, each device can only store a subset of all features. Assume that each mobile device can store up to μF bits ($\mu < N$) and that the total storage of K devices can cover the whole dataset, that is, $\mu K \geq N$.

Computation tasks admitting the structure of MapReduce can be decomposed as

$$\phi_k(d_k; f_1, \ldots, f_N) = h_k(g_{k,1}(d_k; f_1), \ldots, g_{k,N}(d_k; f_N)), \tag{6.1}$$

where $g_{k,n}(d_k; f_n)$ is the Map function with output w_k, n is an intermediate value with E bits, and h_k is the Reduce function that maps all intermediate values to the computation result ϕ_k. As illustrated in Fig. 6.1, the computation procedure can be concluded as the following four phases.

- **Dataset placement:** Before computing the tasks, the dataset will be distributedly deployed across K devices based on a predetermined file placement strategy $\mathcal{F}_1, \ldots, \mathcal{F}_K$.
- **Map:** Based on the input d_k and locally stored files $f_{\mathcal{F}_K}$, every device k computes intermediate values $\{w_{k,n} : n \in \mathcal{F}_k\}$.
- **Shuffle:** Note that the intermediate values $\{w_{k,n} : n \notin \mathcal{F}_k\}$ are also required to compute each task ϕ_k. In this phase, devices exchange these intermediate values with each other.
- **Reduce:** The output of each computation task ϕ_k is obtained by computing the Reduce function $\phi_k(d_k; f_1, \ldots, f_N) = h_k(w_{k,1}, \ldots, w_{k,N})$ based on all required intermediate values.

The heavy communication load is one of the main bottlenecks in distributed computing systems. The limited spectral resources make it more challenging to exchange intermediate values through wireless links, which hinders the scaling up of wireless MapReduce-based distributed computing [3]. It is thus critical to improve the communication efficiency of data shuffling to enable on-device cooperative inference.

In the following, we provide the detailed procedure of designing a fast data shuffling scheme in wireless MapReduce system as a representative.

6.2. A communication-efficient data shuffling scheme

In this section, we model data shuffling as a side-information aided message delivery problem and provide a communication-efficient data shuffling scheme with concurrent transmission.

6.2.1 Communication model

Suppose the intermediate values $\{w_{1,1}, \ldots, w_{1,N}, \ldots, w_{K,N}\}$ are a library of independent messages $W_1, \ldots, W_T$ with $T = KN$, that is, we denote the intermediate value $w_{k,n}$ by $W_{(k-1)N+n}$. Each mobile device k has only access to $\{W_t, t \in \mathcal{T}_k\}$ locally after the Map phase and requires messages $\{W_t, t \in \mathcal{R}_k\}$ from others. Let $\mathcal{T}_k = \{(j-1)N + n : j = 1, \ldots, K, n \in \mathcal{F}_k\}$ and $\mathcal{R}_k = \{(k-1)N + n : n \notin \mathcal{F}_k\}$ be the index set of messages available at MU k and messages required by MU k, respectively. Thus the Shuffle phase is a message delivery problem with side information $\mathcal{T}_k$'s. We consider a communication model consisting of two stages, uplink multiple access (MAC) and downlink broadcasting (BC). In this system, there is an M-antenna wireless access point (AP) that collects the mixed signal from all L-antenna

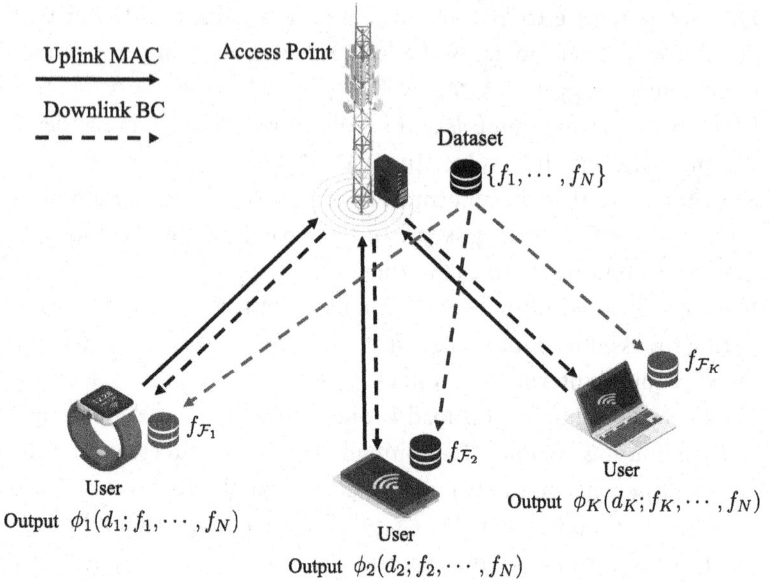

Figure 6.2 Coded computing system.

mobile devices in uplink MAC stage and broadcasts it to each device in downlink BC stage, as illustrated in Fig. 6.2.

We denote the aggregated transmit signal at device k over r channel uses by

$$\boldsymbol{x}_k = [\boldsymbol{x}_k[i]] = \begin{bmatrix} \boldsymbol{x}_k[1] \\ \vdots \\ \boldsymbol{x}_k[L] \end{bmatrix} \in \mathbb{C}^{Lr}, \tag{6.2}$$

where $\boldsymbol{x}_k[i] \in \mathbb{C}^r$ is the transmitted signal corresponding to the ith antenna over r channel uses. We assume the quasi-static fading channel model where channel coefficients remain unchanged over r channel uses. Let $H_k^{\mathsf{up}}[s, i]$ be the uplink channel coefficient between the ith antenna of device k and the sth antenna of the AP. The channel coefficient matrix between device k and the AP is formed by $H_k^{\mathsf{up}}[s, i]$ for all $s = 1, \ldots, M$ and $i = 1, \ldots, L$, which is denoted as $\boldsymbol{H}_k^{\mathsf{up}} \in \mathbb{C}^{M \times L}$. Thus the received signal at the AP in uplink MAC stage can be represented as

$$\boldsymbol{y} = \sum_{k=1}^{K} (\boldsymbol{H}_k^{\mathsf{up}} \otimes \boldsymbol{I}_r)\boldsymbol{x}_k + \boldsymbol{n}^{\mathsf{up}}, \tag{6.3}$$

$$\boldsymbol{y} = [\boldsymbol{y}[s]] = \begin{bmatrix} \boldsymbol{y}[1] \\ \vdots \\ \boldsymbol{y}[M] \end{bmatrix} \in \mathbb{C}^{Mr}, \boldsymbol{n}^{\mathsf{up}} = [\boldsymbol{n}^{\mathsf{up}}[s]] = \begin{bmatrix} \boldsymbol{n}^{\mathsf{up}}[1] \\ \vdots \\ \boldsymbol{n}^{\mathsf{up}}[M] \end{bmatrix}, \tag{6.4}$$

where $\boldsymbol{y}[s] \in \mathbb{C}^r$ and $\boldsymbol{n}^{\mathsf{up}}[s] \in \mathbb{C}^r$ are the signal and the complex additive isotropic white Gaussian noise corresponding to the sth antenna, respectively, and $\otimes$ denotes the Kronecker product. Likewise, the received signal in downlink BC stage at the kth mobile device is given by

$$\boldsymbol{z}_k = (\boldsymbol{H}_k^{\mathsf{down}} \otimes \boldsymbol{I}_r)\boldsymbol{y} + \boldsymbol{n}_k^{\mathsf{down}}, \tag{6.5}$$

where the downlink channel coefficient matrix $\boldsymbol{H}_k^{\mathsf{down}} \in \mathbb{C}^{L\times M}$ between the AP and the kth device and the downlink complex additive isotropic white Gaussian noise $\boldsymbol{n}_k^{\mathsf{down}} \in \mathbb{C}^{Lr}$ are respectively given by

$$\boldsymbol{H}_k^{\mathsf{down}} = \begin{bmatrix} H_k^{\mathsf{down}}[1,1] & \dots & H_k^{\mathsf{down}}[1,M] \\ \vdots & \ddots & \vdots \\ H_k^{\mathsf{down}}[L,1] & \dots & H_k^{\mathsf{down}}[L,M] \end{bmatrix} \in \mathbb{C}^{L\times M}, \tag{6.6}$$

$$\boldsymbol{n}_k^{\mathsf{down}} = \begin{bmatrix} \boldsymbol{n}_k^{\mathsf{down}}[1] \\ \vdots \\ \boldsymbol{n}_k^{\mathsf{down}}[L] \end{bmatrix} \in \mathbb{C}^{Lr}. \tag{6.7}$$

Thus the overall input–output relationship of the presented communication model for data shuffling can be written as

$$\boldsymbol{z}_k = \sum_{i=1}^{K} (\boldsymbol{H}_k^{\mathsf{down}} \otimes \boldsymbol{I}_r)(\boldsymbol{H}_i^{\mathsf{up}} \otimes \boldsymbol{I}_r)\boldsymbol{x}_i + (\boldsymbol{H}_k^{\mathsf{down}} \otimes \boldsymbol{I}_r)\boldsymbol{n}^{\mathsf{up}} + \boldsymbol{n}_k^{\mathsf{down}} \tag{6.8}$$

$$= \sum_{i=1}^{K} (\boldsymbol{H}_{ki} \otimes \boldsymbol{I}_r)\boldsymbol{x}_i + \boldsymbol{n}_k, \tag{6.9}$$

by denoting the equivalent channel coefficient matrix as $\boldsymbol{H}_{ki} = \boldsymbol{H}_k^{\mathsf{down}}\boldsymbol{H}_i^{\mathsf{up}} \in \mathbb{C}^{L\times L}$ and the effective additive noise as $\boldsymbol{n}_k = (\boldsymbol{H}_k^{\mathsf{down}} \otimes \boldsymbol{I}_r)\boldsymbol{n}^{\mathsf{up}} + \boldsymbol{n}_k^{\mathsf{down}}$. The data shuffling problem is now equivalent to a message delivery problem over a K-user multiple-input–multiple-output (MIMO) interference channel with side information.

6.2.2 Achievable data rates and DoF

In this chapter, we choose the degree-of-freedom (DoF) as the performance metric for designing communication-efficient data shuffling schemes. DoF is a first-order characterization of the channel capacity and has been widely used in interference channels [4–6]. Let $R_k(W_l)$ be the achievable data rate for message W_l at device k; that is, there exists a coding scheme such that the transmission rate of message W_l is $R_k(W_l)$, and W_l can be decoded at device k with arbitrarily small probability of error as the codeword length approaches infinity [7]. Denote the signal-to-noise ratio (SNR) at receiver k for message W_l by $\mathrm{SNR}_{k,l}$. Then the DoF is given by [4]

$$\mathrm{DoF}_{k,l} \triangleq \limsup_{\mathrm{SNR}_{k,l}\to\infty} \frac{R_k(W_l)}{\log(\mathrm{SNR}_{k,l})}. \tag{6.10}$$

Without loss of generality, we will maximize the achievable symmetric DoF, denoted by $\mathrm{DoF}_{\mathrm{sym}}$, that is, the largest achievable DoF for all $k \in \{1, \ldots, K\}$, $l \in \mathcal{R}_k$, in the following parts of this chapter, which can be readily extended to asymmetric cases.

6.3. A low-rank optimization framework for communication-efficient data shuffling

By leveraging interference alignment technique, in this section, we develop a low-rank optimization framework for designing linear transceivers to maximize the achievable DoF.

6.3.1 Interference alignment conditions

In this chapter, we consider a linear coding scheme due to its low complexity and optimality in terms of DoFs for interference alignment [4] and other applications. Let $\boldsymbol{s}_j \in \mathbb{C}^d$ denote the representative vector of message W_j, where d is the number of datastreams, and each datastream carries one DoF. Let $\boldsymbol{V}_{kj} \in \mathbb{C}^{rL\times d}$ be the precoding matrix of mobile device k to transmit message j, and let $\boldsymbol{U}_{kl} \in \mathbb{C}^{d\times Lr}$ be the decoding matrix of mobile device k for message W_l, $l \in \mathcal{R}_k$. The transmitted signal of device k is given by

$$\boldsymbol{x}_k = \sum_{j\in\mathcal{T}_k} \boldsymbol{V}_{kj}\boldsymbol{s}_j, \tag{6.11}$$

and each required message W_l will be estimated based on

$$\tilde{\boldsymbol{z}}_{kl} = \boldsymbol{U}_{kl}\boldsymbol{z}_k = \boldsymbol{U}_{kl}\sum_{i=1}^{K}(\boldsymbol{H}_{ki}\otimes\boldsymbol{I}_r)\sum_{j\in\mathcal{T}_i}\boldsymbol{V}_{ij}\boldsymbol{s}_j + \boldsymbol{U}_{kl}\boldsymbol{n}_k. \tag{6.12}$$

A key observation is that $\tilde{z}_{kl}$ is a noisy signal that contains the linear combination of the whole message set, which can be divided into three parts: desired message, locally available messages, and interferences, that is,

$$\tilde{z}_{kl} = \mathcal{I}_1(\underbrace{s_l}_{\text{desired message}}) + \mathcal{I}_2(\underbrace{\{s_j : j \in \mathcal{T}_k\}}_{\text{locally available messages}}) + \mathcal{I}_3(\underbrace{\{s_j : j \notin \mathcal{T}_k \cup \{l\}\}}_{\text{interferences}}) + \tilde{n}_{kl}, \tag{6.13}$$

$$\mathcal{I}_1(s_l) = \sum_{i:l \in \mathcal{T}_i} U_{kl}(H_{ki} \otimes I_r) V_{il} s_l, \tag{6.14}$$

$$\mathcal{I}_2(\{s_j : j \in \mathcal{T}_k\}) = \sum_{j \in \mathcal{T}_k} \sum_{i:j \in \mathcal{T}_i} U_{kl}(H_{ki} \otimes I_r) V_{ij} s_j, \tag{6.15}$$

$$\mathcal{I}_3(\{s_j : j \notin \mathcal{T}_k \cup \{l\}\}) = \sum_{j \notin \mathcal{T}_k \cup \{l\}} \sum_{i:j \in \mathcal{T}_i} U_{kl}(H_{ki} \otimes I_r) V_{ij} s_j. \tag{6.16}$$

The locally available messages can be eliminated directly, whereas the interference becomes the main bottleneck for data shuffling.

To handle the cochannel interference, we leverage the powerful interference alignment technique [4] for transceiver design. The basic principle of interference alignment is to align and cancel the interferences at unintended receivers while preserving the required signals at intended receivers. Specifically, the following interference alignment conditions are established:

$$\det\left(\sum_{i:l \in \mathcal{T}_i} U_{kl}(H_{ki} \otimes I_r) V_{il}\right) \neq 0, \forall l \in \mathcal{R}_k, k = 1, \ldots, K, \tag{6.17}$$

$$\sum_{i:j \in \mathcal{T}_i} U_{kl}(H_{ki} \otimes I_r) V_{ij} = \mathbf{0}, \forall j \notin \mathcal{T}_k \cup \{l\}, l \in \mathcal{R}_k, k = 1, \ldots, K. \tag{6.18}$$

With transceivers satisfying conditions (6.17) and (6.18), each message W_l could be transmitted with d datastreams over r channel uses without cochannel interference and estimated as

$$\tilde{s}_l = \mathcal{I}_1^{-1}\left(\tilde{z}_{kl} - \mathcal{I}_2(\{s_j : j \in \mathcal{T}_k\})\right) \tag{6.19}$$

for all $l \in \mathcal{R}_k$, $k = 1, \ldots, K$. Thus the achievable symmetric DoF is d/r, that is,

$$\text{DoF}_{\text{sym}} = d/r. \tag{6.20}$$

Given the number of datastreams d, the achievable symmetric DoF can be maximized through finding transceivers with minimum number of channel uses r.

6.3.2 Low-rank optimization approach

Denote

$$\boldsymbol{V}_{kj} = \begin{bmatrix} \boldsymbol{V}_{kj}[1] \\ \vdots \\ \boldsymbol{V}_{kj}[L] \end{bmatrix} \in \mathbb{C}^{rL\times d}, \ \tilde{\boldsymbol{V}}_{ij} = \begin{bmatrix} \boldsymbol{V}_{ij}[1] & \dots & \boldsymbol{V}_{ij}[L] \end{bmatrix} \in \mathbb{C}^{r\times dL}, \tag{6.21}$$

$$\boldsymbol{U}_{kl} = \begin{bmatrix} \boldsymbol{U}_{kl}[1] & \dots & \boldsymbol{U}_{kl}[L] \end{bmatrix} \in \mathbb{C}^{d\times Lr}, \tilde{\boldsymbol{U}}_{kl} = \begin{bmatrix} \boldsymbol{U}_{kl}[1] \\ \vdots \\ \boldsymbol{U}_{kl}[L] \end{bmatrix} \in \mathbb{C}^{dL\times r}, \tag{6.22}$$

where $\boldsymbol{V}_{kj}[n] \in \mathbb{C}^{r\times d}$, $\boldsymbol{U}_{kl}[m] \in \mathbb{C}^{d\times r}$. Note that

$$\boldsymbol{U}_{kl}(\boldsymbol{H}_{ki} \otimes \boldsymbol{I}_r)\boldsymbol{V}_{ij} = \sum_{m=1}^{L}\sum_{n=1}^{L} H_{ki}[m,n]\boldsymbol{U}_{kl}[m]\boldsymbol{V}_{ij}[n], \tag{6.23}$$

where $H_{ki}[m,n]$ is the (m,n)th entry of matrix $\boldsymbol{H}_{ki}$. Thus we can encode the transceivers in a matrix $\boldsymbol{X}$ by defining

$$\boldsymbol{X}_{k,l,i,j} = [\boldsymbol{X}_{k,l,i,j}[m,n]] = [\boldsymbol{U}_{kl}[m]\boldsymbol{V}_{ij}[n]] = \tilde{\boldsymbol{U}}_{kl}\tilde{\boldsymbol{V}}_{ij}, \tag{6.24}$$

$$\boldsymbol{X} = [\boldsymbol{X}_{k,l,i,j}] = \begin{bmatrix} \tilde{\boldsymbol{U}}_{11} \\ \vdots \\ \tilde{\boldsymbol{U}}_{1T} \\ \vdots \\ \tilde{\boldsymbol{U}}_{KT} \end{bmatrix} \begin{bmatrix} \tilde{\boldsymbol{V}}_{11} & \dots & \tilde{\boldsymbol{V}}_{1T} & \dots & \tilde{\boldsymbol{V}}_{KT} \end{bmatrix} = \tilde{\boldsymbol{U}}\tilde{\boldsymbol{V}}, \tag{6.25}$$

where $\tilde{\boldsymbol{U}} \in \mathbb{C}^{LdKT\times r}$ and $\tilde{\boldsymbol{V}} \in \mathbb{C}^{r\times LdKT}$. Without loss of generality, we set $\sum_{i:l\in\mathcal{T}_i} \boldsymbol{U}_{kl}(\boldsymbol{H}_{ki} \otimes \boldsymbol{I}_r)\boldsymbol{V}_{il} = \boldsymbol{I}$ for condition (6.17) to facilitate algorithm design. The interference alignment conditions (6.17) and (6.18) can be rewritten as

$$\sum_{i:l\in\mathcal{T}_i}\sum_{m=1}^{L}\sum_{n=1}^{L} H_{ki}[m,n]\boldsymbol{X}_{k,l,i,l}[m,n] = \boldsymbol{I}, \tag{6.26}$$

$$\sum_{i:j\in\mathcal{T}_i}\sum_{m=1}^{L}\sum_{n=1}^{L} H_{ki}[m,n]\boldsymbol{X}_{k,l,i,j}[m,n] = \boldsymbol{0}, \ j \notin \mathcal{T}_k \cup \{l\} \tag{6.27}$$

for all $l \in \mathcal{R}_k$, $k = 1, \dots, K$.

The notation of these affine constraints of matrix $\boldsymbol{X}$ can be simplified as $\mathcal{A}(\boldsymbol{X}) = \boldsymbol{b}$, where $\mathcal{A} : \mathbb{C}^{D\times D} \mapsto \mathbb{C}^S$ is a linear operator related to $\boldsymbol{H}_{ki}$. A key observation is that the rank of matrix $\boldsymbol{X}$ is equal to the number of channel uses r due to $\boldsymbol{X} = \tilde{\boldsymbol{U}}\tilde{\boldsymbol{V}}$. This motivates us to maximize the achievable symmetric DoF via the following low-rank optimization approach:

$$\begin{aligned} \mathscr{P}_{6.1} : \underset{\boldsymbol{X}\in\mathbb{C}^{D\times D}}{\text{minimize}} \quad & \text{rank}(\boldsymbol{X}) \\ \text{subject to} \quad & \mathcal{A}(\boldsymbol{X}) = \boldsymbol{b}, \end{aligned} \tag{6.28}$$

where $D = LdKT$. Note that this problem is always feasible since each requested intermediate value can be delivered via orthogonal transmission. It is a computationally difficult nonconvex optimization problem due to the rank function, for which we will present convex and nonconvex approaches to induce low-rankness in the following section.

6.4. Numerical algorithms

Low-rank optimization has garnered much attention from a wide variety of areas such as machine learning, signal processing, and wireless communications [5,6,8]. To address the nonconvexity of the rank function, researchers have paid enormous efforts on developing convex and nonconvex algorithms.

6.4.1 Nuclear norm relaxation

Nuclear norm relaxation is a well-known approach for addressing low-rank optimization problems. The resulted nuclear norm minimization problem for problem $\mathscr{P}_{6.1}$ is given by

$$\begin{aligned} \mathscr{P}_{6.1.\text{Nuc}} : \underset{\boldsymbol{X}\in\mathbb{C}^{D\times D}}{\text{minimize}} \quad & \|\boldsymbol{X}\|_* \\ \text{subject to} \quad & \mathcal{A}(\boldsymbol{X}) = \boldsymbol{b}. \end{aligned} \tag{6.29}$$

The nuclear norm $\|\boldsymbol{X}\|_*$ is defined as the sum of all singular values, which is the convex envelope of the rank function under unit norm constraint $\|\boldsymbol{X}\|_2 \leq 1$ [9]. Therefore it is the tightest convex relaxation for rank functions. The nuclear norm relaxation problem can be equivalently rewritten as a semidefinite program (SDP):

$$\underset{\boldsymbol{X},\boldsymbol{W}_1,\boldsymbol{W}_2}{\text{minimize}} \quad \text{Tr}(\boldsymbol{W}_1) + \text{Tr}(\boldsymbol{W}_2)$$

$$\text{subject to} \quad \mathcal{A}(\boldsymbol{X}) = \boldsymbol{b}, \\ \begin{bmatrix} \boldsymbol{W}_1 & \boldsymbol{X} \\ \boldsymbol{X}^{\mathsf{H}} & \boldsymbol{W}_2 \end{bmatrix} \succeq \boldsymbol{0}. \tag{6.30}$$

This problem can be solved by the interior point method, which returns a high-precision solution within a few iterations, whereas the computation cost for each iteration is $O((S+D^2)^3)$ due to the Newton step [10]. With the first-order method such as ADMM [11,12], the computational cost of each iteration can be reduced to $O(SD^2+D^3)$.

Unfortunately, the poor structure of the affine constraint in problem $\mathscr{P}_{6.1}$ makes the performance of nuclear norm relaxation approach unsatisfactory. For instance, consider the two-user single-antenna on-device distributed computing system where $K=N=2$ and $\mu=d=L=M=1$. Each device stores a distinct file and requests the computed intermediate value from the other device. The nuclear norm relaxation problem for this example is given by

$$\underset{\boldsymbol{X}}{\text{minimize}} \quad \|\boldsymbol{X}\|_* \\ \text{subject to} \quad \boldsymbol{X} = \begin{bmatrix} \star & \star & 1/H_{12} & 0 \\ 0 & 1/H_{21} & \star & \star \end{bmatrix}. \tag{6.31}$$

Here $\star$ represents the corresponding entry of a matrix $\boldsymbol{X}$ that can be chosen as an arbitrary value. Note that we have removed the entire rows and columns of $\boldsymbol{X}$ which are all $\star$. We can readily obtain that the optimal rank is 1. However, the solution returned by the nuclear norm relaxation approach is a full-rank matrix (i.e., rank is 2). The poor performance of nuclear norm relaxation approach will also be demonstrated via simulations in Chapter 6.5.

6.4.2 Iteratively reweighted least squares

Another approach for inducing low-rankness is the iteratively reweighted least squares (IRLS) approach [13]. It is realized by studying the Schatten p-norm ($0<p<1$) for low-rank optimization, which is defined by

$$\|\boldsymbol{X}\|_p = \left(\sum_{i=1}^{D} \sigma_i^p(\boldsymbol{X})\right)^{1/p}. \tag{6.32}$$

The Schatten p-norm is nonconvex for $0<p<1$. The IRLS algorithm is implemented by alternately solving a weighted Frobenius norm minimization problem and updating the weights as follows:

$$\boldsymbol{X}^{[t]} = \underset{\boldsymbol{X}}{\operatorname{argmin}}\{\operatorname{Tr}(\boldsymbol{W}^{[k-1]}\boldsymbol{X}^{\mathsf{H}}\boldsymbol{X}) : \mathcal{A}(\boldsymbol{X}) = \boldsymbol{b}\} \tag{6.33}$$

$$\boldsymbol{W}^{[t]} = (\boldsymbol{X}^{[t]^{\mathsf{H}}}\boldsymbol{X}^{[t]} + \gamma^{[k]}\boldsymbol{I})^{\frac{p}{2}-1}, \tag{6.34}$$

where $\gamma^{[k]} > 0$ is a smoothing parameter. It is based on the fact that

$$\|\boldsymbol{X}\|_p^p = \operatorname{Tr}((\boldsymbol{X}^{\mathsf{H}}\boldsymbol{X})^{\frac{p}{2}-1}\boldsymbol{X}^{\mathsf{H}}\boldsymbol{X}). \tag{6.35}$$

6.4.3 Difference-of-convex (DC) programming approach

Recently, the work of [14] proposed a novel difference-of-convex functions (DC) representation of the rank function. It is based on the following key observation:

"the $(k+1)$th largest singular value for a rank k matrix $\boldsymbol{X}$" $= 0$.

Therefore, for a rank k matrix $\boldsymbol{X} \in \mathbb{C}^{D\times D}$, the sum of all singular values (i.e., the nuclear norm) is equal to the sum of the largest k singular values (i.e., the Ky Fan k-norm). We present the definition of the Ky Fan k-norm of a matrix as follows.

Definition 1. Ky Fan k-norm [15]: The Ky Fan k-norm is defined as the sum of the largest-k singular values:

$$|||\boldsymbol{X}|||_k = \sum_{i=1}^{k} \sigma_i(\boldsymbol{X}), \tag{6.36}$$

where $\sigma_i(\boldsymbol{X})$ is the ith largest singular value of a matrix $\boldsymbol{X}$.

We can thus obtain the DC representation for the rank function as

$$\operatorname{rank}(\boldsymbol{X}) = \min\{k : \|\boldsymbol{X}\|_* - |||\boldsymbol{X}|||_k = 0, 0 < k \leq D\} \tag{6.37}$$

since both the nuclear norm and the Ky Fan k-norm are convex functions. Based on this representation, the DC program for solving problem $\mathscr{P}_{6.1}$ is given by

$$\begin{aligned} \mathscr{P}_{6.1.\text{DC-Nuc}} : \underset{\boldsymbol{X}\in\mathbb{C}^{D\times D}}{\text{minimize}} \quad & \|\boldsymbol{X}\|_* - |||\boldsymbol{X}|||_k \\ \text{subject to} \quad & \mathcal{A}(\boldsymbol{X}) = \boldsymbol{b}. \end{aligned} \tag{6.38}$$

By solving problem $\mathscr{P}_{6.1.\text{DC-Nuc}}$ for $k = 1, \ldots, K$ until the objective value achieves zero, we can find the solution $\boldsymbol{X}$ with the minimum rank satisfying the affine constraint.

The DC algorithm for addressing the DC program $\mathscr{P}_{6.1.\text{DC-Nuc}}$ is realized by iteratively performing primal and dual step [16], which guarantees the convergence to critical points from arbitrary initial feasible points. Specifically, we denote problem $\mathscr{P}_{6.1.\text{DC-Nuc}}$ as

$$\alpha = \inf_{\boldsymbol{X} \in \mathcal{X}} \quad f(\boldsymbol{X}) = g(\boldsymbol{X}) - h(\boldsymbol{X}), \tag{6.39}$$

where $g(\boldsymbol{X}) = \|\boldsymbol{X}\|_* + I_{(\mathcal{A}(\boldsymbol{X})=\boldsymbol{b})}(\boldsymbol{X})$ and $h(\boldsymbol{X}) = |||\boldsymbol{X}|||_k$. The indicator function I is

$$I_{(\mathcal{A}(\boldsymbol{X})=\boldsymbol{b})}(\boldsymbol{X}) = \begin{cases} 0, & \mathcal{A}(\boldsymbol{X}) = \boldsymbol{b}, \\ +\infty & \text{otherwise.} \end{cases} \tag{6.40}$$

According to the Fenchel duality [17], we have

$$\alpha = \inf_{\boldsymbol{Y} \in \mathcal{Y}} \quad h^*(\boldsymbol{Y}) - g^*(\boldsymbol{Y}), \tag{6.41}$$

where g^* is the conjugate functions of g,

$$g^*(\boldsymbol{Y}) = \sup_{\boldsymbol{X} \in \mathcal{X}} \quad \langle \boldsymbol{X}, \boldsymbol{Y} \rangle - g(\boldsymbol{X}). \tag{6.42}$$

The inner product is given by $\langle \boldsymbol{X}, \boldsymbol{Y} \rangle = \text{Tr}(\boldsymbol{X}^{\mathsf{H}} \boldsymbol{Y})$. Iterations of the DC algorithm are applied to update the primal and dual variables with successive convex approximation:

$$\boldsymbol{Y}^{[t]} = \arg \inf_{\boldsymbol{Y} \in \mathcal{Y}} \; h^*(\boldsymbol{Y}) - [g^*(\boldsymbol{Y}^{[t-1]}) + \langle \boldsymbol{Y} - \boldsymbol{Y}^{[t-1]}, \boldsymbol{X}^{[t]} \rangle], \tag{6.43}$$

$$\boldsymbol{X}^{[t+1]} = \arg \inf_{\boldsymbol{X} \in \mathcal{X}} \; g(\boldsymbol{X}) - [h(\boldsymbol{X}^{[t]}) + \langle \boldsymbol{X} - \boldsymbol{X}^{[t]}, \boldsymbol{Y}^{[t]} \rangle]. \tag{6.44}$$

By the Fenchel biconjugation theorem [17] the iterations can be simplified to

$$\boldsymbol{Y}^{[t]} \in \partial h(\boldsymbol{X}^{[t]}), \tag{6.45}$$

$$\boldsymbol{X}^{[t+1]} = \arg \inf_{\boldsymbol{X} \in \mathcal{X}} \; g(\boldsymbol{X}) - [h(\boldsymbol{X}^{[t]}) + \langle \boldsymbol{X} - \boldsymbol{X}^{[t]}, \boldsymbol{Y}^{[t]} \rangle]. \tag{6.46}$$

The subgradient of the Ky Fan k-norm is given by

$$\partial |||\boldsymbol{X}_t|||_k = \{\boldsymbol{U} \text{diag}(\boldsymbol{q}) \boldsymbol{V}^{\mathsf{H}}, \boldsymbol{q} = [\underbrace{1, \ldots, 1}_{k}, \underbrace{0, \ldots, 0}_{D-k}]\}. \tag{6.47}$$

Therefore the DC algorithm for problem $\mathscr{P}_{6.1.\text{DC-Nuc}}$ can be concluded as

$$\boldsymbol{Y}^{[t]} \in \partial |||\boldsymbol{X}_t|||_k \tag{6.48}$$

$$\boldsymbol{X}^{[t+1]} = \arg\inf_{\boldsymbol{X}\in\mathcal{X}} \{\|\boldsymbol{X}\|_* - \langle \boldsymbol{X}, \boldsymbol{Y}^{[t]}\rangle : \mathcal{A}(\boldsymbol{X}) = \boldsymbol{b}\}. \tag{6.49}$$

Although the DC approach based on the difference of nuclear norm and the Ky Fan k-norm can improve the performance of inducing low-rank solutions, we observe that it requires solving a nuclear norm minimization problem in each iteration, which results in high computation complexity.

6.4.4 Computationally efficient DC approach

To reduce the high computation costs of the DC approach presented in Chapter 6.4.3, in this subsection, we present a novel DC representation of the rank function and develop a computationally efficient DC approach. It is based on the following definition of the Ky Fan 2-k norm.

Definition 2. Ky Fan 2-k norm [18]: For any integer $1 \le k \le D$, the Ky Fan 2-k norm of a matrix $\boldsymbol{X} \in \mathbb{C}^{D\times D}$ is a unitarily invariant norm given by the square root of the sum of squares of the largest k singular values of $\boldsymbol{X}$:

$$|||\boldsymbol{X}|||_{k,2} = \left(\sum_{i=1}^{k} \sigma_i^2(\boldsymbol{X})\right)^{1/2}. \tag{6.50}$$

Based on this definition, we have

$$\text{rank}(\boldsymbol{X}) \le k \Leftrightarrow \|\boldsymbol{X}\|_F = |||\boldsymbol{X}|||_{k,2} \tag{6.51}$$

for a matrix $\boldsymbol{X} \in \mathbb{C}^{D\times D}$ and $0 < k \le D$. Furthermore, we obtain the following DC representation of the rank function:

$$\text{rank}(\boldsymbol{X}) = \min\{k : \|\boldsymbol{X}\|_F^2 - |||\boldsymbol{X}|||_{k,2}^2 = 0, k \le \min\{m, n\}\}. \tag{6.52}$$

This novel DC representation enables us to find the minimum rank by solving a sequence of DC programs:

$$\begin{aligned} \mathscr{P}_{6.1.\text{DC-Fro}} : \underset{\boldsymbol{X}\in\mathbb{C}^{D\times D}}{\text{minimize}} \quad & \|\boldsymbol{X}\|_F^2 - |||\boldsymbol{X}|||_{k,2}^2 \\ \text{subject to} \quad & \mathcal{A}(\boldsymbol{X}) = \boldsymbol{b} \end{aligned} \tag{6.53}$$

for $k = 1, \ldots, D$ until the objective value decreases to zero. According to Chapter 6.4.3, the iterations of DC algorithm for solving problem

$\mathscr{P}_{6.1.\text{DC-Fro}}$ are given by

$$\boldsymbol{Y}^{[t]} \in \partial |||\boldsymbol{X}^{[t]}|||_{k,2}^2 \tag{6.54}$$

$$\boldsymbol{X}^{[t+1]} = \arg \inf_{\boldsymbol{X} \in \mathcal{X}} \{\|\boldsymbol{X}\|_F^2 - \langle \boldsymbol{X}, \boldsymbol{Y}^{[t]} \rangle : \mathcal{A}(\boldsymbol{X}) = \boldsymbol{b}\}. \tag{6.55}$$

The subgradient of the square of the Ky Fan 2-k norm can be computed by the following proposition.

Proposition 1. *The subgradient of* $|||\boldsymbol{X}|||_{k,2}^2$ *can be computed as two times the best rank k approximation of matrix* $\boldsymbol{X}$*:*

$$\partial |||\boldsymbol{X}|||_{k,2}^2 := 2\boldsymbol{U}\boldsymbol{\Sigma}_k \boldsymbol{V}^{\mathsf{H}}. \tag{6.56}$$

$\boldsymbol{X} = \boldsymbol{U}\boldsymbol{\Sigma}\boldsymbol{V}^{\mathsf{H}}$ *is the singular value decomposition (SVD).* $\boldsymbol{\Sigma}_k$ *keeps the largest k diagonal elements of* $\boldsymbol{\Sigma}$ *and sets others as zeros.*

Proof. The square of the Ky Fan 2-k norm of a matrix $\boldsymbol{X}$ is given by

$$|||\boldsymbol{X}|||_{k,2}^2 = |||\boldsymbol{\sigma}(\boldsymbol{X})|||_{k,2}^2 = \sum_{i=1}^{k} \sigma_i^2(\boldsymbol{X}), \tag{6.57}$$

where $\boldsymbol{\sigma} = [\sigma_i(\boldsymbol{X})] \in \mathbb{R}^D$ is the vector formed by all singular values. $|||\boldsymbol{\sigma}(\boldsymbol{X})|||_{k,2}$ denotes the Ky Fan 2-k norm of a vector $\boldsymbol{\sigma}(\boldsymbol{X})$. As discussed in [19], for the Ky Fan 2-k norm of a vector, the subgradient of $|||\boldsymbol{\sigma}(\boldsymbol{X})|||_{k,2}^2$ with respect to $\boldsymbol{\sigma}(\boldsymbol{X})$ is

$$\boldsymbol{c} \in \mathbb{R}^D : c_i = \begin{cases} 2\sigma_i(\boldsymbol{X}), & i <= k, \\ 0, & i > k. \end{cases} \tag{6.58}$$

The theorem of subdifferential of orthogonally invariant norm [20] tells us that

$$\{\boldsymbol{U}\text{diag}(\boldsymbol{d})\boldsymbol{V}^{\mathsf{H}} : \boldsymbol{X} = \boldsymbol{U}\boldsymbol{\Sigma}\boldsymbol{V}^{\mathsf{H}}, \boldsymbol{d} \in \partial |||\boldsymbol{\sigma}(\boldsymbol{X})|||_{k,2}\} \subseteq \partial |||\boldsymbol{X}|||_{k,2}. \tag{6.59}$$

Then we have

$$2\boldsymbol{U}\boldsymbol{\Sigma}_k \boldsymbol{V}^{\mathsf{H}} \in \partial |||\boldsymbol{X}|||_{k,2}^2, \tag{6.60}$$

where $\boldsymbol{\Sigma}_k$ is given by

$$(i,j)\text{-th entry of } \boldsymbol{\Sigma}_k := \begin{cases} \sigma_i(\boldsymbol{X}), & i = j, i <= k, \\ 0 & \text{otherwise.} \end{cases} \tag{6.61}$$

□

Note that iterations (6.54) and (6.55) can be computed more efficiently than the DC approach based on the difference of the nuclear norm and the Ky Fan k-norm given in Eq. (6.45) and Eq. (6.46), since the primal update for the presented efficient DC method only requires solving a quadratic program. Furthermore, we are able to simplify iterations (6.54) and (6.55) as

$$\begin{aligned} \boldsymbol{X}^{[t+1]} = \underset{\boldsymbol{X} \in \mathbb{C}^{D\times D}}{\arg\min} \quad & \|\boldsymbol{X} - \frac{1}{2}\partial \|\|\boldsymbol{X}^{[t]}\|\|_{k,2}^2 \|_F^2 \\ \text{subject to} \quad & \mathcal{A}(\boldsymbol{X}) = \boldsymbol{b}, \end{aligned} \tag{6.62}$$

which has a closed-form solution as the projection onto the affine constraint. Thus we can conclude the iterations for the computationally efficient DC approach as

$$\boldsymbol{X}^{[t+1]} = (\boldsymbol{I} - \mathcal{A}^{+}\mathcal{A})(\frac{1}{2}\partial \|\|\boldsymbol{X}^{[t]}\|\|_{k,2}^2) + \mathcal{A}^{+}(\boldsymbol{b}). \tag{6.63}$$

Here $\mathcal{A}^{+} = \mathcal{A}^{\mathsf{H}}(\mathcal{A}\mathcal{A}^{\mathsf{H}})^{-1}$ is the pseudoinverse of $\mathcal{A}$. The computational complexity of the subdifferential is $O(D^3)$, which is equal to computing the subdifferential of the Ky Fan k-norm. However, the primal update of the efficient DC approach is only $O(SD^2)$ because the pseudoinverse can be computed and stored in advance. It is much more efficient than solving a nuclear norm minimization problem.

6.5. Simulation results

This section conducts extensive numerical experiments to evaluate the performance of the numerical algorithms proposed in Chapter 6.4:

- Nuclear norm relaxation (referred to as **"Nuclear norm"**): As presented in Chapter 6.4.1, we implement the nuclear norm relaxation approach with interior point method with CVX toolbox [21] to obtain high-precision solutions.
- Iteratively reweighted least squares (referred to as **"IRLS"**): We adopt the iteratively reweighted least squares algorithm [13] introduced in Chapter 6.4.2 with $p = 0.5$.
- DC approach based on the difference between the nuclear norm and Ky Fan k-norm (referred to as **"DC-Nuc"**): This DC approach is proposed in [14] and presented in Chapter 6.4.3.

- Computationally efficient DC approach based on the difference between the square of the Frobenius norm and the square of the Ky Fan 2-k norm (referred to as **"Efficient DC"**): As demonstrated in Chapter 6.4.4, the computation of "Efficient DC" per iteration is much cheaper than "DC-Nuc". We will demonstrate its satisfactory performance through simulations.

We consider symmetric systems in all simulations, that is, the AP and all mobile users are equipped with $L = M$ antennas. We randomly generate the channel matrices with independent and identically distributed (i.i.d.) coefficients according to complex Gaussian distribution, that is, $\boldsymbol{H}_{ki} \sim \mathcal{CN}(\boldsymbol{0}, \boldsymbol{I})$. We consider the single datastream case in all simulations, that is, $d = 1$.

6.5.1 Convergence behaviors

Consider the on-device cooperative inference system with five single-antenna mobile devices. Suppose that the dataset consists of 10 files and each device stores 5 files. We compare the convergence rate and convergence time of "IRLS", "DC-Nuc", and "Efficient DC" algorithm given $r = 13$, that is, the number of iterations and the computation time for convergence. The convergence behaviors are illustrated in Fig. 6.3 with $\sigma_{r+1}(\boldsymbol{X})$ as the cost function. It demonstrates that the "DC-Nuc" converges with the fewest steps of iterations, whereas the "Efficient DC" algorithm converges within shortest time due to its cheaper computational costs.

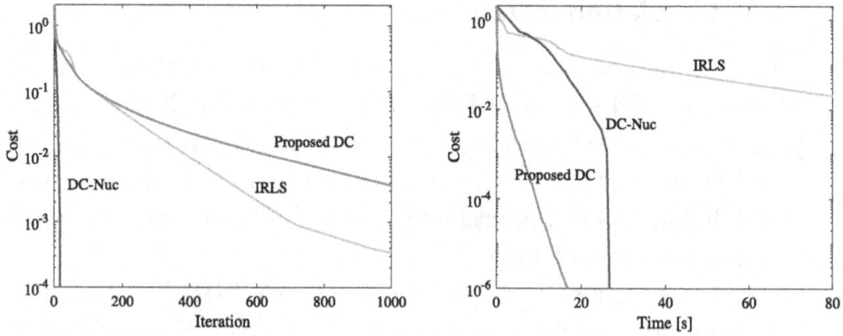

(a) Convergence Rate (b) Convergence Time

Figure 6.3 Convergence rate and time of each algorithm.

6.5.2 Achievable DoF over local storage size

Consider the on-device distributed cooperative system with five single-antenna mobile devices and a single-antenna AP. The whole dataset consists of nine files. We compare the achievable DoF for each algorithm averaged over 100 channel realizations, whereas each device stores 5–9 files. The simulation results are demonstrated in Fig. 6.4. We can observe that the achievable DoF has considerable performance gain when the storage size of each device increases. The "Efficient DC" algorithm has comparable performance with the "DC-Nuc" algorithm with much cheaper computations and considerably outperforms other approaches.

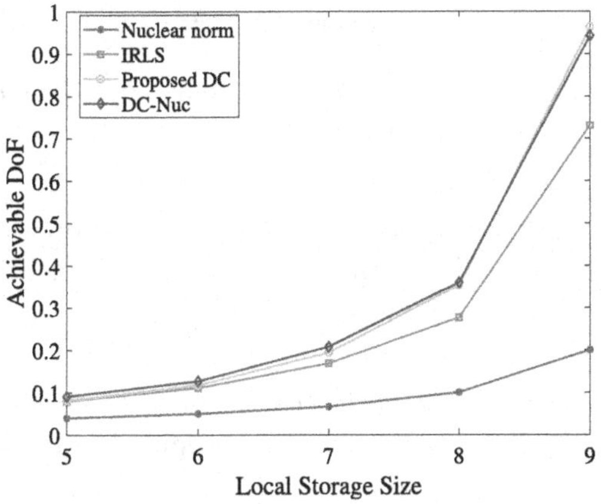

Figure 6.4 The maximum achievable symmetric DoF over local storage size μ of each mobile user.

6.5.3 Scalability

As we discussed in Chapter 6.1, the limited communication bandwidth is one of the main bottlenecks for on-device cooperative inference system. It is thus critical to evaluate the scalability of the presented communication-efficient data shuffling scheme. We consider the on-device cooperative inference system with single-antenna mobile devices. Suppose that the dataset consists of five files, and the storage size of each device is only up to two files. Consider the uniform placement scheme such that each file in the dataset is stored by $\mu K/N = 2K/5$ mobile devices with $\mu = 2$. We illustrate the achievable DoF over the number of mobile devices in Fig. 6.5 averaged over 100 channel realizations. Due to the high computation complexity of "DC-Nuc", we do not include the "DC-Nuc" algorithm into

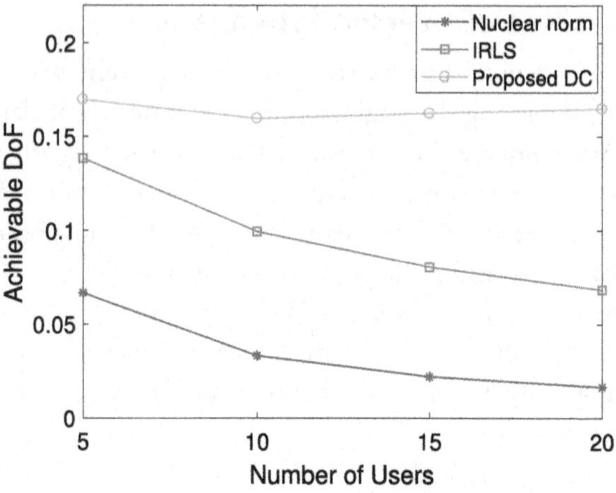

Figure 6.5 The achievable DoF with different algorithms over the number of mobile users.

simulations. The simulation results demonstrate that the achievable DoF yielded by "Efficient DC" algorithm almost remains unchanged with increased number of devices, whereas other approaches fail to be scalable. Although the requested messages to be exchanged in the system increase as the number of devices grows, the opportunities of collaboration among devices also increase since each message is computed by more devices. The scalability of the "Efficient DC" approach results from its great power of exploiting the collaboration opportunities among devices.

6.6. Summary

In this chapter, we studied the on-device cooperative inference system. To address the critical communication challenge for exchanging intermediate values among devices, we proposed a communication-efficient data shuffling scheme with concurrent transmissions. The achievable DoF was maximized via developing a low-rank optimization formulation. A number of convex and nonconvex algorithms were presented, whereas the novel DC algorithm based on the difference between the square of Frobenius norm and the square of the Ky Fan 2-k norm achieved satisfactory DoFs with cheaper computations. Furthermore, this computationally efficient DC approach yielded almost the same achievable DoF when the number of involved devices in the system increased.

References

[1] S. Han, H. Mao, W.J. Dally, Deep compression: compressing deep neural networks with pruning, trained quantization and Huffman coding, in: Int. Conf. Learn. Representations (ICLR), 2016.
[2] J. Dean, S. Ghemawat, MapReduce: simplified data processing on large clusters, Commun. ACM 51 (1) (2008) 107–113.
[3] S. Li, Q. Yu, M.A. Maddah-Ali, A.S. Avestimehr, A scalable framework for wireless distributed computing, IEEE/ACM Trans. Netw. 25 (Oct. 2017) 2643–2654.
[4] V.R. Cadambe, S.A. Jafar, Interference alignment and degrees of freedom of the k-user interference channel, IEEE Trans. Inf. Theory 54 (Aug. 2008) 3425–3441.
[5] Y. Shi, J. Zhang, K.B. Letaief, Low-rank matrix completion for topological interference management by Riemannian pursuit, IEEE Trans. Wirel. Commun. 15 (Jul. 2016) 4703–4717.
[6] K. Yang, Y. Shi, Z. Ding, Generalized low-rank optimization for topological cooperation in ultra-dense networks, IEEE Trans. Wirel. Commun. 18 (May 2019) 2539–2552.
[7] T.M. Cover, J.A. Thomas, Elements of Information Theory, John Wiley & Sons, 2012.
[8] M.A. Davenport, J. Romberg, An overview of low-rank matrix recovery from incomplete observations, IEEE J. Sel. Top. Signal Process. 10 (Jun. 2016) 608–622.
[9] S.M. Fazel, Matrix rank minimization with applications, PhD thesis, Stanford University, 2003.
[10] S. Boyd, L. Vandenberghe, Convex Optimization, Cambridge Univ. Press, 2004.
[11] Y. Shi, J. Zhang, B. O'Donoghue, K.B. Letaief, Large-scale convex optimization for dense wireless cooperative networks, IEEE Trans. Signal Process. 63 (Sept. 2015) 4729–4743.
[12] B. O'Donoghue, E. Chu, N. Parikh, S. Boyd, Conic optimization via operator splitting and homogeneous self-dual embedding, J. Optim. Theory Appl. 169 (Jun 2016) 1042–1068.
[13] K. Mohan, M. Fazel, Iterative reweighted algorithms for matrix rank minimization, J. Mach. Learn. Res. 13 (Nov. 2012) 3441–3473.
[14] J.-y. Gotoh, A. Takeda, K. Tono, DC formulations and algorithms for sparse optimization problems, Math. Program. 169 (May 2018) 141–176.
[15] G. Watson, On matrix approximation problems with Ky Fan k norms, Numer. Algorithms 5 (5) (1993) 263–272.
[16] P.D. Tao, L.T.H. An, Convex analysis approach to DC programming: theory, algorithms and applications, Acta Math. Vietnam. 22 (1) (1997) 289–355.
[17] R.T. Rockafellar, Convex Analysis, Princeton University Press, 2015.
[18] X.V. Doan, S. Vavasis, Finding the largest low-rank clusters with Ky Fan 2-k-norm and ℓ_1-norm, SIAM J. Optim. 26 (1) (2016) 274–312.
[19] K. Tono, A. Takeda, J.-y. Gotoh, Efficient DC algorithm for constrained sparse optimization, preprint, arXiv:1701.08498, 2017.
[20] G.A. Watson, Characterization of the subdifferential of some matrix norms, Linear Algebra Appl. 170 (1992) 33–45.
[21] M. Grant, S. Boyd, CVX: Matlab software for disciplined convex programming, version 2.1, http://cvxr.com/cvx, Mar. 2014.

CHAPTER SEVEN

Computation offloading for edge cooperative inference

7.1. Background

7.1.1 Computation offloading

Cloud computing led to a rapid growth of many computation intensive services, such as the online shopping service provided by Amazon and cloud storage service provided by Dropbox. However, the inherent limitation of cloud computing limits the development of low-latency and computation-intensive services. To meet the ever-increasing computation demands from mobile applications and alleviate the extremely high communication traffic required by cloud computing, the concept of mobile edge computing (MEC) [1–3] was proposed to push the computation and storage resources to the network edge.

To achieve ubiquitous computing, computation offloading is a key enabling technology by coordinating the computation resources between mobile devices and proximal servers (e.g., mobile base stations). There are basically two different categories of computation task offloading models, *binary offloading* and *partial offloading*. For a highly integrated task that could not be partitioned, we determine whether to execute the task on the device locally or offload the task to an edge server, which is called the binary offloading model [4,5]. There is another category of computation tasks composed of separated components, which allow us to partition the task into multiple parts and offload a part of the task to edge servers for remote execution. This type of computation models is called the partial offloading model, which requires the optimization of subtask allocation to multiple edge nodes including end device and edge servers [6,7]. In addition, there are also a number of works considering the stochastic arrival of computational tasks [8], for which long-term performance in terms of average energy consumption and computation latency are particularly relevant.

Energy consumption and computation latency are two main concerns for designing offloading strategies. For example, Bi and Zhang [4] proposed to jointly design the binary offloading strategy and transmission time allocation with the purpose of maximizing the computation rate for wireless

Mobile Edge Artificial Intelligence
https://doi.org/10.1016/B978-0-12-823817-2.00017-6

powered MEC systems. Huang et al. [5] developed a deep reinforcement learning-based offloading framework to maximize the computation rate by learning binary offloading decisions for wireless powered MEC systems. Wang et al. [6] designed a partial offloading scheme by jointly optimizing the computational speed, transmit power, and offloading ratio of mobile devices to minimize the energy consumption and latency. Chen et al. [7] considered the partial offloading scheme for minimizing energy consumption and latency in relay-assisted computation offloading systems.

7.1.2 Edge inference via computation offloading

Deploying AI models at network edges has the potential of providing low-latency and high-security intelligent services. However, there are a lot of constraints for performing inference directly on mobile devices, especially for computationally intensive deep learning inference tasks. Therefore it is promising to offload the inference task to proximal edge servers equipped with more powerful computation resources than mobile devices. In recent years, this type of edge inference systems, termed as *computation offloading-based edge inference systems*, have attracted much attention.

One important strategy is to offload the entire computation task to edge servers [1], termed as server-based edge inference. It is particularly suitable for IoT devices with limited computation resources. For this type of systems, the entire AI model is deployed on the edge server, and each mobile device simply uploads the raw input data to the edge server for inference. To improve the uplink communication efficiency, the work [9] proposed to transmit only the key frames data to reduce the required communication bandwidth. The work [10] proposed a DNN-based data compression scheme to compress the input image to a smaller size than traditional methods such as JPEG without degrading the accuracy of image recognition.

Another important strategy of computation offloading-based edge inference considers the hierarchical structure of computation tasks. That is, by splitting the tasks and offloading a portion of tasks to edge servers, the inference results could be obtained by the the partial model parameters and the input intermediate values from mobile devices, which can be termed as device-edge joint inference. The work [11] proposed to split the procedure of image classification and deploy the feature extraction part on mobile devices and the remaining part on the edge server to reduce the total execution time. The hierarchical structure over mobile devices, edge servers, and the cloud servers has been studied in the work [12], which proposed an early exit scheme to reduce the computation redundancy. In addition, the work [13] proposed to jointly design the model split strategy and early exit strategy to achieve low-latency inference based on the computational resources and network conditions.

In this chapter, we present a representative computation offloading-based edge inference framework by designing an energy-efficient binary offloading strategy to multiple edge servers under target quality-of-service constraints.

7.2. Energy-efficient wireless cooperative transmission for edge inference

The methods mentioned above for edge inference are based on the given computational capabilities of edge servers. We notice that cooperative transmission [14] is a well-known approach to reduce the cochannel interference and improve the spectral efficiency. It motivates an energy-efficient wireless cooperative transmission approach for computation offloading-based edge inference. By performing each task at multiple edge servers and cooperatively transmitting the inference results to mobile devices, the quality-of-service (QoS) for delivering the inference result could be improved, which is critical to support low-latency services. As illustrated in Fig. 7.1, consider the edge inference system where each mobile user (MU) uploads its input data (e.g., a piece of sketch) to the APs. By performing each inference task with a pretrained DNN model (e.g., Nvidia GauGan [15] AI system for creating photorealistic landscapes from sketches), the inference results (e.g., a landscape image) are available at multiple APs and can be transmitted to MUs via cooperative transmission. Note that this scheme is applicable for not only the server-based edge inference but also for the device-edge joint inference system. We discuss this in the remark of Chapter 7.2.4.

7.2.1 Communication model

Consider an edge inference network with N edge computing enabled APs, each equipped with L antennas and K single-antenna MUs, as illustrated in Fig. 7.1. The deep learning inference task for MU k can be denoted as $\phi_k(d_k)$ with input d_k. Due to low-latency and privacy concerns, we predownload the trained DNN models from the cloud center to the APs and perform the DNN inference tasks on the edge computing enabled APs. After collecting all input data d_k from MUs, each AP selectively performs

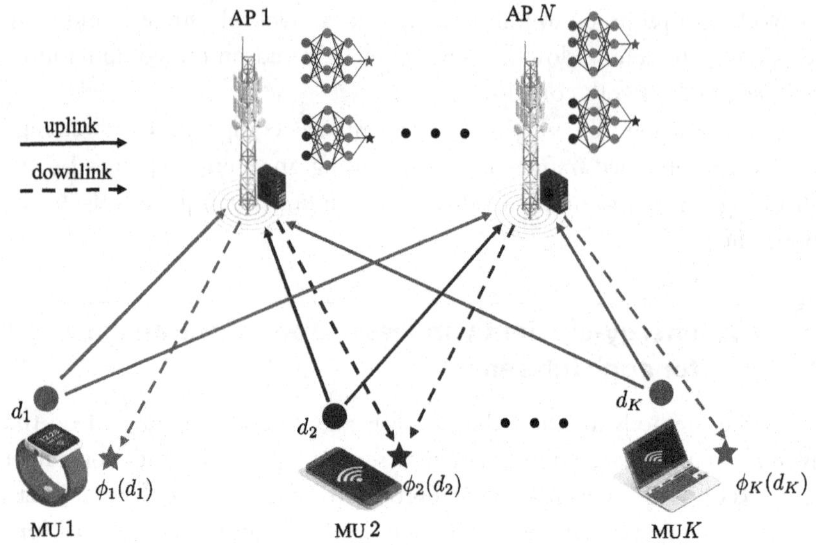

Figure 7.1 System model of edge inference for DNNs.

a subset of all inference tasks and cooperatively transmits the inference results to MUs for low-latency intelligent services. Though both the uplink and downlink transmissions are important in such a system, in this chapter, we focus on the tradeoff between computation and cooperative downlink transmission, that is, cooperation opportunities increase when each task is executed by more APs and can be exploited to improve the downlink transmission efficiency. However, it requires a higher energy consumption because of replication in computing. To address this problem, in this chapter, we will jointly design the task selection and downlink beamforming strategy.

We denote by $s_k \in \mathbb{C}$ the encoded scalar for the inference result $\phi_k(d_k)$ to be transmitted with unit power, that is, $\mathbb{E}[|s_k|^2] = 1$. Let $\boldsymbol{v}_{nk} \in \mathbb{C}^L$ be the beamforming vector of the nth AP for s_k. Assuming that all inputs d_k are collected at each AP, the received signal at the kth MU in downlink transmission is given by

$$y_k = \sum_{n=1}^{N}\sum_{l=1}^{K} \boldsymbol{h}_{kn}^{\mathsf{H}} \boldsymbol{v}_{nl} s_l + z_k, \tag{7.1}$$

where $\boldsymbol{h}_{kn} \in \mathbb{C}^L$ denotes the channel coefficient vector between AP n and MU k, and $z_k \sim \mathcal{CN}(0, \sigma_k^2)$ denotes the complex additive isotropic white

Gaussian noise. All data symbols s_k and the noise are assumed to be mutually independent. Let $\mathcal{A} \subseteq \{(n, k) : n = 1, \ldots, N, k = 1, \ldots, K\}$ be a task allocation on APs, that is, if $(n, k) \in \mathcal{A}$, then the inference task ϕ_k is executed at the nth AP. It is interesting that the group sparsity pattern of the aggregative beamforming vector

$$\boldsymbol{v} = [\boldsymbol{v}_{11}^{\mathsf{H}}, \ldots, \boldsymbol{v}_{N1}^{\mathsf{H}}, \ldots, \boldsymbol{v}_{NK}^{\mathsf{H}}]^{\mathsf{H}} \in \mathbb{C}^{NKL} \tag{7.2}$$

indicates the task allocation strategy. Specifically, if the kth inference task is not performed at the nth AP, that is, $(n, k) \in \mathcal{A}$, then the beamforming vector $\boldsymbol{v}_{nk}$ can be set as the zero vector. Denote the group sparsity pattern of $\boldsymbol{v}$ as

$$\mathcal{T}(\boldsymbol{v}) = \{(n, k) | \boldsymbol{v}_{nk} \neq \boldsymbol{0}\}. \tag{7.3}$$

The signal-to-interference-plus-noise ratio (SINR) of the received signal at device k is given by

$$\mathrm{SINR}_k(\boldsymbol{v}; \boldsymbol{h}_k) = \frac{|\boldsymbol{h}_k^{\mathsf{H}} \boldsymbol{v}_k|^2}{\sum_{l \neq k} |\boldsymbol{h}_k^{\mathsf{H}} \boldsymbol{v}_l|^2 + \sigma_k^2}, \tag{7.4}$$

where $\boldsymbol{h}_k$ and $\boldsymbol{v}_k$ are respectively given by

$$\boldsymbol{h}_k = [\boldsymbol{h}_{k1}^{\mathsf{H}}, \ldots, \boldsymbol{h}_{kN}^{\mathsf{H}}]^{\mathsf{H}} \in \mathbb{C}^{NL}, \tag{7.5}$$

$$\boldsymbol{v}_k = \begin{bmatrix} \boldsymbol{v}_{1k}^{\mathsf{H}} & \cdots & \boldsymbol{v}_{Nk}^{\mathsf{H}} \end{bmatrix}^{\mathsf{H}} \in \mathbb{C}^{NL}. \tag{7.6}$$

Denote the aggregative channel coefficient vector as

$$\boldsymbol{h} = [\boldsymbol{h}_1^{\mathsf{H}}, \ldots, \boldsymbol{h}_K^{\mathsf{H}}]^{\mathsf{H}} \in \mathbb{C}^{NKL}. \tag{7.7}$$

Each AP n has the maximum transmit power constraint

$$\mathbb{E}\left[\sum_{l=1}^{K} \|\boldsymbol{v}_{nl} s_l\|_2^2\right] = \sum_{l=1}^{K} \|\boldsymbol{v}_{nl}\|_2^2 \leq P_n^{\mathsf{Tx}}, n = 1, \ldots, N, \tag{7.8}$$

with $P_n^{\mathsf{Tx}} > 0$ as the maximum transmit power.

7.2.2 Power consumption model

Though deep learning has been widely leveraged in intelligent systems, the high energy consumption is still one of the major issues. Indeed, the energy consumption of deep learning inference is dominated by the memory access procedure. The energy consumption of a memory access operation in 32-bit DRAM (i.e., dynamic random access memory) is 640 pJ, whereas the energy consumption of a cache access operation in 32-bit SRAM (i.e., static random access memory) is 5 pJ, and a 32-bit floating point add operation only consumes 0.9 pJ, as exemplified by [16]. For inference task with DNN models, the large size of DNNs probably cannot fit the local storage of resource-constrained mobile devices. It leads to more DRAM memory access operations and much higher energy consumption. Thus we leverage the computation offloading technique for performing edge inference tasks with large DNN models.

Suppose the power consumption for the nth AP to perform task ϕ_k is P^{c}_{nk}. The total computation power consumption is given by

$$P^{\mathrm{c}} = \sum_{n,k} P^{\mathrm{c}}_{nk} I_{(n,k)\in\mathcal{T}(\boldsymbol{v})}, \tag{7.9}$$

where the indicator function equals 1 if $(n, k) \in \mathcal{T}(\boldsymbol{v})$ and 0 otherwise. The total power consumption for the edge inference system consists of computation power and communication power given by

$$P = \sum_{n,k} \frac{1}{\eta_n} \|\boldsymbol{v}_{nk}\|_2^2 + \sum_{n,k} P^{\mathrm{c}}_{nk} I_{(n,k)\in\mathcal{T}(\boldsymbol{v})}, \tag{7.10}$$

where η_n denotes the power amplifier efficiency of the nth AP.

Due to the widespread use of DNNs, especially deep convolutional neural networks (CNNs) for intelligent services, much attention has been garnered in energy-efficient structure design of neural networks [16]. A critical topic is estimating the energy consumption of performing DNN inference, for which the work of [17] has developed an estimation tool. The energy consumption consists of the computation part and the data movement part [18]. The computation part is obtained by counting the number of multiply-and-accumulate (MAC) operations in each layer multiplying the energy consumption of each MAC operation. The data movement part is given by counting the number of memory accesses at each level of memory (e.g., DRAM, SRAM) and weighing them with the energy consumption of memory access in the corresponding level.

We provide an effective estimation procedure for the computation power of image classification with classic CNN, a.k.a., AlexNet with five convolutional layers and three fully connected layers on Eyeriss chip [18].

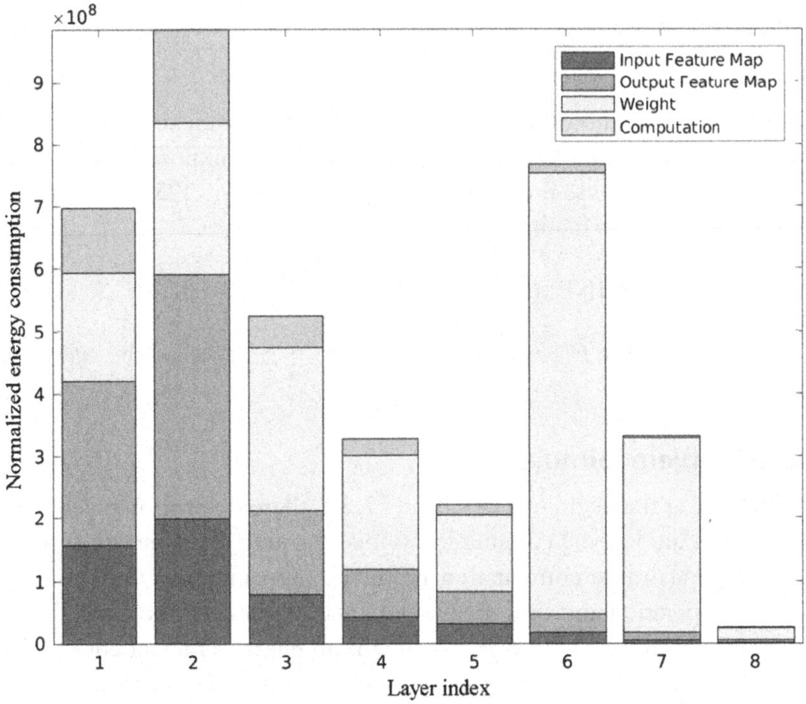

Figure 7.2 Energy consumption estimation of the AlexNet [19].

The input of the energy consumption estimation tool is network configuration information, whereas the output is the energy breakdown (including computation, input feature map, output feature map, and weight) of each layer measured by the energy consumption of one MAC cooperation. The estimation results are illustrated in Fig. 7.2. The computation power consumption can be determined through dividing the energy consumption by the computation time.

7.2.3 Channel uncertainty model

In reality, there is an inevitable uncertainty error in the acquired channel state information (CSI) $\boldsymbol{h}$ for downlink transmission. This may be due to training-based channel estimation [20], limited feedback precision [21], CSI acquisition delays [22], and so on. For a number of high-stake intelligent applications, including smart vehicles and robots, robustness is one of the key requirements. We take the additive error model of channel imperfection into consideration,

$$h = \hat{h} + e, \tag{7.11}$$

where $\hat{h} \in \mathbb{C}^{NKL}$ denotes the estimated aggregative channel coefficient vector, and $e \in \mathbb{C}^{NKL}$ denotes the random errors with unknown distribution and zero mean. We use the probabilistic QoS constraints [23] to characterize the robustness to random errors:

$$\Pr(\mathrm{SINR}_k(v; h_k) \geq \gamma_k) \geq 1 - \zeta, \ \ k = 1, \ldots, K, \tag{7.12}$$

where ζ denotes the *tolerance level* and "$\mathrm{SINR}_k \geq \gamma_k$" is called the *safe condition.*

7.2.4 Problem formulation

As discussed at the beginning of Chapter 7.2.1, there is a critical tradeoff between computation and communication. Performing the same task at more APs consumes more computation power but also increases the opportunity of cooperation and thus has the potential of reducing the transmission power consumption. Therefore we provide an energy-efficient edge inference approach by minimizing the total network power consumption under the probabilistic QoS constraint at each MU and the maximum transmit power constraint at each AP. It can be formulated as the following group sparse beamforming problem with joint chance constraints:

$$\begin{aligned} \mathscr{P}_{7.1.\mathrm{CCP}}: \min_{v \in \mathbb{C}^{NKL}} \quad & \sum_{n,k} \frac{1}{\eta_n} \|v_{nk}\|_2^2 + \sum_{n,k} P_{nk}^{\mathrm{c}} I_{(n,k) \in \mathcal{T}(v)} \\ \text{s.t.} \quad & \Pr(\mathrm{SINR}_k(v; h_k) \geq \gamma_k) \geq 1 - \zeta, k = 1, \ldots, K \qquad (7.13) \\ & \sum_{k=1}^{K} \|v_{nk}\|_2^2 \leq P_n^{\mathrm{Tx}}, n \in [N]. \qquad (7.14) \end{aligned}$$

Remark 1. The privacy concern for data is also a key point for high-stake applications where the end users may not be willing to directly send their raw data input to the APs. To avoid the data exposure, there are a number of works considering the device-edge joint inference scheme with hierarchical structure, such as [13]. By partitioning a DNN model and deploying it across the mobile device and the AP we are able to protect the data privacy since only the output before the partition point is available to APs. Note that the presented framework is also applicable to this privacy-preserving hierarchical structure. In this case the input data d_k become the locally computed intermediate values of the layers before the partition point. The computation task ϕ_k becomes the task of computing the inference result with the subsequent layers.

7.3. Computationally tractable approximation for probabilistic QoS constraints

In this section, we present a number of computationally tractable approximations to address the probabilistic QoS constraints. In particular, we provide a statistical learning approach to find a robust optimization counterpart for the probabilistic QoS constraints of problem $\mathscr{P}_{\text{CCP}}$, which has notable advantages over the scenario generation approach and the stochastic programming approach.

7.3.1 Analysis of probabilistic QoS constraints

The general idea of achieving a high probability of satisfying QoS constraints is as follows [23]. By collecting a number of independent and identically distributed (i.i.d.) samples of the imperfect CSI we are able to learn the underlying uncertainty model from the samples to combat against CSI errors with unknown distribution. Specifically, we denote the set of collected D i.i.d. samples as $\mathcal{D} = \{\tilde{\boldsymbol{h}}^{(1)}, \ldots, \tilde{\boldsymbol{h}}^{(D)}\}$. The target is to find an aggregative beamforming vector $\boldsymbol{v}$ to guarantee that the safe conditions $\text{SINR}_k \geq \gamma_k$ are satisfied with a probability not less than $1 - \zeta$. Due to the unknown prior distribution of CSI errors, the statistical guarantee that we can obtain is usually given by certain tolerance level $1 - \epsilon$ with certain confidence level $1 - \delta$, that is,

$$\text{“the confidence level of} \Pr(\text{SINR}_k(\boldsymbol{v}; \boldsymbol{h}_k) \geq \gamma_k) \geq 1 - \epsilon\text{”} \geq 1 - \delta, \quad (7.15)$$

given $\boldsymbol{v}, D, 0 < \epsilon < 1$, and $0 < \delta < 1$. This statistical guarantee leads to an upper bound for the violation probability of the safe condition:

$$\Pr(\text{SINR}_k(\boldsymbol{v}; \boldsymbol{h}_k) < \gamma_k) < \delta + \epsilon(1 - \delta). \quad (7.16)$$

By choosing the tolerance level ϵ and the confidence level δ such that $\zeta > \delta + \epsilon(1 - \delta)$, we can guarantee that the safe condition (7.12) holds. We leave the discussions on the collection of i.i.d. imperfect CSI samples to Chapter 7.3.5.

The joint chance constraints (7.13) are usually computationally difficult [24]. Moreover, we have no prior information about the uncertainty.

A natural idea of addressing the issue is finding computationally tractable approximations for the joint chance constraints. We will introduce several known approaches to obtain computationally tractable approximations for the probabilistic QoS constraints (7.13) in the following, and the statistical guarantee for each approach (if available) is given by (7.15).

7.3.2 Scenario generation approach

The well-known scenario generation approach [24] is realized by approximating the probabilistic QoS constraints (7.13) as deterministic QoS constraints for all channel samples:

$$\begin{aligned}
\mathscr{P}_{7.1.\mathrm{SG}}: \min_{\boldsymbol{v}\in\mathbb{C}^{NKL}} \quad & \sum_{n,k}\frac{1}{\eta_n}\|\boldsymbol{v}_{nk}\|_2^2+\sum_{n,k}P_{nk}^{\mathrm{c}}I_{(n,k)\in\mathcal{T}(\boldsymbol{v})} \\
\text{s.t.} \quad & \mathrm{SINR}_k(\boldsymbol{v};\tilde{\boldsymbol{h}}_k^{(i)})\geq\gamma_k, i=1,\ldots,D, k=1,\ldots,K \quad (7.17)\\
& \sum_{k=1}^{K}\|\boldsymbol{v}_{nk}\|_2^2\leq P_n^{\mathrm{Tx}}, n\in[N]. \quad (7.18)
\end{aligned}$$

However, the scenario generation approach is conservative because it guarantees the robustness in the minimax sense. The feasible region volume for problem $\mathscr{P}_{7.1.\mathrm{SG}}$ decreases when increasing the number of channel samples D, which may lead to a high probability of infeasibility. The required sample size D to satisfy the statistical guarantee (7.15) is given by

$$\sum_{i=1}^{NKL-1}\binom{D}{i}\epsilon^i(1-\epsilon)^{D-i}\leq\delta. \quad (7.19)$$

Therefore another disadvantage of the scenario generation approach is that the required sample size given statistical guarantee is roughly linear with $1/\epsilon$ and NKL when ϵ is small.

7.3.3 Stochastic programming approach

The stochastic programming approach [25] can be used to overcome the overconservativeness of the scenario generation approach. For problem $\mathscr{P}_{7.1.\mathrm{CCP}}$, we can adopt the stochastic DC program approach by using a DC approximation for the joint chance constraints and adopting the successive convex approximation with Monte Carlo approach [23]. The main disadvantage of the stochastic programming approach is its much higher computational cost, which increases linearly with the sample size D. Therefore it is not scalable to large sample size to obtain solutions robust to CSI errors. In addition, the statistical guarantee for this approach is still not available under finite sample size.

7.3.4 Statistical learning-based robust optimization approach

To address these limitations for the existing approaches, we provide a statistical learning-based robust optimization approximation for the joint chance constraints, which yields a group sparse beamforming problem with nonconvex quadratic constraints for further algorithm design. We will firstly introduce the robust optimization approximation for the probabilistic QoS constraint, followed by the procedure of learning the parameters of the high probability region from channel samples.

7.3.4.1 Robust optimization approximation for probabilistic QoS constraints

The basic idea of robust optimization [26] approximation is finding a high probability region for the imperfect CSI (7.13) and imposing safe conditions to be met for all random channel coefficients within the region. It is given by

$$\mathrm{SINR}_k(\boldsymbol{v}; \boldsymbol{h}_k) \geq \gamma_k, \boldsymbol{h}_k \in \mathcal{U}_k, \ \ k = 1, \ldots, K, \tag{7.20}$$

where $\mathcal{U}_k$ denotes the high-probability region of $\boldsymbol{h}_k$. By learning the high-probability region $\mathcal{U}_k$ from the channel samples in $\mathcal{D}$, that is, $\mathcal{U}_k := \mathcal{U}_k(\mathcal{D})$, such that

$$\text{“the confidence level of } \Pr(\boldsymbol{h}_k \in \mathcal{U}_k) \geq 1 - \epsilon \ \text{ holds”} \geq 1 - \delta. \tag{7.21}$$

A more precise description of the confidence is that the high-probability region is random due to the randomness of data $\mathcal{D}$. By repeating the data generation procedure and high-probability region procedure, we aim to make the probabilistic constraint $\Pr(\boldsymbol{h}_k \in \mathcal{U}_k) \geq 1 - \epsilon$ satisfy for at least $1 - \delta$ proportion of trials.

The robust optimization approximation for problem $\mathscr{P}_{7.1.\mathrm{CCP}}$ is given by

$$\begin{aligned} \mathscr{P}_{7.1.\mathrm{RO}} : \underset{\boldsymbol{v},\boldsymbol{h}}{\text{minimize}} \quad & \sum_{n,k} \frac{1}{\eta_n} \|\boldsymbol{v}_{nk}\|_2^2 + \sum_{n,l} P_{nk}^{\mathrm{c}} I_{(n,k)\in\mathcal{T}(\boldsymbol{v})} \\ \text{subject to} \quad & \mathrm{SINR}_k(\boldsymbol{v}; \boldsymbol{h}_k) \geq \gamma_k, \boldsymbol{h}_k \in \mathcal{U}_k, k = 1, \ldots, K \end{aligned}$$

$$\sum_{k=1}^{K} \|\boldsymbol{v}_{nk}\|_2^2 \leq P_n^{\mathsf{Tx}}, n = 1, \ldots, N. \tag{7.22}$$

The high-probability region $\mathcal{U}_k$ is often chosen as some geometric set, and the geometric shape has important influence on the performance and the tractability of problem $\mathscr{P}_{7.1.\text{RO}}$. Ellipsoids and polytopes are two commonly chosen geometric shapes as the basic uncertainty sets because of computational tractability concerns. Furthermore, we can choose the uncertainty set as the unions or intersections of the basic uncertainty sets. In this chapter, we set the uncertainty geometric sets as ellipsoids due to wide applications in modeling CSI uncertainties [27]. Specifically, the ellipsoidal high-probability region $\mathcal{U}_k$ can be parameterized as

$$\mathcal{U}_k = \{\boldsymbol{h}_k : \boldsymbol{h}_k = \hat{\boldsymbol{h}}_k + \boldsymbol{B}_k \boldsymbol{u}_k, \boldsymbol{u}_k^{\mathsf{H}} \boldsymbol{u}_k \leq 1\}, \tag{7.23}$$

where the statistical learning procedure for the parameters $\boldsymbol{B}_k \in \mathbb{C}^{NL \times NL}$ and $\hat{\boldsymbol{h}}_k \in \mathbb{C}^{NL}$ is presented in Chapter 7.3.4.2. To facilitate algorithm design, we will reformulate problem $\mathscr{P}_{7.1.\text{RO}}$ as a group sparse beamforming problem with nonconvex quadratic constraints in Chapter 7.3.4.3.

7.3.4.2 Statistical learning approach for the high-probability region

Condition (7.20) guarantees the feasibility of (7.15). However, the conservativeness of the robust optimization approximation is still a challenging problem to be addressed. Generally speaking, approximation with a smaller feasible region means its higher conservativeness. To obtain a larger feasible region for problem $\mathscr{P}_{7.1.\text{RO}}$, we prefer the high-probability regions $\mathcal{U}_k$ with smaller volumes. Therefore we aim to set the volume of high-probability region such that the confidence is close to $1 - \delta$.

The ellipsoidal model of $\mathcal{U}_k$ in (7.23) can be rewritten as

$$\mathcal{U}_k = \{\boldsymbol{h}_k : (\boldsymbol{h}_k - \hat{\boldsymbol{h}}_k)^T \boldsymbol{\Sigma}_k^{-1} (\boldsymbol{h}_k - \hat{\boldsymbol{h}}_k) \leq s_k\}, \tag{7.24}$$

where $\hat{\boldsymbol{h}}_k$ and $\boldsymbol{\Sigma}_k$ are shape parameters, and $s_k > 0$ is the size parameter. Therein, $\boldsymbol{\Sigma}_k / s_k = \boldsymbol{B}_k \boldsymbol{B}_k^{\mathsf{H}}$. We will adopt the statistical learning approach [26] to construct the high-probability region $\mathcal{U}$, including shape learning and size calibration. First of all, the channel samples $\mathcal{D}$ will be split into two subsets, $\mathcal{D}^1 = \{\tilde{\boldsymbol{h}}^{(1)}, \ldots, \tilde{\boldsymbol{h}}^{(D_1)}\}$ for shape learning and $\mathcal{D}^2 = \{\tilde{\boldsymbol{h}}^{(D_1+1)}, \ldots, \tilde{\boldsymbol{h}}^{(D)}\}$ for size calibration through quantile estimation.

7.3.4.2.1 Shape learning

Denote the set of channel samples for $\boldsymbol{h}_k$ as $\mathcal{D}_k = \mathcal{D}_k^1 \cup \mathcal{D}_k^2 = \{\tilde{\boldsymbol{h}}_k^{(j)}\}_{j=1}^{D}$. The shape parameter $\hat{\boldsymbol{h}}_k$ is chosen as the mean of $\mathcal{D}_k^1$:

$$\hat{\boldsymbol{h}}_k = \frac{1}{D_1}\sum_{j=1}^{D_1} \tilde{\boldsymbol{h}}_k^{(j)}. \tag{7.25}$$

We choose $\boldsymbol{\Sigma}_k$ as a block-diagonal matrix by omitting the correlation between $\boldsymbol{h}_{kn}$ to reduce the complexity. The diagonal elements are set as the sample covariance in $\mathcal{D}_k^1$, that is,

$$\boldsymbol{\Sigma}_k = \begin{bmatrix} \boldsymbol{\Sigma}_{k1} & & \\ & \ddots & \\ & & \boldsymbol{\Sigma}_{kN} \end{bmatrix}, \quad \boldsymbol{\Sigma}_{kn} = \frac{1}{D_1 - 1}\sum_{j=1}^{D_1} (\tilde{\boldsymbol{h}}_{kn}^{(j)} - \hat{\boldsymbol{h}}_{kn})(\tilde{\boldsymbol{h}}_{kn}^{(j)} - \hat{\boldsymbol{h}}_{kn})^{\mathsf{H}}. \tag{7.26}$$

7.3.4.2.2 Size calibration

The second part of data samples, i.e., $\mathcal{D}_k^2$, is used for calibrating the size parameter s_k by estimating a $(1-\epsilon)$-quantile with $1-\delta$ confidence. Specifically, define the transformation

$$\mathcal{G}(\xi) = (\xi - \hat{\boldsymbol{h}}_k)^{\mathsf{H}} \boldsymbol{\Sigma}_k^{-1} (\xi - \hat{\boldsymbol{h}}_k) \tag{7.27}$$

for mapping the data samples in $\mathcal{D}_k^2$ to a real number. We choose s_k as the estimated $(1-\epsilon)$-quantile of $\mathcal{G}(\boldsymbol{h}_k)$ from $\mathcal{D}_k^2$. The $(1-\epsilon)$-quantile $q_{1-\epsilon}$ is defined by

$$\Pr(\mathcal{G}(\xi) \le q_{1-\epsilon}) = 1 - \epsilon. \tag{7.28}$$

Based on $\mathcal{D}_k^2$, we can construct the i.i.d. samples as $\{G_j = \mathcal{G}(\boldsymbol{h}_k^{(D_1+j)})\}$. Given the confidence level $1-\delta$, the size parameter s_k is chosen as an estimated $(1-\epsilon)$-quantile [26]:

$$s_k = G_{(j^\star)}, j^\star = \underset{1\le j \le D-D_1}{\arg\min} \left\{ j : \sum_{k=0}^{j-1} \binom{D-D_1}{k} (1-\epsilon)^k \epsilon^{D-D_1-k} \ge 1-\delta \right\}, \tag{7.29}$$

where $G_{(1)} \le \cdots \le G_{(D-D_1)}$ is a permutation of $\{G_j\}$ in ascending order.

The statistical learning approach via the above two steps yields the high-probability regions $\mathcal{U}_k$, which ensures that for any feasible solution to problem $\mathscr{P}_{7.1.\mathrm{RO}}$, the probabilistic QoS constraints (7.13) are satisfied with confidence at least $1-\delta$. To obtain the required minimum sample size, we find that $j^\star$ exists if and only if

$$\sum_{k=0}^{D-D_1-1} \binom{D-D_1}{k}(1-\epsilon)^k \epsilon^{D-D_1-k} \geq 1-\delta. \tag{7.30}$$

It follows that $1-(1-\epsilon)^{D-D_1} \geq 1-\delta$. Therefore the required minimum sample size is given by $D > D - D_1 \geq \log\delta / \log(1-\epsilon)$ to achieve the target statistical guarantee (7.15). The matrix $\boldsymbol{B}_k$ is given by computing the Cholesky decomposition $\boldsymbol{\Sigma}_k = \boldsymbol{\Delta}_k \boldsymbol{\Delta}_k^{\mathsf{H}}$ and following

$$\boldsymbol{B}_k = \sqrt{s_k}\boldsymbol{\Delta}_k. \tag{7.31}$$

The whole procedure for constructing the high-probability region from channel samples in $\mathcal{D}$ is summarized in Algorithm 9.

Algorithm 9: Learning the high-probability region $\{\mathcal{U}_k\}$.

Input: i.i.d. channel samples $\mathcal{D} = \{\tilde{\boldsymbol{h}}^{(1)}, \ldots, \tilde{\boldsymbol{h}}^{(D)}\}$.
for $k = 1, \ldots K$ **do**
- **Data splitting:** Randomly split the samples of $\boldsymbol{h}_k$, i.e., $\mathcal{D}_k$, into two subsets $\mathcal{D}_k^1$ and $\mathcal{D}_k^2$.
- **Shape learning:** Set the shape parameters $\hat{\boldsymbol{h}}_k$ and $\boldsymbol{\Sigma}_k$ following Eqs. (7.25) and (7.26) based on $\mathcal{D}_k^1$.
- **Size calibration:** Set the size parameter s_k following Eq. (7.29).
- Compute $\boldsymbol{B}_k = \sqrt{s_k}\boldsymbol{\Delta}_k$ via Cholesky decomposition $\boldsymbol{\Sigma}_k = \boldsymbol{\Delta}_k\boldsymbol{\Delta}_k^{\mathsf{H}}$.

end
Output: $\hat{\boldsymbol{h}}_k, \boldsymbol{B}_k, \forall k = 1, \ldots, K$.

7.3.4.3 Problem reformulation for problem $\mathscr{P}_{7.1.RO}$

According to the ellipsoidal model (7.23), we can rewrite the robust optimization approximation (7.20) as

$$\boldsymbol{h}_k^{\mathsf{H}}\left(\frac{1}{\gamma_k}\boldsymbol{v}_k\boldsymbol{v}_k^{\mathsf{H}} - \sum_{l\neq k}\boldsymbol{v}_l\boldsymbol{v}_l^{\mathsf{H}}\right)\boldsymbol{h}_k \geq \sigma_k^2, \tag{7.32}$$

$$\boldsymbol{h}_k = \hat{\boldsymbol{h}}_k + \boldsymbol{B}_k \boldsymbol{u}_k, \boldsymbol{u}_k^{\mathsf{H}} \boldsymbol{u}_k \le 1, \tag{7.33}$$

where $\boldsymbol{u}_k \in \mathbb{C}^{NL}$. According to the S-procedure [28], we can equivalently reformulate Eqs. (7.32) and (7.33) as

$$\boldsymbol{H}_k^{\mathsf{H}} \left(\frac{1}{\gamma_k} \boldsymbol{v}_k \boldsymbol{v}_k^{\mathsf{H}} - \sum_{l \neq k} \boldsymbol{v}_l \boldsymbol{v}_l^{\mathsf{H}} \right) \boldsymbol{H}_k \succeq \boldsymbol{Q}_k, \tag{7.34}$$

$$\lambda_k \ge 0, \tag{7.35}$$

where $\boldsymbol{\lambda} = [\lambda_k] \in \mathbb{R}_+^K$, and $\boldsymbol{H}_k$, $\boldsymbol{Q}_k$ are respectively given by

$$\boldsymbol{H}_k = \begin{bmatrix} \hat{\boldsymbol{h}}_k & \boldsymbol{B}_k \end{bmatrix} \in \mathbb{C}^{NL \times (NL+1)}, \tag{7.36}$$

$$\boldsymbol{Q}_k = \begin{bmatrix} \lambda_k + \sigma_k^2 & \boldsymbol{0} \\ \boldsymbol{0} & -\lambda_k \boldsymbol{I}_{NL} \end{bmatrix} \in \mathbb{C}^{(NL+1) \times (NL+1)}. \tag{7.37}$$

Therefore we reformulate the robust optimization approximation for problem $\mathscr{P}_{\mathrm{CCP}}$ as the following group sparse beamforming problem with nonconvex quadratic constraints:

$$\begin{aligned} \mathscr{P}_{7.1.\mathrm{RGS}}: \underset{\boldsymbol{v} \in \mathbb{C}^{NKL}, \boldsymbol{\lambda} \in \mathbb{R}^K}{\text{minimize}} \quad & \sum_{n,l} \frac{1}{\eta_n} \|\boldsymbol{v}_{nl}\|_2^2 + \sum_{n,l} P_{nl}^{\mathrm{c}} I_{(n,l) \in \mathcal{T}(\boldsymbol{v})} \\ \text{subject to} \quad & \boldsymbol{H}_k^{\mathsf{H}} \left(\frac{1}{\gamma_k} \boldsymbol{v}_k \boldsymbol{v}_k^{\mathsf{H}} - \sum_{l \neq k} \boldsymbol{v}_l \boldsymbol{v}_l^{\mathsf{H}} \right) \boldsymbol{H}_k \succeq \boldsymbol{Q}_k, \ k = 1, \ldots, K, \end{aligned} \tag{7.38}$$

$$\lambda_k \ge 0, \forall k = 1, \ldots, K, \tag{7.39}$$

$$\sum_{l=1}^{K} \|\boldsymbol{v}_{nl}\|_2^2 \le P_n^{\mathrm{Tx}}, \forall n = 1, \ldots, N. \tag{7.40}$$

We observe that the computational cost of solving problem $\mathscr{P}_{7.1.\mathrm{RGS}}$ remains unchanged when increasing the sample size D.

We can adopt the well-known SDR technique [29] to address the nonconvex quadratic constraints by lifting the aggregative beamforming vector as a positive semidefinite (PSD) matrix $\boldsymbol{V} = \boldsymbol{v}\boldsymbol{v}^{\mathsf{H}}$ with rank-one constraint and simply dropping the rank constraint. As discussed in Chapter 6, it has a poor capability of yielding rank-one solutions. The work [27] provides a quadratic variational form of weighted mixed ℓ_1/ℓ_2-norm to induce group sparsity with nonconvex quadratic constraints. In this chapter, we adopt

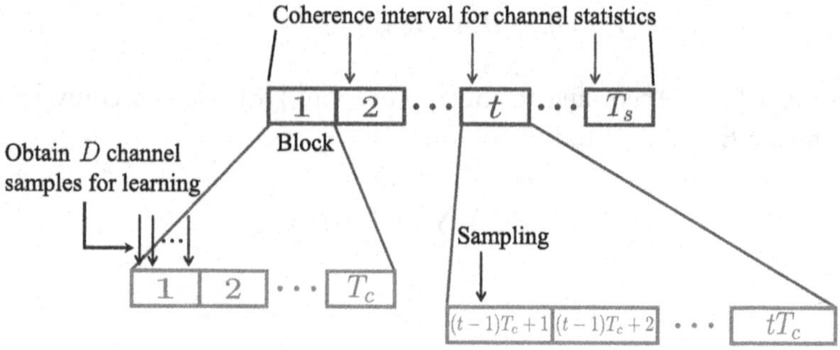

Figure 7.3 Timeline of proposed cost-effective channel sampling strategy.

the iteratively reweighted minimization approach to enhance group sparsity [30,31] thanks to its quadratic form, which allows us to further use the matrix lifting approach to address the nonconvex quadratic constraints. Then we use a DC regularization to induce rank-one solutions. The detailed algorithm for problem $\mathscr{P}_{7.1.\mathrm{RGS}}$ will be presented in Chapter 7.4. Before going into the details of the optimization algorithms, we will introduce how to obtain channel samples $\mathcal{D}$ in the following.

7.3.5 A cost-effective channel sampling strategy

In this chapter, we consider the block fading channel model. We assume that the channel distribution is invariant [32] within T_s blocks, which is called the *coherence interval for channel statistics*. The channel coefficients remain invariant within the block, for which each block is called the *coherence interval for CSI* and consists of T_c time slots. Note that the main issue of collecting D channel samples within each block is the high signaling overhead. To deal with this problem, we provide a cost-effective channel sample strategy as illustrated in Fig. 7.3. Specifically, we collect D i.i.d. samples of the channel coefficients as a set $\mathcal{D}$ at the beginning of the coherence interval for channel statistics. We are able to learn the estimated channel coefficient vector $\hat{\boldsymbol{h}}_k$ from (7.25) and learn $\boldsymbol{B}_k$ as the estimated uncertainty information of the error $\boldsymbol{e}_k$ from (7.31). By combining these two parts as $\boldsymbol{H}_k$ according to (7.36), we obtain the beamformers and the task selection strategy via solving problem $\mathscr{P}_{\mathrm{RGS}}$ for the signal transmission in the first block. For any subsequent block $t > 1$, we set the mean of the collected channel samples as the estimated channel coefficient $\hat{\boldsymbol{h}}[t]$. Then the parameter $\{\boldsymbol{H}_k[t]\}$ for solving problem $\mathscr{P}_{\mathrm{RGS}}(\{\boldsymbol{H}_k[t]\})$ is constructed by combining the estimated channel coefficient in the current block and the estimated uncertainty information in the first block, that is,

$$\boldsymbol{H}_k[t] = \left[\hat{\boldsymbol{h}}_k[t] \quad \boldsymbol{B}_k\right], \ k = 1, \ldots, K. \tag{7.41}$$

This approach is able to considerably reduce the signaling overhead of channel sampling, whose effectiveness will be demonstrated in Chapter 7.5.1 through numerical experiments.

7.4. Reweighted power minimization approach with DC regularization

In this section, we provide a reweighted power minimization approach with DC regularization to solve problem $\mathscr{P}_{7.1.\mathrm{RGS}}$ to achieve satisfactory performance.

7.4.1 Nonconvex quadratic constraints

Fortunately, constraints (7.38) are convex in terms of the positive semidefinite matrix (PSD) $\boldsymbol{V} = \boldsymbol{v}\boldsymbol{v}^{\mathsf{H}}$ despite of their nonconvexity in terms of $\boldsymbol{v}$. It motivates the matrix lifting technique [29] by denoting

$$\boldsymbol{V}_{ij}[s,t] = \boldsymbol{v}_{si}\boldsymbol{v}_{tj}^{\mathsf{H}} \in \mathbb{C}^{L\times L}, \tag{7.42}$$

$$\boldsymbol{V}_{ij} = \begin{bmatrix} \boldsymbol{V}_{ij}[1,1] & \ldots & \boldsymbol{V}_{ij}[1,N] \\ \vdots & \ddots & \vdots \\ \boldsymbol{V}_{ij}[N,1] & \ldots & \boldsymbol{V}_{ij}[N,N] \end{bmatrix} = \boldsymbol{v}_i\boldsymbol{v}_j^{\mathsf{H}} \in \mathbb{C}^{NL\times NL}, \tag{7.43}$$

$$\boldsymbol{V} = \boldsymbol{v}\boldsymbol{v}^{\mathsf{H}} = \begin{bmatrix} \boldsymbol{V}_{11} & \ldots & \boldsymbol{V}_{1K} \\ \vdots & \ddots & \vdots \\ \boldsymbol{V}_{K1} & \ldots & \boldsymbol{V}_{KK} \end{bmatrix} \in \mathbb{S}_+^{NKL}, \tag{7.44}$$

where $\mathbb{S}_+^{NKL}$ is the subspace formed by all Hermitian PSD matrices. With these notations, we equivalently rewrite the nonconvex quadratic constraints (7.38) as

$$\boldsymbol{H}_k^{\mathsf{H}}\left(\frac{1}{\gamma_k}\boldsymbol{V}_{kk} - \sum_{l\neq k}\boldsymbol{V}_{ll}\right)\boldsymbol{H}_k \succeq \mathbf{Q}_k, \tag{7.45}$$

$$\boldsymbol{V} \succeq \mathbf{0}, \operatorname{rank}(\boldsymbol{V}) = 1. \tag{7.46}$$

The transmit power constraint (7.40) and the objective function can also be rewritten in terms of $\boldsymbol{V}$. The reformulated problem for problem $\mathscr{P}_{7.1.\mathrm{RGS}}$ is given by

$$
\begin{aligned}
\mathscr{P}_{7.2}: \underset{\boldsymbol{V},\boldsymbol{\lambda}}{\text{minimize}} \quad & \sum_{n,l}\left(\frac{1}{\eta_n}\mathrm{Tr}(\boldsymbol{V}_{ll}[n,n]) + P_{nl}^{\mathsf{C}} I_{\mathrm{Tr}(\boldsymbol{V}_{ll}[n,n])\neq 0}\right) \\
\text{subject to} \quad & \boldsymbol{H}_k^{\mathsf{H}}\left(\frac{1}{\gamma_k}\boldsymbol{V}_{kk} - \sum_{l\neq k}\boldsymbol{V}_{ll}\right)\boldsymbol{H}_k \succeq \mathbf{Q}_k,\ k=1,\ldots,K, \quad (7.47) \\
& \lambda_k \geq 0, \forall k = 1,\ldots,K, \quad (7.48) \\
& \sum_{l=1}^{K}\mathrm{Tr}(\boldsymbol{V}_{ll}[n,n]) \leq P_n^{\mathsf{Tx}},\ n=1,\ldots,N, \quad (7.49) \\
& \boldsymbol{V}\succeq \mathbf{0},\ \mathrm{rank}(\boldsymbol{V})=1. \quad (7.50)
\end{aligned}
$$

7.4.2 Reweighted power minimization with DC regularization

For the PSD matrix $\boldsymbol{V}$, its rank is one if and only if the largest singular value is nonzero and others are zeros. We thus obtain the DC representation of the rank one constraint as the difference between the trace norm and the spectral norm

$$\mathcal{R}(\boldsymbol{V}) = \mathrm{Tr}(\boldsymbol{V}) - \|\boldsymbol{V}\|_2 = 0. \quad (7.51)$$

For the group sparse objective function, iteratively reweighted minimization approach for enhancing group sparsity has shown its effectiveness in improving the energy efficiency of cloud radio access networks [30,31]. Specifically, the indicator function $I_{\mathrm{Tr}(\boldsymbol{V}_{ll}[n,n])\neq 0}$ in the objective function of problem $\mathscr{P}_{7.2}$ can be approximated by $w_{nl}\mathrm{Tr}(\boldsymbol{V}_{ll}[n,n])$, where the weight is given by

$$w_{nl} = \frac{c}{\mathrm{Tr}(\boldsymbol{V}_{ll}[n,n]) + \tau} \quad (7.52)$$

with two constant parameters $\tau > 0$ and $c > 0$. The iteratively reweighted minimization algorithm is given by alternatively optimizing the aggregative beamforming vector and updating the weight. When $\mathrm{Tr}(\boldsymbol{V}_{ll}[n,n])$ is small (i.e., $\boldsymbol{v}_{nl}$ is close to zero), the reweighted approach gives a larger weight on the corresponding transceiver pair (n, l) and thus prompts its group sparsity. By applying the DC representation (7.51) of rank-one constraint into the iteratively reweighted minimization algorithm, we develop the following reweighted power minimization approach:

$$V^{[j+1]} = \text{solution to}: \tag{7.53}$$

$$\begin{aligned} \mathscr{P}_{7.3.\mathrm{DC}}: \underset{V\succeq 0, \boldsymbol{\lambda}\succeq \mathbf{0}}{\text{minimize}} \quad & \sum_{n,l}\left(\frac{1}{\eta_n} + w_{nl}^{[j]} P_{nl}^{\mathsf{c}}\right)\mathrm{Tr}(V_{ll}[n,n]) + \mu \mathcal{R}(V) \\ \text{subject to} \quad & \boldsymbol{H}_k^{\mathsf{H}}\left(\frac{1}{\gamma_k}V_{kk} - \sum_{l\neq k} V_{ll}\right)\boldsymbol{H}_k \succeq \mathbf{Q}_k,\ k=1,\ldots,K, \\ & \sum_{l=1}^{K}\mathrm{Tr}(V_{ll}[n,n]) \le P_n^{\mathsf{Tx}},\ n=1,\ldots,N, \end{aligned}$$

$$w_{nl}^{[j+1]} = \frac{c}{\mathrm{Tr}(V_{ll}^{[j+1]}[n,n]) + \tau}. \tag{7.54}$$

The DC program $\mathscr{P}_{7.3.\mathrm{DC}}$ for updating V can be addressed by the DC algorithm as demonstrated in Chapter 6.4.3. The tth iteration for solving $\mathscr{P}_{7.3.\mathrm{DC}}$ is given by updating $V^{(t+1)}$ as the solution to the following optimization problem:

$$\underset{V\succeq 0, \boldsymbol{\lambda}\succeq \mathbf{0}}{\text{minimize}} \quad \sum_{n,l}\left(\frac{1}{\eta_n} + w_{nl}^{[j]} P_{nl}^{\mathsf{c}}\right)\mathrm{Tr}(V_{ll}[n,n]) + \mu(\mathrm{Tr}(V) - \mathrm{Tr}(G^{(t)}V))$$

$$\text{subject to} \quad \boldsymbol{H}_k^{\mathsf{H}}\left(\frac{1}{\gamma_k}V_{kk} - \sum_{l\neq k} V_{ll}\right)\boldsymbol{H}_k \succeq \mathbf{Q}_k,\ k=1,\ldots,K, \tag{7.55}$$

$$\sum_{l=1}^{K}\mathrm{Tr}(V_{ll}[n,n]) \le P_n^{\mathsf{Tx}},\ n=1,\ldots,N, \tag{7.56}$$

where $\mathbf{G}^{(t)}$ is the subgradient of $\|V\|_2$ at $V^{(t)}$ and given by $\partial\|V\|_2 = \boldsymbol{u}_1\boldsymbol{u}_1^{\mathsf{H}}$, where $\boldsymbol{u}_1$ is the eigenvector corresponding to the largest eigenvalue of $\boldsymbol{V}$. It guarantees the global convergence to a critical point of problem $\mathscr{P}_{7.3.\mathrm{DC}}$ from any feasible initial point.

When we obtain a rank-one solution V with the presented reweighted power minimization approach, we can extract the aggregative beamforming vector $\boldsymbol{v}$ via the Cholesky decomposition $V = \boldsymbol{v}\boldsymbol{v}^{\mathsf{H}}$. The overall procedure of the reweighted power minimization approach is demonstrated in Algorithm 10.

Algorithm 10: Reweighted power minimization approach for solving problem $\mathscr{P}$.

Initialization: $V^{[0]}$, w_{nl}.
while *not converge* **do**
  $V^{(0)} \leftarrow V^{[j]}$
  while *not converge* **do**
    $V^{(t)} \leftarrow$ solution to (7.56)
  end
  $V^{[j+1]} \leftarrow V^{(t)}$
  update the weights $\{w_{nl}^{[j+1]}\}$ following Eq. (7.52)
end
Computing the Cholesky decomposition $V = vv^{\mathsf{H}}$.
Output: v.

7.5. Simulation results

In this section, we demonstrate the advantages of the proposed approach through numerical experiments.

In our simulations, we consider an edge inference system with fixed-location APs and randomly located MUs. Suppose that $N = 4$ APs equipped with $L = 2$ antennas are located at $(\pm 400\,\text{m}, \pm 400\,\text{m})$ and $K = 4$ single-antenna MUs are uniformly distributed in the square region of $[-800\,\text{m}, 800\,\text{m}] \times [-800\,\text{m}, 800\,\text{m}]$. We generate the imperfect channel coefficient vectors according to $\boldsymbol{h}_{kn} = 10^{-L(d_{kn})/20}(\boldsymbol{c}_{kn} + \boldsymbol{e}_{kn})$, where $L(d_{kn}) = 128.1 + 37.6 \log_{10} d_{kn}$ is the path loss, $\boldsymbol{c}_{kn} \sim \mathcal{CN}(\mathbf{0}, \boldsymbol{I})$ is the Rayleigh fading coefficient, and $\boldsymbol{e}_{kn} \sim \mathcal{CN}(\mathbf{0}, 10^{-4}\boldsymbol{I})$ is the additive error. D_1 and D_2 should be chosen carefully since D_1 affects the accuracy of the shape of high-probability region, and D_2 affects the accuracy of the size of high-probability region. We evenly split the dataset to balance these two sides of learning the high-probability region, that is, $D_1 = D_2 = D/2$. We set the power amplifier efficiency of each AP as $\eta = 1/4$, the average maximum transmit power of each AP as $P^{\mathsf{Tx}} = 1\,\text{W}$, and the computation power consumption for each task as $P^{\mathsf{c}} = 0.6\,\text{W}$. The target SINRs for each device are set to be identical, $\gamma_1 = \cdots = \gamma_K = \gamma$. We set the tolerance and confidence levels as $\epsilon = \delta = 0.05$. We set the regularization parameters as $\tau = 10^{-6}$ and $\mu = 10$.

7.5.1 Benefits of considering CSI uncertainty

We have provided a systematic approach for combating the uncertainty of available CSI and integrated a cost-effective channel sampling strategy to reduce the signaling overhead in Chapter 7.3.5. We conduct numerical experiments to show its advantages under the simple setting of selecting all tasks at each AP. In the training phase, we collect $D = 200$ channel samples within one coherent interval for CSI. In the test phase, only one sample $\boldsymbol{h}^{(1)}$ is collected for constructing $\boldsymbol{H}_k$ as given in Eq. (7.41). The beamformer design with the provided approach is given by the solution to

$$\begin{aligned}
\mathscr{P}_{7.4.\mathrm{RO}}: \underset{\boldsymbol{V}\succeq\mathbf{0},\boldsymbol{\lambda}\succeq\mathbf{0}}{\text{minimize}} \quad & \sum_{n,l}\left(\frac{1}{\eta_n}\mathrm{Tr}(\boldsymbol{V}_{ll}[n,n]) + P^{\mathsf{c}}_{nl}\right) \\
\text{subject to} \quad & \boldsymbol{H}_k^{\mathsf{H}}\left(\frac{1}{\gamma_k}\boldsymbol{V}_{kk} - \sum_{l\neq k}\boldsymbol{V}_{ll}\right)\boldsymbol{H}_k \succeq \mathbf{Q}_k,\ k = 1,\ldots,K, \\
& \sum_{l=1}^{K}\mathrm{Tr}(\boldsymbol{V}_{ll}[n,n]) \leq P_n^{\mathsf{Tx}},\ n = 1,\ldots,N,
\end{aligned} \tag{7.57}$$

whereas the beamformer design without considering the CSI uncertainty is given by the solution to

$$\begin{aligned}
\mathscr{P}_{7.4.\mathrm{CB}}: \underset{\boldsymbol{V}\succeq\mathbf{0}}{\text{minimize}} \quad & \sum_{n,l}\left(\frac{1}{\eta_n}\mathrm{Tr}(\boldsymbol{V}_{ll}[n,n]) + P^{\mathsf{c}}_{nl}\right) \\
\text{subject to} \quad & \boldsymbol{h}_k^{(1)\mathsf{H}}\left(\frac{1}{\gamma_k}\boldsymbol{V}_{kk} - \sum_{l\neq k}\boldsymbol{V}_{ll}\right)\boldsymbol{h}_k^{(1)} \geq \sigma_k^2,\ k = 1,\ldots,K, \\
& \sum_{l=1}^{K}\mathrm{Tr}(\boldsymbol{V}_{ll}[n,n]) \leq P_n^{\mathsf{Tx}},\ n = 1,\ldots,N,
\end{aligned} \tag{7.58}$$

where we use the SDR technique for both approaches for fairness. For one realization of the training set (i.e., $\mathcal{D}$ with 200 channel samples), we generate 200 channel realizations for test. This procedure is repeated over 200 times, and we compute the achieved SINR for both approaches over 40,000 trials. The achieved SINR is computed by $\mathrm{SINR}_k(\boldsymbol{v}; \tilde{\boldsymbol{h}})$ with the ground truth aggregative channel coefficient vector $\tilde{\boldsymbol{h}}$. We count the number of trials that the target QoS is met for each mobile user and illustrate the results in Table 7.1. It demonstrates that the robust optimization approximation approach integrated with the cost-effective sampling strategy can considerably improve the robustness of QoS.

Table 7.1 Number of trials that target QoS is satisfied.

User index	**1**	**2**	**3**	**4**
Proposed approach $\mathscr{P}_{7.4.\mathrm{RO}}$	39,946	39,946	39,946	39,946
Without considering uncertainty $\mathscr{P}_{7.4.\mathrm{CB}}$	15,205	15,123	15,197	15,214

7.5.2 Advantages of overcoming the overconservativeness

Here we use simulations to show the overconservativeness of the scenario generation approach and the advantages of the robust optimization approximation approach in addressing probabilistic QoS constraints. We consider the following feasibility problem $\mathscr{P}_{7.5.\mathrm{RO}}$ yielded by the robust optimization approximation approach:

$$\begin{aligned}\mathscr{P}_{7.5.\mathrm{RO}}: \text{find} \quad & \boldsymbol{V} \succeq \boldsymbol{0}, \boldsymbol{\lambda} \geq \boldsymbol{0} \\ \text{subject to} \quad & \boldsymbol{H}_k^{\mathsf{H}}\left(\frac{1}{\gamma_k}\boldsymbol{V}_{kk} - \sum_{l\neq k}\boldsymbol{V}_{ll}\right)\boldsymbol{H}_k \succeq \mathbf{Q}_k, \ k = 1, \ldots, K, \\ & \sum_{l=1}^{K}\mathrm{Tr}(\boldsymbol{V}_{ll}[n, n]) \leq P_n^{\mathrm{Tx}}, \ n \in [N],\end{aligned} \tag{7.59}$$

and the following feasibility problem $\mathscr{P}_{7.5.\mathrm{SG}}$ yielded by the scenario generation approach:

$$\begin{aligned}\mathscr{P}_{7.5.\mathrm{SG}}: \text{find} \quad & \boldsymbol{V} \succeq \boldsymbol{0} \\ \text{subject to} \quad & \boldsymbol{h}_k^{(i)\mathsf{H}}\left(\frac{1}{\gamma_k}\boldsymbol{V}_{kk} - \sum_{l\neq k}\boldsymbol{V}_{ll}\right)\boldsymbol{h}_k^{(i)} \geq \sigma_k^2, \ k = 1, \ldots K, \ i = 1, \ldots, D, \\ & \sum_{l=1}^{K}\mathrm{Tr}(\boldsymbol{V}_{ll}[n, n]) \leq P_n^{\mathrm{Tx}}, \quad n = 1, \ldots, N,\end{aligned} \tag{7.60}$$

where the SDR technique is adopted for both approaches. For each trial, we generate $D = 200$ channel samples and check the feasibility of each approach. We run 25 trials and count the probability of returning feasible solutions. The simulation results are illustrated in Fig. 7.4. The higher probability of feasibility using the robust optimization approximation approach indicates that it is able to overcome the overconservativeness of the scenario generation approach.

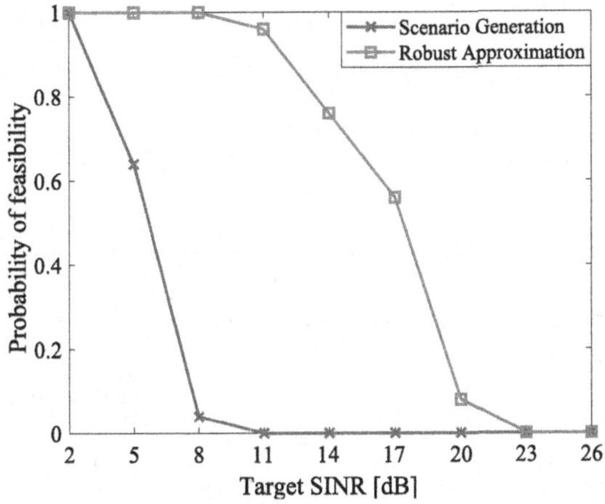

Figure 7.4 Comparisons of the probability of feasibility for the robust optimization approximation approach and the scenario generation approach.

7.5.3 Total power consumption

We then evaluate the total power consumption of different algorithms/settings for solving problem $\mathscr{P}_{7.2}$ in edge inference:

- **"mixed ℓ_1/ℓ_2+SDR"**: As provided in [27], we adopt the quadratic variational form of the weighted mixed ℓ_1/ℓ_2-norm to induce the group sparsity and adopt the SDR technique for the nonconvex quadratic constraints.
- **"reweighted+SDR"**: As provided in [30] for energy-efficient downlink transmission in cloud-RAN, we adopt the iteratively reweighted minimization algorithm for inducing the group sparsity. We use the SDR technique to address the nonconvex quadratic constraints in this approach.
- **"CB+SDR"**: In this setting, we simply select all tasks at each AP and use coordinated beamforming to minimize the transmission power consumption under probabilistic QoS constraints.

We choose $D = 200$ and $c = 1/\ln(1+\tau^{-1})$ in our simulations. We illustrate the total power consumption and total number of computed tasks at APs averaged over 100 trials in Figs. 7.5 and 7.6, respectively. We conclude that less power is consumed with the reweighted power minimization approach than others due to its better capability of inducing group sparse solutions.

Therefore we conclude that using the provided statistical learning-based robust optimization approximation approach and the reweighted power minimization algorithm enjoys considerable advantages in improving the

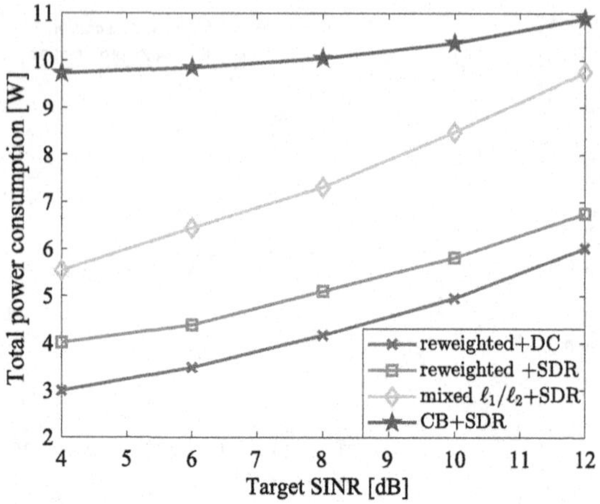

Figure 7.5 Total power consumption over target SINR.

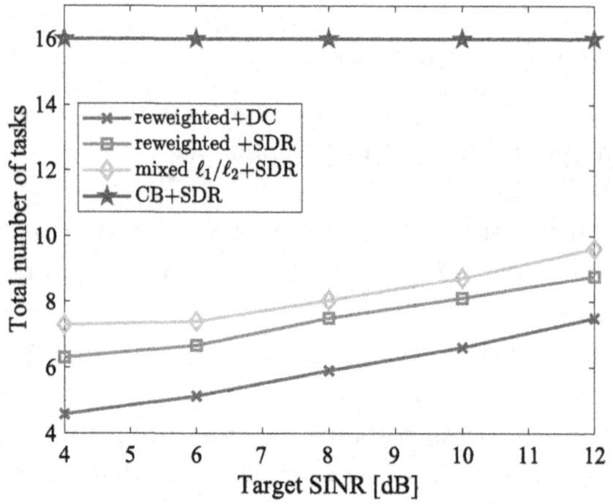

Figure 7.6 Total number of computed tasks over target SINR.

energy efficiency and providing robust downlink transmission service for the computation offloading based edge inference system.

7.6. Summary

In this chapter, we investigated computation offloading-based edge cooperative inference systems. We exploited the wireless cooperative transmission scheme for improving the communication efficiency of computation offloading-based edge inference systems. We presented an energy-efficient and robust downlink transmission framework to enable computationally intensive deep learning inference tasks at the edge computing nodes. By performing joint task selection and beamforming design, we minimized the total power consumption including computation power and transmission power under probabilistic QoS constraints. We provided a statistical learning-based robust optimization approximation for the probabilistic QoS constraints and reformulated the resulting problem as a group sparse beamforming problem with nonconvex quadratic constraints. We further developed a reweighted power minimization algorithm by adopting the iteratively reweighted minimization approach to induce group sparsity and a DC regularization to address the nonconvex quadratic constraints, which had lower power consumption than other state-of-the-art approaches.

References

[1] Y. Mao, C. You, J. Zhang, K. Huang, K.B. Letaief, A survey on mobile edge computing: the communication perspective, IEEE Commun. Surv. Tutor. 19 (2017) 2322–2358.

[2] P. Mach, Z. Becvar, Mobile edge computing: a survey on architecture and computation offloading, IEEE Commun. Surv. Tutor. 19 (2017) 1628–1656.

[3] N. Abbas, Y. Zhang, A. Taherkordi, T. Skeie, Mobile edge computing: a survey, IEEE Int. Things J. 5 (Feb. 2018) 450–465.

[4] S. Bi, Y.J. Zhang, Computation rate maximization for wireless powered mobile-edge computing with binary computation offloading, IEEE Trans. Wirel. Commun. 17 (Jun. 2018) 4177–4190.

[5] L. Huang, S. Bi, Y.-J.A. Zhang, Deep reinforcement learning for online computation offloading in wireless powered mobile-edge computing networks, IEEE Trans. Mob. Comput. 19 (Nov. 2019) 2581–2593.

[6] Y. Wang, M. Sheng, X. Wang, L. Wang, J. Li, Mobile-edge computing: partial computation offloading using dynamic voltage scaling, IEEE Trans. Commun. 64 (Oct. 2016) 4268–4282.

[7] X. Chen, Y. Cai, Q. Shi, M. Zhao, B. Champagne, L. Hanzo, Efficient resource allocation for relay-assisted computation offloading in mobile-edge computing, IEEE Int. Things J. 7 (3) (2020) 2452–2468.

[8] J. Kwak, Y. Kim, J. Lee, S. Chong, Dream: dynamic resource and task allocation for energy minimization in mobile cloud systems, IEEE J. Sel. Areas Commun. 33 (Dec. 2015) 2510–2523.

[9] G. Mohanarajah, V. Usenko, M. Singh, R. D'Andrea, M. Waibel, Cloud-based collaborative 3D mapping in real-time with low-cost robots, IEEE Trans. Autom. Sci. Eng. 12 (Apr. 2015) 423–431.

[10] Z. Liu, T. Liu, W. Wen, L. Jiang, J. Xu, Y. Wang, G. Quan, DeepN-JPEG: a deep neural network favorable JPEG-based image compression framework, in: Proceedings of the 55th Annual Design Automation Conference, ACM, 2018, pp. 1–6.

[11] J. Hauswald, T. Manville, Q. Zheng, R. Dreslinski, C. Chakrabarti, T. Mudge, A hybrid approach to offloading mobile image classification, in: 2014 IEEE International Conference on Acoustics, Speech and Signal Processing (ICASSP), 2014, pp. 8375–8379.

[12] S. Teerapittayanon, B. McDanel, H.-T. Kung, Distributed deep neural networks over the cloud, the edge and end devices, in: Proc. IEEE Int. Conf. Dist. Comput. Syst. (ICDCS), 2017, pp. 328–339.
[13] E. Li, L. Zeng, Z. Zhou, X. Chen, Edge AI: on-demand accelerating deep neural network inference via edge computing, IEEE Trans. Wirel. Commun. 19 (1) (Jan. 2020) 447–457.
[14] D. Gesbert, S. Hanly, H. Huang, S.S. Shitz, O. Simeone, W. Yu, Multi-cell MIMO cooperative networks: a new look at interference, IEEE J. Sel. Areas Commun. 28 (9) (2010) 1380–1408.
[15] T. Park, M.-Y. Liu, T.-C. Wang, J.-Y. Zhu, Semantic image synthesis with spatially-adaptive normalization, in: Proc. IEEE Conf. Comput. Vision Pattern Recognition (CVPR), 2019, pp. 2337–2346.
[16] S. Han, H. Mao, W.J. Dally, Deep compression: compressing deep neural networks with pruning, trained quantization and Huffman coding, in: Proc. Int. Conf. Learn. Representations (ICLR), 2016.
[17] CNN energy estimation website, http://energyestimation.mit.edu.
[18] T.-J. Yang, Y.-H. Chen, V. Sze, Designing energy-efficient convolutional neural networks using energy-aware pruning, in: Proc. IEEE Conf. Comput. Vision Pattern Recognition (CVPR), Jul. 2017, pp. 5687–5695.
[19] A. Krizhevsky, I. Sutskever, G.E. Hinton, ImageNet classification with deep convolutional neural networks, in: Proc. Adv. Neural Inf. Process. Syst. (NIPS), 2012, pp. 1097–1105.
[20] F. Yang, P. Cai, H. Qian, X. Luo, Pilot contamination in massive MIMO induced by timing and frequency errors, IEEE Trans. Wirel. Commun. 17 (Jul. 2018) 4477–4492.
[21] J. Mo, R.W. Heath, Limited feedback in single and multi-user MIMO systems with finite-bit ADCs, IEEE Trans. Wirel. Commun. 17 (May 2018) 3284–3297.
[22] M.A. Maddah-Ali, D. Tse, Completely stale transmitter channel state information is still very useful, IEEE Trans. Inf. Theory 58 (Jul. 2012) 4418–4431.
[23] Y. Shi, J. Zhang, K.B. Letaief, Optimal stochastic coordinated beamforming for wireless cooperative networks with CSI uncertainty, IEEE Trans. Signal Process. 63 (4) (2015) 960–973.
[24] A. Nemirovski, A. Shapiro, Convex approximations of chance constrained programs, SIAM J. Optim. 17 (4) (2006) 969–996.
[25] M. Razaviyayn, M. Sanjabi, Z.-Q. Luo, A stochastic successive minimization method for nonsmooth nonconvex optimization with applications to transceiver design in wireless communication networks, Math. Program. 157 (2) (2016) 515–545.
[26] L.J. Hong, Z. Huang, H. Lam, Learning-based robust optimization: procedures and statistical guarantees, preprint, arXiv:1704.04342, 2017.
[27] Y. Shi, J. Zhang, K.B. Letaief, Robust group sparse beamforming for multicast green cloud-RAN with imperfect CSI, IEEE Trans. Signal Process. 63 (Sept. 2015) 4647–4659.
[28] S. Boyd, L. Vandenberghe, Convex Optimization, Cambridge Univ. Press, 2004.
[29] Z.-Q. Luo, N.D. Sidiropoulos, P. Tseng, S. Zhang, Approximation bounds for quadratic optimization with homogeneous quadratic constraints, SIAM J. Optim. 18 (1) (2007) 1–28.
[30] B. Dai, W. Yu, Energy efficiency of downlink transmission strategies for cloud radio access networks, IEEE J. Sel. Areas Commun. 34 (Apr. 2016) 1037–1050.
[31] Y. Shi, J. Cheng, J. Zhang, B. Bai, W. Chen, K.B. Letaief, Smoothed l_p-minimization for green cloud-ran with user admission control, IEEE J. Sel. Areas Commun. 34 (Apr. 2016) 1022–1036.
[32] A. Liu, X. Chen, W. Yu, V.K.N. Lau, M. Zhao, Two-timescale hybrid compression and forward for massive MIMO aided C-RAN, IEEE Trans. Signal Process. 67 (May 2019) 2484–2498.

PART THREE

Edge training

CHAPTER EIGHT

Over-the-air computation for federated learning

8.1. Background of federated learning and over-the-air computation

8.1.1 Federated learning

With the advancement of AI and big data analytics, the importance of data is more and more recognized by large companies and states across the world. Data have been thought as a new type of production factor in addition to traditional factors including land, labor, and capital. Operators have been enacting stricter and stricter regulations to protect data privacy, such as the General Data Protection Regulation (GDPR) [1] issued by the European Union and the Personal Information Security Specification[1] issued by China's National Information Security Standardization Technical Committee (TC260). The increasing emphasis on user privacy and data security makes it a worldwide great challenge to design AI systems and algorithms with protection of data privacy and security. Recently, an emerging frontier field called *federated learning* [2,3] has drawn much attention from both industry and academia, which studies the privacy-preserving collaborative machine learning frameworks while leaving data at their providers locally. It is based on the key observation that real-world data usually exist in isolated data silos in most applications and data owners are often reluctant or not allowed to share their raw data to others.

In traditional AI engines, all data are collected by one party and stored in the cloud center. It is challenging to build collaborative AI models from the isolated data islands for federated learning [4]. According to the data availability of multiple parties, federated learning can be categorized into three types, *horizontal federated learning*, *vertical federated learning*, and *federated transfer learning*, as illustrated in Fig. 8.1. Horizontal federated learning is referred to as the federated learning with distributed data samples across multiple parties. Different participants collaboratively build machine learning models

[1] https://www.tc260.org.cn/upload/2018-01-24/1516799764389090333.pdf.

Mobile Edge Artificial Intelligence
https://doi.org/10.1016/B978-0-12-823817-2.00019-X

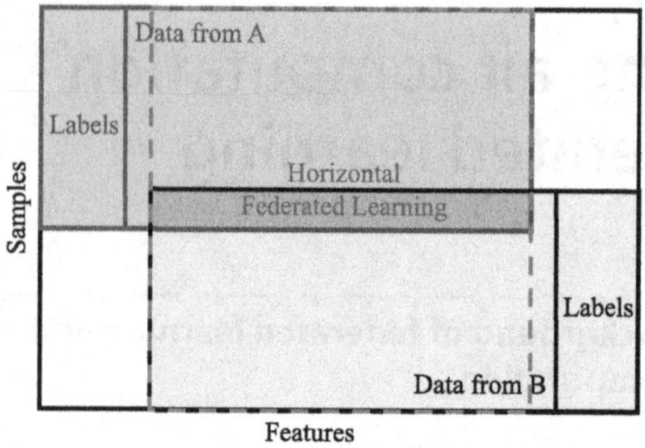

(a) Horizontal federated learning

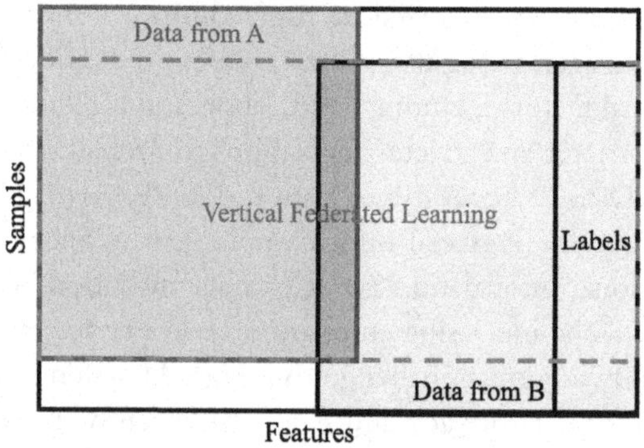

(b) Vertical federated learning

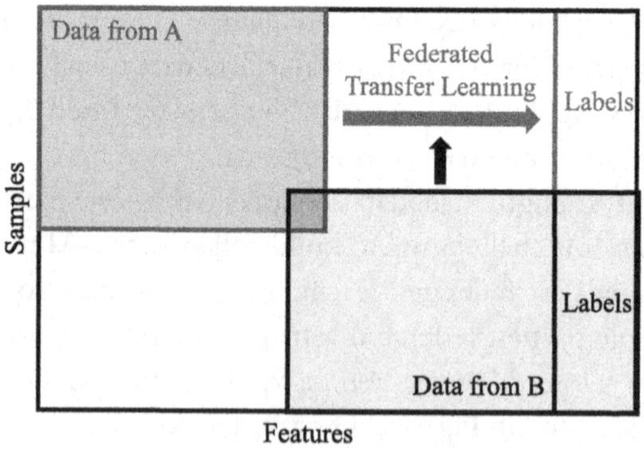

(c) Federated transfer learning

Figure 8.1 Illustration of different categories of federated learning.

based on different data samples sharing the same feature space. For example, Bonawitz et al. [5] developed a horizontal federated learning system on a large number of Android mobile phones, each holding a portion of data samples. In vertical federated learning, different participating nodes hold a portion of features for a common set of data samples. Vertical federated learning has found its great value in industrial applications such as credit risk management[2] and advertising.[3] Transfer learning [6] can be applied to the scenarios in which the data of different parties differ in both sample and feature spaces. It can be used for opening up a new business that has a different group of target users.

Communication efficiency is one of the main bottlenecks in federated learning system, which requires frequent communication between mobile devices or between distant data centers. In addition, the necessity of adopting security models, such as secure multiparty computation (MPC) and homomorphic encryption, leads to high computation and communication costs out of privacy and security concerns. To address these issues, there are an increasing number of researches on enabling secure and efficient federated learning. In early works, horizontal structure of federated learning has been extensively studied. The concept of federated optimization was firstly proposed in [7], which refers to the distributed optimization that learns a centralized model from decentralized nodes, each with a subset of data samples. The work [8] proposed the federated averaging (FedAvg) algorithm to improve the communication efficiency by periodically aggregating the local updates from each node for horizontal federated learning. For vertical federated learning structure, a line of works have proposed numerous model-dependent federated learning architectures and algorithms. Based on the secure MPC framework, researchers designed privacy-preserving K-means [9], support vector machine (SVM) [10], and logistic regression [11]. In recent years, it is widely recognized to adopt homomorphic encryption to achieve secure intermediate value computation for vertical federated learning, such as stochastic gradient descent for logistic regression [12], stochastic quasi-Newton method for logistic regression [13], decision tree [14], and gradient boosting machine [15].

Generally, it often requires intensive computing resources to train an AI model. The advancements of computational capabilities of edge devices and mobile edge computing [16] make it promising to perform training tasks

[2] https://www.jddglobal.com/products/union-learn.

[3] https://github.com/bytedance/fedlearner.

at network edges, which is critical for providing low-latency and privacy-sensitive AI services. In this chapter, we study a representative edge training framework, that is, the federated learning on mobile devices with horizontal structure, which pools the collected data and computation resources from distributed mobile devices to collaboratively train an AI model.

8.1.2 Over-the-air computation

The ever-increasing number of wireless devices such as mobile phones and IoT devices poses great challenge for the 5G system. To address this issue, massive MIMO technique improves the capability of supporting massive connectivity from the point of view of communication. A growing body of works realize the huge potential of task-specific designs instead of isolated communication to provide service for massive devices. Toward this direction, wireless data aggregation [17] becomes one of the most concerned tasks to support ubiquitous intelligent services that are either data intensive (e.g., distributed learning) or latency critical (e.g., vehicle platooning), which are major missions for the futuristic communication systems.

Wireless data aggregation is a class of joint computation and communication tasks for distributed mobile devices. The high communication bandwidth required by traditional communication paradigm motivates the proposal of new technology, over-the-air computation (which is often abbreviated to AirComp) [18], to efficiently compute a function of distributed data from wireless devices by joint communication and computation design. In general, the basic principle of over-the-air computation is to utilize the waveform superposition property of a wireless multiple access channel to realize over-the-air aggregation of data simultaneously transmitted by devices. Functions that are computable over-the-air fall into the category of *nomographic functions*, which can be expressed as post-processing functions of the sum of multiple preprocessed values [19].

The functions that are computable over the air fall into the category of *nomographic functions* [19]. Supposing there are K devices, a monographic function is given in the form

$$y = \psi(\sum_{i=1}^{K} \phi_i(d_i)), \tag{8.1}$$

where ψ denotes the postprocessing function, and ϕ_i denotes the local preprocessing function on the data value d_i at device i. Typical functions range from the arithmetic mean, weighted sum, geometric mean, and polynomial to the Euclidean norm. The detailed procedure of turning the air into a computer by exploiting the principles of over-the-air computation for wireless data aggregation will be provided in Chapter 8.3.1 and Fig. 8.3.

The basic principle of over-the-air computation is not new and has been studied over the past decades. The researches of over-the-air computation vary from different point of views, including information theory [18], signal processing [19], transceivers design for multiple functions computation [20], robust against channel state information errors [21], synchronization issues [22], and digital modulation [23]. In recent years, researchers creatively discover the connection between over-the-air computation and machine learning over wireless devices [24–26]. It is motivated by the linear combination nature of aggregating local updates from distributed mobile devices. Yang et al. [24] observed that the model aggregation for federated machine learning is computable over-the-air, and proposed the joint device selection and beamforming design to improve the learning performance using over-the-air computation based fast model aggregation approach. Amiri et al. [25] studied the collaborative machine learning at the wireless edge and explored the principle of over-the-air computation to improve the communication efficiency of data aggregation for distributed stochastic gradient descent algorithm. Zhu et al. [26] characterized the tradeoff between communication and federated learning performance by adopting a channel inversion power control scheme to control the transmit power of the involved devices in over-the-air computation-based local updates aggregation. In the following, we will provide a representative framework of using over-the-air computation to achieve fast model aggregation of federated machine learning.

8.2. System model

We illustrate the federated learning system consisting of one N-antenna base station (BS) and M single-antenna mobile devices in Fig. 8.2. The BS serves as the aggregation center that coordinates the information exchange of mobile devices to support the following distributed learning task:

$$\underset{\boldsymbol{z}\in\mathbb{R}^d}{\text{minimize}} \quad f(\boldsymbol{z}) = \frac{1}{T}\sum_{j=1}^{T} f_j(\boldsymbol{z}), \tag{8.2}$$

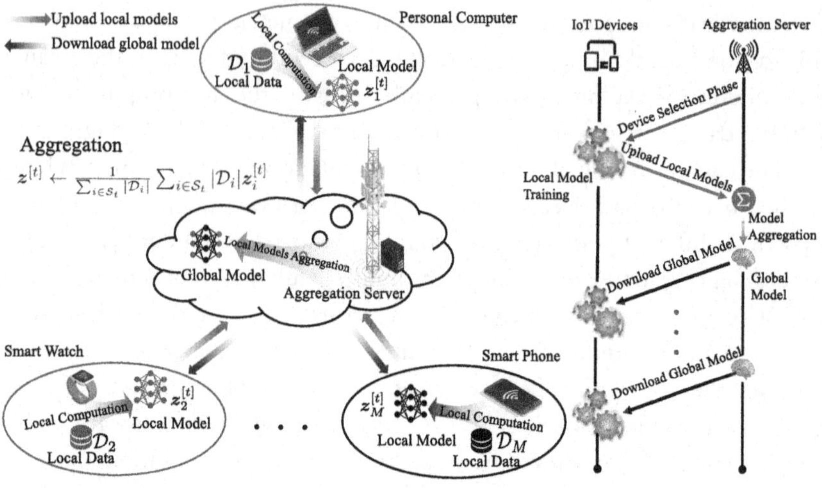

Figure 8.2 Illustration of a federated learning system.

where $z \in \mathbb{R}^d$ is the machine learning model parameter vector. The function f_j can usually be parameterized as $\ell(z; x_j, y_j)$, where (x_j, y_j) represents the jth input–output data pair, and T is the training data size in the system. The dataset can be denoted as $\mathcal{D} = \{(x_j, y_j) : j = 1, \ldots, T\}$. This machine learning model has been widely used in linear regression, support vector machine, deep neural networks, and so on.

Note that each mobile device i has only access to a subset of the overall dataset in the federated learning system, which is denoted $\mathcal{D}_i \subseteq \mathcal{D}$. Without uploading the local dataset to the center node, the training procedure can be accomplished via periodically aggregating updates from all devices [8]. Specifically, in the tth communication round:

1. A subset of devices $S_t \subseteq \{1, 2, \ldots, M\}$ is selected;
2. The BS sends the global model z^{t-1} to selected devices through downlink broadcast channel;
3. Each selected device performs local computation (e.g., running a step of stochastic gradient descent algorithm) and obtains a local updated model $z_i^{[t]}$ based on the global model;
4. All selected devices transmit their local updates to the BS, which serves as the aggregation center. The BS computes their weighted average as the updated global model $z^{[t]}$.

This typical federated learning framework is called the federated averaging (FedAvg) algorithm, which is presented in Algorithm 11.

Algorithm 11: Federated averaging (FedAvg) algorithm.

Initialize $\boldsymbol{w}_0$.
for *each round* $t = 1, 2, \ldots$ **do**
  $\mathcal{S}_t \leftarrow$ select a subset of M devices;
  The BS broadcasts the global model $\boldsymbol{z}^{[t-1]}$ to devices in $\mathcal{S}_t$.
  for *each mobile device* $i \in \mathcal{S}_t$ ***in parallel*** **do**
    $\boldsymbol{z}_i^{[t]} \leftarrow \text{LocalUpdate}(\mathcal{D}_i, \boldsymbol{z}^{[t-1]})$
  end
  $\boldsymbol{z}^{[t]} \leftarrow \frac{1}{\sum_{i \in \mathcal{S}_t} |\mathcal{D}_i|} \sum_{i \in \mathcal{S}_t} |\mathcal{D}_i| \boldsymbol{z}_i^{[t]}$ **(aggregation)**
end

However, the information exchange across mobile devices for on-device distributed federated learning, that is, the model aggregation over wireless networks, is quite challenging due to the limited communication bandwidth. Thus we will present an over-the-air computation-based fast model aggregation approach for on-device federated learning in the following part.

8.3. Fast model aggregation via over-the-air computation

The model aggregation procedure requires the wireless transmission from multiple mobile devices to BS and the computation of the weighted average of locally updated model parameters. By exploiting the signal superposition property of a wireless multiple access channel, over-the-air computation [18] is an efficient way to compute a function value of the data from distributed nodes through joint communication and computation design. Fortunately, the weighted average function falls into the category of functions that are computable over-the-air. Compared with traditional orthogonal transmission, over-the-air computation is able to significantly improve the communication efficiency via allowing concurrent transmissions from multiple mobile devices. Thus, in this section, we present the over-the-air computation-based fast model aggregation approach for on-device federated learning. We begin with a simple single-antenna case (i.e., $N = 1$) of over-the-air computation, followed by the over-the-air computation approach for model aggregation with a multiple-antenna BS.

8.3.1 A simple single-antenna case

The aggregation function of over-the-air computation from M mobile devices can be expressed as

$$z = \psi\left(\sum_{i=1}^{M} \phi_i(z_i)\right), \tag{8.3}$$

where z_i is the message available at device i, ϕ_i is the preprocessing function to be performed at each device i, and ψ is the postprocessing function at the BS. We use $s_i \in \mathbb{C}$ to denote the independent symbol scalar for each $\phi_i(z_i)$, which is assumed to be with unit power, that is, $\mathbb{E}(|s_i|^2) = 1$. Denoting the transmit scalar as $b_i \in \mathbb{C}$, the received signal at the BS is given by

$$y = \sum_{i=1}^{M} h_i b_i s_i + n, \tag{8.4}$$

where $h_i \in \mathbb{C}$ is the channel coefficient between the ith mobile device and the BS, and $n \sim \mathcal{CN}(0, 1)$ is the additive white Gaussian noise. By estimating the target function $g = \sum_{i=1}^{M} s_i$ at the BS and performing postprocessing on the estimated result, the BS can obtain the aggregation result without knowing each s_i individually, thereby reducing the required communication bandwidth. Specifically, the estimated target function value is given by

$$\hat{g} = \frac{1}{\sqrt{\eta}} m^* y = \frac{1}{\sqrt{\eta}} m^* \Big(\sum_{i=1}^{M} h_i b_i s_i + n\Big), \tag{8.5}$$

where $\eta > 0$ is a normalizing factor, and m is the decoding scalar at the BS. The function distortion of $\hat{g}$ can be measured by the mean-squared error (MSE):

$$\mathsf{MSE}(\hat{g}, g) = \mathbb{E}\left(|\hat{g} - g|^2\right) = \sum_{i=1}^{M} \left|\frac{m^* h_i}{\sqrt{\eta}} b_i - 1\right|^2 + \sigma^2 \frac{|m|^2}{\eta}. \tag{8.6}$$

We find that the MSE remains unchanged for the transceiver pair ($b_i e^{j\theta}$, $m e^{j\theta}$) with any phase shift θ. Therefore we can simply choose m as a real scalar. The optimal transmit scalar is given by the solution to

$$\frac{m^* h_i}{\sqrt{\eta}} b_i - 1 = 0, \tag{8.7}$$

that is, the following zero-forcing transmitter

$$b_i = \sqrt{\eta}\frac{(m^* h_i)^*}{|m^* h_i|^2} = \frac{\sqrt{\eta}}{m} \cdot \frac{1}{h_i}. \tag{8.8}$$

Therefore, in the single-antenna case, the optimal transceiver pair can be chosen as

$$b_i = \frac{P_0}{h_i}, \quad m = \frac{1}{P_0}, \tag{8.9}$$

where P_0 is a normalizing factor determined by the maximum transmit power at each device.

The whole procedure of over-the-air computation for single-antenna case is illustrated in Fig. 8.3.

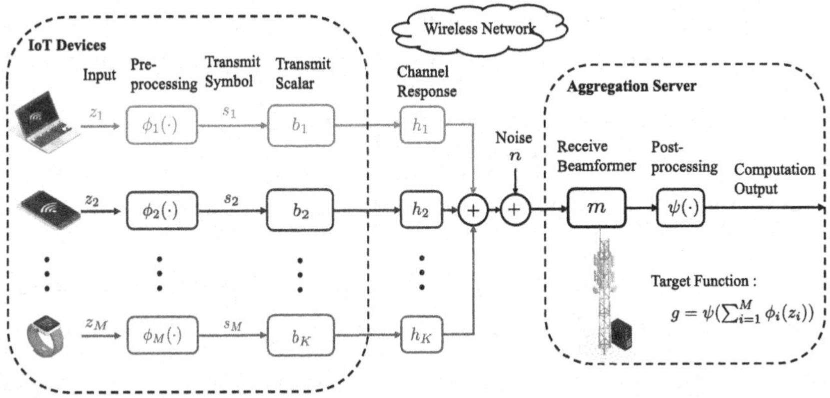

Figure 8.3 Illustration of over-the-air computation approach for computing a function of distributed devices.

8.3.2 Over-the-air computation for model aggregation with a multiantenna BS

For a general on-device distributed federated learning system with an N-antenna BS and M single-antenna mobile devices, the model aggregation function in each communication round is given by

$$\boldsymbol{z} = \psi\left(\sum_{i \in \mathcal{S}} \phi_i \cdot \boldsymbol{z}_i\right), \tag{8.10}$$

where vector $\boldsymbol{z}_i$ is the local updated model at device i, and $\mathcal{S} \subseteq \{1, \ldots, M\}$ is the set of selected devices. Note that the preprocessing function is a scaling factor $\phi_i = |\mathcal{D}_i|$, and the postprocessing function is also a scalar $\psi = \frac{1}{\sum_{i\in\mathcal{S}}|\mathcal{D}_i|}$. Let $\boldsymbol{s}_i := \boldsymbol{z}_i \in \mathbb{C}^d$ be the representative symbol vector with unit variance, that is, $\mathbb{E}(\boldsymbol{s}_i\boldsymbol{s}_i^{\mathsf{H}}) = \boldsymbol{I}$. The target function to be estimated for the BS at each time slot $j \in \{1, \ldots, d\}$ can be denoted as

$$g = \sum_{i\in\mathcal{S}} \phi_i s_i \tag{8.11}$$

by omitting the time indexes of $g^{(j)}$ and $s_j^{(j)}$.

At each time slot, the BS receives the signal

$$\boldsymbol{y} = \sum_{i\in\mathcal{S}} \boldsymbol{h}_i b_i s_i + \boldsymbol{n}, \tag{8.12}$$

where $\boldsymbol{h}_i \in \mathbb{C}^N$ is the channel coefficient vector, and $\boldsymbol{n} \sim \mathcal{CN}(\boldsymbol{0}, \sigma^2\boldsymbol{I})$ is the additive white Gaussian noise vector. The maximum transmit power constraint is given by

$$\mathbb{E}(|b_i s_i|^2) = |b_i|^2 \leq P^{\mathsf{Tx}}. \tag{8.13}$$

The BS obtains the estimated target function before postprocessing as

$$\hat{g} = \frac{1}{\sqrt{\eta}}\boldsymbol{m}^{\mathsf{H}}\boldsymbol{y} = \frac{1}{\sqrt{\eta}}\boldsymbol{m}^{\mathsf{H}}\sum_{i\in\mathcal{S}} \boldsymbol{h}_i b_i s_i + \frac{\boldsymbol{m}^{\mathsf{H}}\boldsymbol{n}}{\sqrt{\eta}}, \tag{8.14}$$

where b_i and $\boldsymbol{m}$ are transceivers, and η is the normalizing factor.

The function distortion of $\hat{g}$ measured by MSE is given by

$$\mathsf{MSE}(\hat{g}, g) = \mathbb{E}\left(|\hat{g} - g|^2\right) = \sum_{i=1}^{M}\left|\frac{\boldsymbol{m}^{\mathsf{H}}\boldsymbol{h}_i}{\sqrt{\eta}}b_i - 1\right|^2 + \sigma^2\frac{\|\boldsymbol{m}\|^2}{\eta}. \tag{8.15}$$

We observe that $\mathsf{MSE}(\hat{g}, g) \geq \sigma^2\|\boldsymbol{m}\|^2/\eta$. The equality holds if and only if $\boldsymbol{m}^{\mathsf{H}}\boldsymbol{h}_i b_i/\sqrt{\eta} - 1 = 0$. Therefore the optimal transmitter scalar is given by

$$b_i = \sqrt{\eta}\frac{(\boldsymbol{m}^{\mathsf{H}}\boldsymbol{h}_i)^{\mathsf{H}}}{|\boldsymbol{m}^{\mathsf{H}}\boldsymbol{h}_i|^2}. \tag{8.16}$$

According to the power constraint (8.13), we obtain that

$$\eta = \min_{i\in\mathcal{S}} P^{\mathsf{Tx}}\frac{|\boldsymbol{m}^{\mathsf{H}}\boldsymbol{h}_i|^2}{\phi_i^2}. \tag{8.17}$$

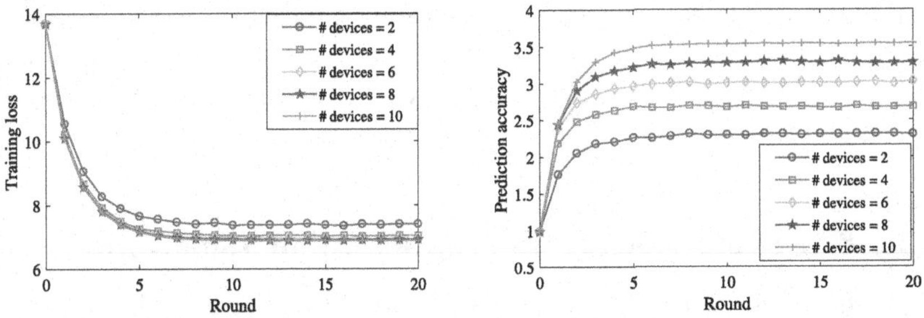

(a) Training loss **(b)** Relative prediction accuracy

Figure 8.4 The training loss and relative prediction accuracy averaged over 10 realizations by randomly selecting different number of devices for FedAvg. An SVM classifier is trained using the CIFAR-10 dataset. We perform one step of the stochastic gradient descent algorithm [27] as the local updated model for each device.

Thus the MSE can be rewritten in terms of the receiver beamforming vector $\boldsymbol{m}$ as follows:

$$\mathsf{MSE}(\hat{g}, g) = \frac{\|\boldsymbol{m}\|^2\sigma^2}{\eta} = \frac{\sigma^2}{P^{\mathsf{Tx}}} \max_{i\in\mathcal{S}} \phi_i^2 \frac{\|\boldsymbol{m}\|^2}{|\boldsymbol{m}^{\mathsf{H}}\boldsymbol{h}_i|^2}. \tag{8.18}$$

8.3.3 Problem formulation

The aggregation error is determined by both the receiver beamforming vector $\boldsymbol{m}$ and the set of selected devices $\mathcal{S}$ as shown in (8.18). For on-device federated learning, we observe two facts:

(a) Selecting more devices in each communication round can improve the learning performance (as shown in Fig. 8.4).

(b) Large aggregation error can induce a notable drop of the model prediction accuracy.

As such, we propose to maximize the number of selected devices while guaranteeing small aggregation error to improve the learning performance of federated learning with over-the-air computation-based fast model aggregation approach. It can be formulated as follows:

$$\mathscr{P}_{8.1}: \underset{\mathcal{S},\boldsymbol{m}\in\mathbb{C}^N}{\text{maximize}} \ |\mathcal{S}| \quad \text{subject to} \ \left(\max_{i\in\mathcal{S}} \phi_i^2 \frac{\|\boldsymbol{m}\|^2}{|\boldsymbol{m}^{\mathsf{H}}\boldsymbol{h}_i|^2}\right) \leq \gamma, \tag{8.19}$$

where the global model aggregation MSE requirement is denoted as $\gamma > 0$. The cardinality $|\mathcal{S}|$ of $\mathcal{S}$ represents the number of selected mobile devices. Due to the combinatorial optimization variable $\mathcal{S}$ and continuous optimization variable $\boldsymbol{m}$, problem $\mathscr{P}_{8.1}$ is a highly intractable mixed combinatorial optimization problem, since the objective function is combinatorial, and the constraint is nonconvex. To address these issues, we will present a sparse and low-rank optimization framework in the following section.

8.4. Sparse and low-rank optimization framework

In this section, we reformulate the mixed combinatorial optimization problem as a sparse and low-rank optimization problem to facilitate algorithm design for model aggregation of on-device distributed federated learning.

Problem $\mathscr{P}_{8.1}$ can be rewritten as

$$\begin{aligned} \underset{\mathcal{S},\boldsymbol{m}\in\mathbb{C}^N}{\text{maximize}} \quad & |\mathcal{S}| \\ \text{subject to} \quad & F_i(\boldsymbol{m}) = \|\boldsymbol{m}\|^2 - \gamma_i\|\boldsymbol{m}^{\mathsf{H}}\boldsymbol{h}_i\|^2 \leq 0, \ i \in \mathcal{S} \\ & \boldsymbol{m} \neq \boldsymbol{0}. \end{aligned} \tag{8.20}$$

By introducing the parameter $\tau > 0$ we can further rewrite it as

$$\begin{aligned} \underset{\mathcal{S},\boldsymbol{m}\in\mathbb{C}^N}{\text{maximize}} \quad & |\mathcal{S}| \\ \text{subject to} \quad & F_i(\boldsymbol{m})/\tau = \|\boldsymbol{m}\|^2/\tau - \gamma_i\|\boldsymbol{m}^{\mathsf{H}}\boldsymbol{h}_i\|^2/\tau \leq 0, i \in \mathcal{S} \\ & \|\boldsymbol{m}\|^2 \geq \tau, \tau > 0. \end{aligned} \tag{8.21}$$

By redefining $\boldsymbol{m}/\sqrt{\tau} \mapsto \boldsymbol{m}$ we can eliminate the parameter τ and equivalently rewrite problem (8.21) as

$$\begin{aligned} \underset{\mathcal{S},\boldsymbol{m}\in\mathbb{C}^N}{\text{maximize}} \quad & |\mathcal{S}| \\ \text{subject to} \quad & \|\boldsymbol{m}\|^2 - \gamma_i\|\boldsymbol{m}^{\mathsf{H}}\boldsymbol{h}_i\|^2 \leq 0, i \in \mathcal{S} \\ & \|\boldsymbol{m}\|^2 \geq 1. \end{aligned} \tag{8.22}$$

Problem (8.22) admits the typical form of maximizing the number of feasible constraints $\|\boldsymbol{m}\|^2 - \gamma_i\|\boldsymbol{m}^{\mathsf{H}}\boldsymbol{h}_i\|^2 \leq 0$. It can be addressed by minimizing the sparsity of variable $\boldsymbol{x} \in \mathbb{R}_+^M$ [28,29], that is,

$$\begin{aligned} \underset{\boldsymbol{x}\in\mathbb{R}_+^M,\boldsymbol{m}\in\mathbb{C}^N}{\text{minimize}} \quad & \|\boldsymbol{x}\|_0 \\ \text{subject to} \quad & \|\boldsymbol{m}\|^2 - \gamma_i\|\boldsymbol{m}^{\mathsf{H}}\boldsymbol{h}_i\|^2 \leq x_i, \forall i, \end{aligned}$$

$$\|\boldsymbol{m}\|^2 \geq 1. \tag{8.23}$$

The feasibility of selecting each device under MSE requirement is indicated by the sparsity pattern of $\boldsymbol{x}$, that is, device i can be selected under the MSE requirement if $x_i = 0$.

The constraints of problem (8.23) are nonconvex quadratic. To address this issue, we can use the well-known matrix lifting technique [30]. The receive beamforming vector can be lifted as $\boldsymbol{M} = \boldsymbol{m}\boldsymbol{m}^{\mathsf{H}}$, thereby obtaining the following sparse and low-rank optimization problem reformulation:

$$\begin{aligned} \mathscr{P}_{8.2} : \underset{\boldsymbol{x}\in\mathbb{R}_+^M, \boldsymbol{M}\in\mathbb{C}^{N\times N}}{\text{minimize}} \quad & \|\boldsymbol{x}\|_0 \\ \text{subject to} \quad & \text{Tr}(\boldsymbol{M}) - \gamma_i \boldsymbol{h}_i^{\mathsf{H}} \boldsymbol{M} \boldsymbol{h}_i \leq x_i, \forall i, \\ & \boldsymbol{M} \succeq \boldsymbol{0}, \text{Tr}(\boldsymbol{M}) \geq 1, \\ & \text{rank}(\boldsymbol{M}) = 1. \end{aligned} \tag{8.24}$$

Problem $\mathscr{P}_{8.2}$ is still nonconvex due to the sparse objective function and the low-rank constraint. In spite of its nonconvexity, sparse and low-rank optimization has garnered much attention in many fields such as signal processing, machine learning, high-dimensional statistics, and so on. In the next section, we present convex and nonconvex approaches to solve this problem.

8.5. Numerical algorithms

In this section, we provide convex and nonconvex methods for solving the computationally difficult sparse and low-rank optimization problem $\mathscr{P}_{8.2}$. The convex method enjoys low computation complexity, but the nonconvex method can enhance the sparsity, which selects more devices and improves the performance of federated learning.

8.5.1 Convex relaxation approach

As we discussed in the previous chapters, the nonconvex sparse objective function, the ℓ_0-norm, can be efficiently solved by its convex surrogate ℓ_1-norm. By using the ℓ_1-norm, problem $\mathscr{P}_{8.2}$ is transformed as the sum-of-infeasibilities [28, Chapter 11.4] problem in optimization theory. The nonconvex rank-one constraint in semidefinite program can be addressed by simply discarding the rank constraint, which is called the semidefinite relaxation (SDR) technique [31]. Thus we can convexify problem $\mathscr{P}_{8.2}$ with ℓ_1-norm relaxation and SDR as

$$\begin{aligned} \underset{\boldsymbol{x}\in\mathbb{R}_+^M, \boldsymbol{M}\in\mathbb{C}^{N\times N}}{\text{minimize}} \quad & \|\boldsymbol{x}\|_1 \\ \text{subject to} \quad & \mathrm{Tr}(\boldsymbol{M}) - \gamma_i \boldsymbol{h}_i^{\mathsf{H}} \boldsymbol{M} \boldsymbol{h}_i \le x_i, \forall i, \\ & \boldsymbol{M} \succeq \boldsymbol{0}, \mathrm{Tr}(\boldsymbol{M}) \ge 1. \end{aligned} \tag{8.25}$$

8.5.2 Iteratively reweighted minimization approach

To enhance the sparsity inducing performance of convex relaxation, smoothed ℓ_p-minimization [29] is proposed as a tight nonconvex approximation for the ℓ_0-norm. The smoothed ℓ_p-norm approximation of a vector $\boldsymbol{x}$ is given by

$$f_p(\boldsymbol{x}) = \sum_i (x_i^2 + \varepsilon^2)^{p/2}. \tag{8.26}$$

Although it is still nonconvex, it can be solved by iteratively reweighted ℓ_2-minimization, that is, alternatively updating a weight parameter $\boldsymbol{w}$ and optimization variables $\boldsymbol{x}$, $\boldsymbol{M}$ in the tth iteration as follows:

$$\begin{aligned} \boldsymbol{x}^{[t]}, \boldsymbol{M}^{[t]} = \quad & \underset{\boldsymbol{x}\in\mathbb{R}_+^M, \boldsymbol{M}\in\mathbb{C}^{N\times N}}{\arg\min} \quad \sum_i w_i^{[t-1]} x_i^2 \\ & \text{subject to} \quad \mathrm{Tr}(\boldsymbol{M}) - \gamma_i \boldsymbol{h}_i^{\mathsf{H}} \boldsymbol{M} \boldsymbol{h}_i \le x_i, \forall i, \\ & \qquad\qquad\quad \boldsymbol{M} \succeq \boldsymbol{0}, \mathrm{Tr}(\boldsymbol{M}) \ge 1. \end{aligned} \tag{8.27}$$

$$w_i^{[t]} = \frac{p}{2}\left[\left(x_i^{[t]}\right)^2 + \varepsilon^2\right]^{\frac{p}{2}-1}. \tag{8.28}$$

Note that the smoothing parameter $\varepsilon > 0$ should be chosen carefully because the convergence behavior of the reweighted approach is usually sensitive [32,33] to it.

8.5.3 DC programming approach

In this subsection, we present a DC programming approach for enhancing sparsity and inducing rank-one solutions, which avoids the parameter sensitivity of reweighted approach and considerably improves the capability of yielding rank-one solutions of SDR technique. We will first provide the DC representation for sparse objective function and rank-one constraint, followed by a unified DC program framework for solving problem $\mathscr{P}_{8.2}$.

8.5.3.1 DC representations

The work [34] has proposed an interesting DC representation of the cardinality constraint for sparse optimization. It is based on the key observation that

"the $(k+1)$th largest absolute value for a k-sparsity vector $\boldsymbol{x}$" $= 0$.

Therefore the sum of the largest k absolute values, which is called the Ky Fan k-norm of $\boldsymbol{x}$ (represented by $|||\boldsymbol{x}|||_k$), equals its ℓ_1-norm.

Definition 3. Ky Fan k-norm [35]: For vector $\boldsymbol{x} \in \mathbb{C}^M$, its Ky Fan k-norm is given by the sum of the largest k absolute values, that is,

$$|||\boldsymbol{x}|||_k = \sum_{i=1}^{k} |x_{\pi(i)}|, \tag{8.29}$$

where π represents a permutation of $\{1, \ldots, M\}$ based on the descending order of the absolute values of entries of $\boldsymbol{x}$, that is, $|x_{\pi(1)}| \geq \cdots \geq |x_{\pi(M)}|$.

Thus we obtain the DC representation for sparse function as follows:

$$\|\boldsymbol{x}\|_0 = \min\{k : \|\boldsymbol{x}\|_1 - |||\boldsymbol{x}|||_k = 0, 0 \leq k \leq M\}. \tag{8.30}$$

This framework can be extended to the rank constraint. The DC representation for the rank-one constraint of a PSD matrix $\boldsymbol{M}$ is given by

$$\text{rank}(\boldsymbol{M}) = 1 \Leftrightarrow \text{Tr}(\boldsymbol{M}) - \|\boldsymbol{M}\|_2 = 0, \tag{8.31}$$

since only the largest singular value is nonzero.

8.5.3.2 DC program framework

Based on the above-introduced DC representations, we provide a unified DC program framework for solving problem $\mathscr{P}_{8.2}$. The device selection in problem $\mathscr{P}_{8.2}$ is addressed by a two-step procedure, consisting of inducing a sparse solution $\boldsymbol{x}^{\star}$ in the first step and performing a sequence of feasibility detection in the second step according to the priority extracted from $\boldsymbol{x}$. Specifically, we solve the following DC program in the first step to induce a sparse solution:

$$\mathscr{P}_{8.2.\text{DC-S1}} : \underset{\boldsymbol{x},\boldsymbol{M}}{\text{minimize}} \quad \|\boldsymbol{x}\|_1 - |||\boldsymbol{x}|||_k + \text{Tr}(\boldsymbol{M}) - \|\boldsymbol{M}\|_2$$

$$\begin{aligned} \text{subject to} \quad & \mathrm{Tr}(\boldsymbol{M}) - \gamma_i \boldsymbol{h}_i^{\mathsf{H}} \boldsymbol{M} \boldsymbol{h}_i \le x_i, \forall i = 1, \dots, M \\ & \boldsymbol{M} \succeq \boldsymbol{0}, \quad \mathrm{Tr}(\boldsymbol{M}) \ge 1, \boldsymbol{x} \succeq \boldsymbol{0}. \end{aligned} \tag{8.32}$$

By successively solving it for $k = 0, \dots, M$, we obtain a sparse vector $\boldsymbol{x}^\star$ such that the objective value achieves zero, which also guarantees the rank-one constraint of $\boldsymbol{M}$. The solution $\boldsymbol{x}^\star$ characterizes the gap between achievable MSE and the target MSE requirement for each device. Thus we set a higher priority for the device k with a higher value of $x_k^\star$. Let π be the permutation such that the elements $x_{\pi(k)}^\star$ are arranged in descending order, that is, $x_{\pi(1)}^\star \ge \dots \ge x_{\pi(M)}^\star$. We will solve a sequence of DC program

$$\begin{aligned} \mathscr{P}_{8.2.\text{DC-S2}}: \underset{\boldsymbol{M}}{\text{minimize}} \quad & \mathrm{Tr}(\boldsymbol{M}) - \|\boldsymbol{M}\|_2 \\ \text{subject to} \quad & \mathrm{Tr}(\boldsymbol{M}) - \gamma_i \boldsymbol{h}_i^{\mathsf{H}} \boldsymbol{M} \boldsymbol{h}_i \le 0, \forall i \in \mathcal{S}^{[k]} \\ & \boldsymbol{M} \succeq \boldsymbol{0}, \quad \mathrm{Tr}(\boldsymbol{M}) \ge 1 \end{aligned} \tag{8.33}$$

for detecting the feasibility of the selected device $\mathcal{S}^{[k]} = \{\pi(k), \pi(k+1), \dots, \pi(M)\}$. If zero is achievable for the objective value, then we can obtain an exact rank-one solution $\boldsymbol{M}^\star$ from problem $\mathscr{P}_{8.2.\text{DC-S2}}$, and the devices in $\mathcal{S}^{[k]}$ can be selected while satisfying the MSE requirement. A feasible receiver beamforming vector $\boldsymbol{m}$ can be extracted via Cholesky decomposition $\boldsymbol{M}^\star = \boldsymbol{m}\boldsymbol{m}^{\mathsf{H}}$. Although DC programs $\mathscr{P}_{8.2.\text{DC-S1}}$ and $\mathscr{P}_{8.2.\text{DC-S2}}$ are still nonconvex, they can be solved by iteratively performing primal and dual steps, which is called the DC algorithm [36] and converges to critical points with arbitrarily feasible initial point. The dual step in each iteration can be efficiently performed by computing the subgradient of the concave part (i.e., $-|||\boldsymbol{x}|||_k - \|\boldsymbol{M}\|_2$ and $-\|\boldsymbol{M}\|_2$). Therefore the DC algorithm can be concluded as iteratively linearizing the concave part of problem $\mathscr{P}_{8.2.\text{DC-S1}}$ and problem $\mathscr{P}_{8.2.\text{DC-S2}}$ with subgradients. The subgradients are given by

$$i\text{-th entry of } \partial |||\boldsymbol{x}|||_k = \begin{cases} \mathrm{sign}(x_i), & |x_i| \ge |x_{(k)}|, \\ 0, & |x_i| < |x_{(k)}|, \end{cases} \tag{8.34}$$

according to [34] and

$$\partial \|\boldsymbol{M}\|_2 = \boldsymbol{v}_1 \boldsymbol{v}_1^{\mathsf{H}}, \tag{8.35}$$

where $\boldsymbol{v}_1$ is the eigenvector of the largest eigenvalue according to the subdifferential of orthogonal invariant norm in [37].

The overall DC program framework is concluded in Algorithm 12.

Algorithm 12: Unified DC program framework for the device selection problem $\mathscr{P}_{8.2}$ in federated learning.

Step 1: inducing sparsity
$k \leftarrow 0$
while *objective value of* $\mathscr{P}_{8.2.DC\text{-}S1}$ *is not zero* **do**
  Obtain solution $\boldsymbol{x}^\star$ to the DC program $\mathscr{P}_{S1}$
  $k \leftarrow k+1$
end

Step 2: detecting feasibility
Arrange $\boldsymbol{x}^\star$ in descending order as $x^\star_{\pi(1)} \geq \cdots \geq x^\star_{\pi(M)}$
$k \leftarrow 1$
while *objective value of* $\mathscr{P}_{8.2.DC\text{-}S2}$ *is not zero* **do**
  $\mathcal{S}^{[k]} \leftarrow \{\pi(k), \pi(k+1), \ldots, \pi(M)\}$
  Obtain solution $\boldsymbol{M}^\star$ to the DC program $\mathscr{P}_{8.2.DC\text{-}S2}$
  $k \leftarrow k+1$
end
Output: $\boldsymbol{m}$ via Cholesky decomposition $\boldsymbol{M}^\star = \boldsymbol{m}\boldsymbol{m}^{\mathsf{H}}$, and selected devices $\mathcal{S}^{[k]} = \{\pi(k), \pi(k+1), \ldots, \pi(M)\}$

8.6. Simulation results

We conduct extensive experiments to evaluate the performance of convex and nonconvex approaches for device selection of federated learning. We randomly generate channel vectors $\boldsymbol{h}_i$ with i.i.d. complex normal distribution, that is, $\boldsymbol{h}_i \sim \mathcal{CN}(\boldsymbol{0}, \boldsymbol{I})$. We set the average transmit signal-to-noise ratio (SNR) P^{Tx}/σ^2 as 20 dB. We choose the same number of data points for each device and set the preprocessing and postprocessing scalars as $\phi_i = 1$ and $\psi = 1/|\mathcal{S}|$, respectively.

8.6.1 Number of selected devices under MSE requirement

We compare the number of selected devices of the following approaches:

- Convex relaxation (**ℓ_1+SDR**): We use ℓ_1-norm relaxation for inducing sparsity in Step 1 and SDR for addressing the rank-one constraint in both Steps 1 and 2.
- Iteratively reweighted minimization (**Reweighted+SDR**): We adopt the iteratively reweighted minimization method to induce sparsity in Step 1 and SDR technique to induce rank-one solutions in both steps.

- Unified DC program framework (**DC**): We evaluate the performance of the presented unified DC program framework for inducing sparsity of $\boldsymbol{x}$ and addressing the rank-one constraint of $\boldsymbol{M}$.

Consider a federated learning system with $M = 20$ mobile devices and an $N = 6$-antenna BS. The number of selected devices yielded by each algorithm is averaged over 500 channel realizations and illustrated in Fig. 8.5. It demonstrated that the DC program framework is able to select much more devices thanks to its great power in accurately detecting the rank-one constraint.

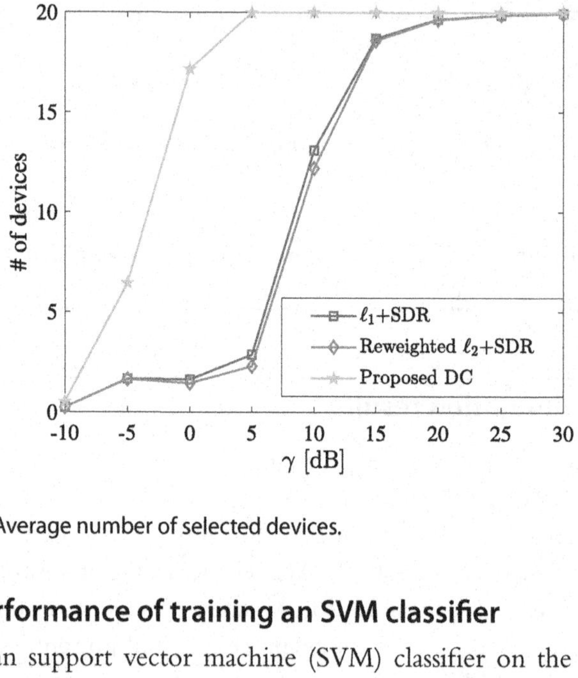

Figure 8.5 Average number of selected devices.

8.6.2 Performance of training an SVM classifier

We train an support vector machine (SVM) classifier on the CIFAR-10 dataset [27] using the federated learning system with an $N = 6$-antenna BS and $M = 20$ mobile devices. CIFAR-10 is a well-known image classification dataset consisting of 10 classes of objects. In addition to the three candidate approaches, "ℓ_1+SDR", "Reweighted+SDR", and "DC", we also evaluate the performance of a benchmark approach by simply selecting all devices without any aggregation error. The training loss and relative prediction error averaged over 10 channel realizations are demonstrated in Fig. 8.6. Here the target MSE is set as $\gamma = 5$ dB, and the sizes of training and test sets are set as $50,000$ and $10,000$, respectively. Then the numerical results demonstrate that the training loss is the lowest and the prediction ac-

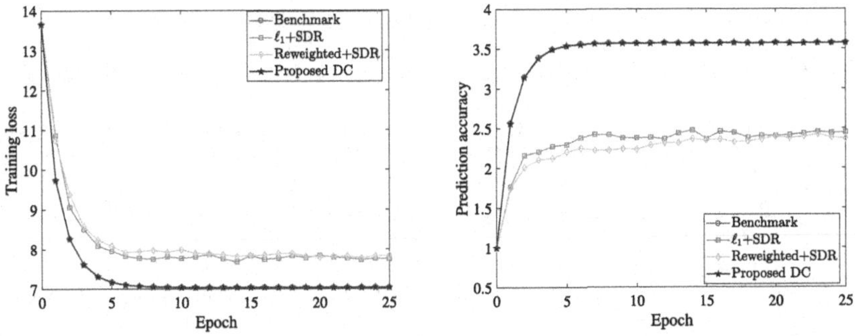

(a) Training loss **(b)** Relative prediction accuracy

Figure 8.6 The training loss and relative prediction accuracy for training an SVM classifier. The relative prediction accuracy is given by the prediction accuracy of each algorithm divided by it using random classification.

curacy is the highest for the DC approach because more devices are selected in each communication round.

8.7. Summary

In this chapter, we studied a typical edge training system to accomplish federated learning tasks. We presented a novel over-the-air computation-based fast model aggregation approach for on-device distributed federated learning. We formulated a device selection problem to improve the statistical learning performance, which was then reformulated as a sparse and low-rank optimization problem for algorithm design. Despite the convex relaxation method for addressing the sparse and low-rank optimization problem, we proposed a novel DC program framework for inducing sparsity and low-rankness. We conducted numerical experiments to compare the performance of these methods. Results demonstrated the advantages of the proposed DC approach compared with the convex method.

References

[1] Regulation (EU) 2016/679 of the European Parliament and of the Council of 27 April 2016 on the protection of natural persons with regard to the processing of personal data and on the free movement of such data, and repealing Directive 95/46/EC (General Data Protection Regulation), Offic. J. Europ. Union L 119 (Apr. 2016) 1–88, https://eur-lex.europa.eu/legal-content/EN/TXT/HTML/?uri=OJ:L:2016:119:FULL&from=EN.

[2] J. Konečný, H.B. McMahan, D. Ramage, Federated optimization: distributed optimization beyond the datacenter, in: NIPS Optimization for Machine Learning Workshop, 2015.

[3] Q. Yang, Y. Liu, T. Chen, Y. Tong, Federated machine learning: concept and applications, ACM Trans. Intell. Syst. Technol. 10 (2) (2019) 12.
[4] Q. Yang, Y. Liu, Y. Cheng, Y. Kang, T. Chen, H. Yu, Federated learning, Synth. Lect. Artif. Intell. Mach. Learn. 13 (3) (2019) 1–207.
[5] K. Bonawitz, H. Eichner, W. Grieskamp, D. Huba, A. Ingerman, V. Ivanov, C. Kiddon, J. Konecny, S. Mazzocchi, H.B. McMahan, et al., Towards federated learning at scale: system design, preprint, arXiv:1902.01046, 2019.
[6] S.J. Pan, Q. Yang, A survey on transfer learning, IEEE Trans. Knowl. Data Eng. 22 (Oct. 2010) 1345–1359.
[7] J. Konečný, H.B. McMahan, F.X. Yu, P. Richtárik, A.T. Suresh, D. Bacon, Federated learning: strategies for improving communication efficiency, preprint, arXiv: 1610.05492, 2016.
[8] B. McMahan, E. Moore, D. Ramage, S. Hampson, B.A. y Arcas, Communication-efficient learning of deep networks from decentralized data, in: Proc. Int. Conf. Artif. Intell. Stat. (AISTATS), 2017, pp. 1273–1282.
[9] J. Vaidya, C. Clifton, Privacy-preserving k-means clustering over vertically partitioned data, in: Proc. ACM SIGKDD Int. Conf. Knowl. Discovery Data Mining (KDD), ACM, 2003, pp. 206–215.
[10] H. Yu, J. Vaidya, X. Jiang, Privacy-preserving SVM classification on vertically partitioned data, in: Pacific-Asia Conf. Knowl. Discovery Data Mining, Springer, 2006, pp. 647–656.
[11] A. Gascón, P. Schoppmann, B. Balle, M. Raykova, J. Doerner, S. Zahur, D. Evans, Secure linear regression on vertically partitioned datasets, IACR Cryptol. ePrint Arch. 2016 (2016) 892.
[12] S. Hardy, W. Henecka, H. Ivey-Law, R. Nock, G. Patrini, G. Smith, B. Thorne, Private federated learning on vertically partitioned data via entity resolution and additively homomorphic encryption, preprint, arXiv:1711.10677, 2017.
[13] K. Yang, T. Fan, T. Chen, Y. Shi, Q. Yang, A quasi-Newton method based vertical federated learning framework for logistic regression, in: NeurIPS Workshops on Federated Learning for Data Privacy and Confidentiality, 2019.
[14] J. Vaidya, C. Clifton, Privacy-preserving decision trees over vertically partitioned data, in: IFIP Annu. Conf. Data Appl. Security Privacy, Springer, 2005, pp. 139–152.
[15] K. Cheng, T. Fan, Y. Jin, Y. Liu, T. Chen, Q. Yang, SecureBoost: a lossless federated learning framework, preprint, arXiv:1901.08755, 2019.
[16] Y. Mao, C. You, J. Zhang, K. Huang, K.B. Letaief, A survey on mobile edge computing: the communication perspective, IEEE Commun. Surv. Tutor. 19 (2017) 2322–2358.
[17] G. Zhu, J. Xu, K. Huang, Over-the-air computing for 6G – turning air into a computer, preprint, arXiv:2009.02181, 2020.
[18] B. Nazer, M. Gastpar, Computation over multiple-access channels, IEEE Trans. Inf. Theory 53 (Oct. 2007) 3498–3516.
[19] M. Goldenbaum, H. Boche, S. Stańczak, Harnessing interference for analog function computation in wireless sensor networks, IEEE Trans. Signal Process. 61 (Oct. 2013) 4893–4906.
[20] L. Chen, N. Zhao, Y. Chen, F.R. Yu, G. Wei, Over-the-air computation for IoT networks: computing multiple functions with antenna arrays, IEEE Int. Things J. (2018).
[21] F. Ang, L. Chen, N. Zhao, Y. Chen, F.R. Yu, Robust design for massive CSI acquisition in analog function computation networks, IEEE Trans. Veh. Technol. 68 (Mar. 2019) 2361–2373.
[22] O. Abari, H. Rahul, D. Katabi, M. Pant, Airshare: distributed coherent transmission made seamless, in: IEEE Int. Conf. Comput. Commun. (INFOCOM), April 2015, pp. 1742–1750.

[23] F. Wu, L. Chen, N. Zhao, Y. Chen, F.R. Yu, G. Wei, NOMA-enhanced computation over multi-access channels, IEEE Trans. Wirel. Commun. (2020).
[24] K. Yang, T. Jiang, Y. Shi, Z. Ding, Federated learning via over-the-air computation, IEEE Trans. Wirel. Commun. 19 (Jan. 2020) 2022–2035.
[25] M. Mohammadi Amiri, D. Gündüz, Machine learning at the wireless edge: distributed stochastic gradient descent over-the-air, IEEE Trans. Signal Process. 68 (2020) 2155–2169.
[26] G. Zhu, Y. Wang, K. Huang, Broadband analog aggregation for low-latency federated edge learning, IEEE Trans. Wirel. Commun. 19 (Jan. 2020) 491–506.
[27] A. Krizhevsky, G. Hinton, Learning multiple layers of features from tiny images, Tech. Rep. 4, University of Toronto, 2009.
[28] S. Boyd, L. Vandenberghe, Convex Optimization, Cambridge Univ. Press, 2004.
[29] Y. Shi, J. Cheng, J. Zhang, B. Bai, W. Chen, K.B. Letaief, Smoothed L_p-minimization for green cloud-RAN with user admission control, IEEE J. Sel. Areas Commun. 34 (Apr. 2016) 1022–1036.
[30] N.D. Sidiropoulos, T.N. Davidson, Z.-Q. Luo, Transmit beamforming for physical-layer multicasting, IEEE Trans. Signal Process. 54 (Jun. 2006) 2239–2251.
[31] Z.-Q. Luo, N.D. Sidiropoulos, P. Tseng, S. Zhang, Approximation bounds for quadratic optimization with homogeneous quadratic constraints, SIAM J. Optim. 18 (1) (2007) 1–28.
[32] R. Chartrand, W. Yin, Iteratively reweighted algorithms for compressive sensing, in: Proc. IEEE Int. Conf. Acoustics Speech Signal Process. (ICASSP), 2008, pp. 3869–3872.
[33] H. Wang, F. Zhang, Q. Wu, Y. Hu, Y. Shi, Nonconvex and nonsmooth sparse optimization via adaptively iterative reweighted methods, arXiv:1810.10167, 2018.
[34] J.-y. Gotoh, A. Takeda, K. Tono, DC formulations and algorithms for sparse optimization problems, Math. Program. 169 (May 2018) 141–176.
[35] K. Fan, Maximum properties and inequalities for the eigenvalues of completely continuous operators, Proc. Natl. Acad. Sci. USA 37 (11) (1951) 760–766.
[36] P.D. Tao, L.T.H. An, Convex analysis approach to DC programming: theory, algorithms and applications, Acta Math. Vietnam. 22 (1) (1997) 289–355.
[37] G.A. Watson, Characterization of the subdifferential of some matrix norms, Linear Algebra Appl. 170 (1992) 33–45.

CHAPTER NINE

Reconfigurable intelligent surface aided federated learning

9.1. Background on reconfigurable intelligent surface

In the conventional wireless communication architecture, the wireless channel is random and uncontrollable, which becomes the ultimate bottleneck of achieving high-capacity and ultra-reliable communications. The wireless channel fading is mainly due to the reflections, diffractions, and scattering in the surrounding environment. Therefore RIS is proposed to implement a smart radio environment and enhance the wireless channel status by controlling the reflections of wireless signals [1].

The RIS is motivated by the metasurface, which is a two-dimensional planer metamaterial. The metamaterial breaks traditional Snell's law to change the amplitude and phase of reflected wireless signal. Moreover, the metamaterial can be achieved by microelectromechanical system (MEMS), positive-intrinsic-negative (PIN) diodes, graphene, and other digitally controllable materials [2]. Thus the properties of reflected signal are tunable through field-programmable gate array (FPGA) controller. A large number of metamaterial units (a.k.a. reflecting element) compose the RIS in a two-dimensional plane, which arbitrarily controls the wireless signals and is illustrated in Fig. 9.1 [3]. The reflecting element can reflect the incident signal by controlling the amplitude and phase shift for directional signal enhancement or nulling.

To describe the mathematical model of RIS, we denote the incident signal by x_n and the reflected signal by y_n for the nth reflecting element. The complex reflection model is presented as

$$y_n = (\beta_n e^{j\theta_n}) x_n, \; n = 1, 2, \ldots, N, \tag{9.1}$$

where N is the total number of reflecting elements. Particularly, $\beta_n \in [0, 1]$ represents the amplitude attenuation for passive reflection, and $\theta_n \in [0, 2\pi)$ is the phase shift between x_n and y_n. The RIS will achieve various purposes with spatial control by adjusting the reflection coefficients $\beta_n, \theta_n, n = 1, 2, \ldots, N$. For instance, RIS can enhance the signal coverage and assist interference cancellation [4].

https://doi.org/10.1016/B978-0-12-823817-2.00020-6

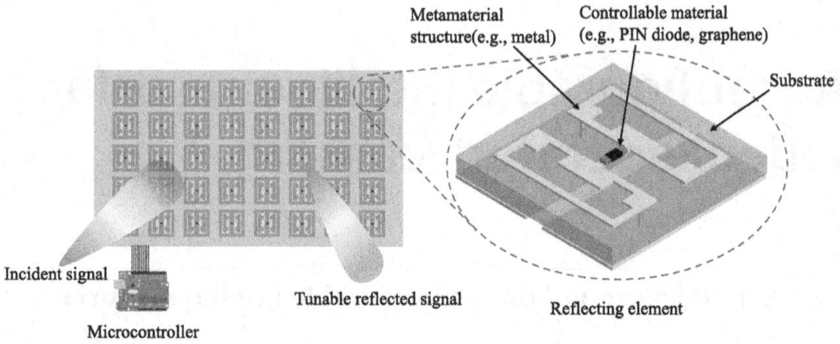

Figure 9.1 Illustration of reconfigurable intelligent surface.

9.2. RIS empowered on-device distributed federated learning

In the last chapter, we have provided a fast model aggregation approach for federated learning based on over-the-air computation. Though we have exploited the wireless signal superposition property to reduce the required spectral resources, the performance is still fundamentally limited by the possible unfavorable signal propagation conditions. RIS [5] emerges as a cost-effective technique improving the spectral efficiency and energy efficiency of wireless communication by reconfiguring the propagation environment of electromagnetic waves. It has a huge potential of integrating RIS with many other advanced techniques such as machine learning and massive MIMO terahertz communications. By deploying RIS in federated learning system [6] it is promising to reduce the model aggregation error of the over-the-air computation approach.

A RIS is a low-cost surface consisting of structured passive scattering elements [7], which enables adjustable phase shifts for the incident signals. By controlling the phase shifts of RIS we can enhance the received signal power and mitigate the cofrequency interferences. The work [8] has proposed a joint active beamforming (i.e., transmit beamforming) and passive beamforming (i.e., the phase shifts of RIS) design approach to minimize the transmission power consumption of APs under target SINR constraints for each user. In the work [9] a joint design of the downlink transmission power and RIS phase shifts is proposed to maximize the energy efficiency. The work [10] has investigated the RIS-empowered nonorthogonal multiple access (NOMA) network to improve energy efficiency. The work [11] has studied the energy beamforming and data aggregation in RIS empowered IoT networks. In this chapter, we develop a more efficient fast model aggregation approach for on-device distributed federated learning by leveraging RIS and over-the-air computation.

9.2.1 System model

Consider the on-device distributed federated learning system consisting of an M-antenna base station and K single-antenna mobile devices as presented in Chapter 8.2. It requires the periodical aggregation of local model updates from each mobile device to accomplish the model training of the target machine learning task (8.2). The global model aggregation in each communication round is given by

$$z = \frac{1}{\sum_{i \in \mathcal{S}} |\mathcal{D}_i|} \sum_{i \in \mathcal{S}} |\mathcal{D}_i| z_i, \tag{9.2}$$

where $\mathcal{D}_i$ is the local dataset of device i. To reduce the high communication overhead of model aggregation, we have provided an over-the-air computation-based fast model aggregation approach to improve the communication efficiency. To overcome the detrimental wireless propagation environment, in this chapter, we adopt a RIS with N reflecting elements to further accelerate the model aggregation procedure as illustrated in Fig. 9.2.

For the over-the-air computation framework for model aggregation given in Chapter 8.3, the preprocessing and postprocessing scalars are given by $\phi_i = |\mathcal{D}_i|$ and $\psi = \frac{1}{\sum_{i \in \mathcal{S}} |\mathcal{D}_i|}$, respectively. Without loss of generality, suppose the transmit information symbol at device i over d time slots for z_i is given by $s_i \in \mathbb{C}^d$ with unit power $\mathbb{E}(s_i s_i^{\mathsf{H}}) = \boldsymbol{I}$. By omitting the time index the target function to be estimated at each time slot is given by

$$g = \sum_{i \in \mathcal{S}} \phi_i s_i. \tag{9.3}$$

Let $\boldsymbol{h}_i^{\mathsf{d}} \in \mathbb{C}^M$ be the channel coefficient vector between the base station and device i, let $\boldsymbol{h}_i^{\mathsf{r}} \in \mathbb{C}^N$ be the channel coefficient vector between the RIS and device i, and let $\mathbf{G} \in \mathbb{C}^{M \times N}$ be the channel coefficient matrix between the base station and RIS. Thus the received signal at the base station is given by

$$\boldsymbol{y} = \sum_{i \in \mathcal{S}} (\mathbf{G}\boldsymbol{\Theta}\boldsymbol{h}_i^{\mathsf{r}} + \boldsymbol{h}_i^{\mathsf{d}}) b_i s_i + \boldsymbol{n}, \tag{9.4}$$

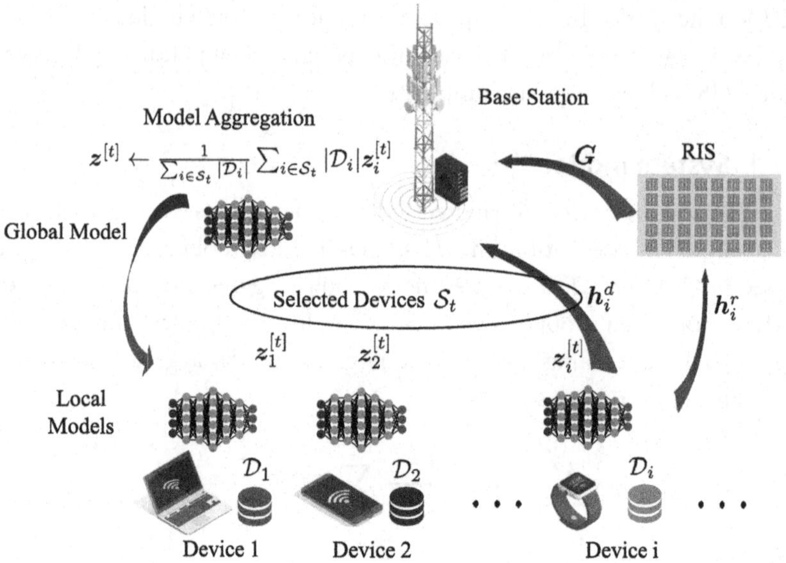

Figure 9.2 RIS empowered on-device federated learning system.

where the diagonal matrix $\mathbf{\Theta} = \text{diag}(e^{j\theta_1}, \ldots, e^{j\theta_N}) \in \mathbb{C}^{N \times N}$ denotes the phase shifts of the RIS and $\theta_n \in [0, 2\pi]$, $b_i \in \mathbb{C}$ denotes the transmit scalar, and $\boldsymbol{n} \sim \mathcal{CN}\left(\mathbf{0}, \sigma^2 \boldsymbol{I}\right)$ is the complex additive white Gaussian noise.

Our target is estimating the target function from the received signal following

$$\hat{g} = \frac{1}{\sqrt{\eta}} \boldsymbol{m}^{\mathsf{H}} \boldsymbol{y} = \frac{1}{\sqrt{\eta}} \boldsymbol{m}^{\mathsf{H}} \sum_{i \in \mathcal{S}} (\mathbf{G}\mathbf{\Theta}\boldsymbol{h}_i^{\mathsf{r}} + \boldsymbol{h}_i^{\mathsf{d}}) b_i s_i + \frac{1}{\sqrt{\eta}} \boldsymbol{m}^{\mathsf{H}} \boldsymbol{n}, \tag{9.5}$$

where $\boldsymbol{m} \in \mathbb{M}$ is the receive beamforming vector, and $\eta > 0$ is a normalizing factor. The estimated global model aggregation result can be computed by performing the postprocessing, that is, $\hat{z} = \psi \cdot \hat{g}$. The model aggregation error measured by MSE is given by

$$\mathsf{MSE}(\hat{g}, g) = \mathbb{E}\left(|\hat{g} - g|^2\right) = \sum_{i \in \mathcal{S}} \left| \frac{1}{\sqrt{\eta}} \boldsymbol{m}^{\mathsf{H}} (\mathbf{G}\mathbf{\Theta}\boldsymbol{h}_i^{\mathsf{r}} + \boldsymbol{h}_i^{\mathsf{d}}) b_i - \phi_i \right|^2 + \frac{\sigma^2 \|\boldsymbol{m}\|^2}{\eta}. \tag{9.6}$$

Similarly, the optimal transmitter scalar for minimizing the MSE is given by

$$b_i = \sqrt{\eta}\phi_i \frac{\left(\boldsymbol{m}^{\mathsf{H}}(\boldsymbol{G}\boldsymbol{\Theta}\boldsymbol{h}_i^{\mathsf{r}} + \boldsymbol{h}_i^{d})\right)^{\mathsf{H}}}{\left\|\boldsymbol{m}^{\mathsf{H}}(\boldsymbol{G}\boldsymbol{\Theta}\boldsymbol{h}_i^{\mathsf{r}} + \boldsymbol{h}_i^{\mathsf{d}})\right\|^2}, \quad i = 1, \ldots, K. \tag{9.7}$$

Due to the constraint of the maximum transmit power $P^{\mathsf{Tx}} > 0$, we have $|b_i|^2 \leq P^{\mathsf{Tx}}$. Therefore the normalizing factor η is given by

$$\eta = P^{\mathsf{Tx}} \min_{i \in \mathcal{S}} \frac{\left\|\boldsymbol{m}^{\mathsf{H}}(\boldsymbol{G}\boldsymbol{\Theta}\boldsymbol{h}_i^{\mathsf{r}} + \boldsymbol{h}_i^{\mathsf{d}})\right\|^2}{\phi_i^2}. \tag{9.8}$$

Thus the MSE can be rewritten in terms of the set of selected devices, receive beamforming vector, and the phase shift matrix:

$$\mathsf{MSE} = \frac{\sigma^2}{P^{\mathsf{Tx}}} \max_{i \in \mathcal{S}} \phi_i^2 \frac{\|\boldsymbol{m}\|^2}{\left\|\boldsymbol{m}^{\mathsf{H}}(\boldsymbol{G}\boldsymbol{\Theta}\boldsymbol{h}_i^{\mathsf{r}} + \boldsymbol{h}_i^{\mathsf{d}})\right\|^2}. \tag{9.9}$$

9.2.2 Problem formulation

As discussed in Chapter 8.3.3, selecting more devices and reducing the MSE for model aggregation can improve the statistical performance of federated learning. Thus we formulate the following combinatorial optimization problem to maximize the number of selected devices under the MSE requirement:

$$\begin{aligned}
\mathscr{P}_{9.1}: \underset{\mathcal{S}, \boldsymbol{m}, \boldsymbol{\Theta}}{\text{maximize}} \quad & |\mathcal{S}| \\
\text{subject to} \quad & \left(\max_{i \in \mathcal{S}} \phi_i^2 \frac{\|\boldsymbol{m}\|^2}{\left\|\boldsymbol{m}^{\mathsf{H}}(\boldsymbol{G}\boldsymbol{\Theta}\boldsymbol{h}_i^{\mathsf{r}} + \boldsymbol{h}_i^{\mathsf{d}})\right\|^2}\right) \leq \gamma, & (9.10)\\
& 0 \leq \theta_n \leq 2\pi, \ n = 1, \ldots, N, & (9.11)
\end{aligned}$$

where $\gamma > 0$ denotes the target MSE. According to the derivation in Chapter 8.4, we can rewrite constraint (9.10) as

$$\begin{aligned}
& F_i(\boldsymbol{m}) = \|\boldsymbol{m}\|^2 - \gamma_i \left\|\boldsymbol{m}^{\mathsf{H}}(\boldsymbol{G}\boldsymbol{\Theta}\boldsymbol{h}_i^{\mathsf{r}} + \boldsymbol{h}_i^{\mathsf{d}})\right\|^2 \leq 0, \ i \in \mathcal{S}, & (9.12)\\
& \boldsymbol{m} \neq \boldsymbol{0}, & (9.13)
\end{aligned}$$

where $\gamma_i = \gamma/\phi_i^2$. It can be further rewritten as

$$F_i(\boldsymbol{m}/\sqrt{\tau}) = F_i(\boldsymbol{m})/\tau \leq 0, \ i \in \mathcal{S}, \tag{9.14}$$

$$\|\boldsymbol{m}\|^2 \geq \tau, \tau > 0. \tag{9.15}$$

By further denoting $\boldsymbol{m} := \boldsymbol{m}/\sqrt{\tau}$ we can equivalently rewrite the constraint (9.10) as

$$\|\boldsymbol{m}\|^2 - \gamma_i \left\| \boldsymbol{m}^{\mathsf{H}}(\mathbf{G}\boldsymbol{\Theta}\boldsymbol{h}_i^{\mathsf{r}} + \boldsymbol{h}_i^{\mathsf{d}}) \right\|^2 \leq 0, \ i \in \mathcal{S}, \tag{9.16}$$

$$\|\boldsymbol{m}\|^2 \geq 1. \tag{9.17}$$

We observe that finding the maximum number of selected devices is equivalent to maximizing the number of feasible constraints in (9.16). Therefore we reformulate problem $\mathscr{P}$ as the following sparse optimization problem:

$$\mathscr{P}_{9.2} : \underset{\boldsymbol{x},\boldsymbol{m},\boldsymbol{\Theta}}{\text{minimize}} \quad \|\boldsymbol{x}\|_0$$

$$\text{subject to} \quad \|\boldsymbol{m}\|^2 - \gamma_i \left\| \boldsymbol{m}^{\mathsf{H}}(\mathbf{G}\boldsymbol{\Theta}\boldsymbol{h}_i^{\mathsf{r}} + \boldsymbol{h}_i^{\mathsf{d}}) \right\|^2 \leq x_i, \forall i, \tag{9.18}$$

$$\|\boldsymbol{m}\|^2 \geq 1, \boldsymbol{x} \succeq \mathbf{0}, \tag{9.19}$$

$$0 \leq \theta_n \leq 2\pi, \ n = 1, \ldots, N. \tag{9.20}$$

Due to the deployment of RIS, the unique computational difficulty of problem $\mathscr{P}_{9.2}$ lies in its nonconvex biquadratic constraints with respect to $\boldsymbol{m}$ and $\boldsymbol{\Theta}$ compared with problem (8.23). We further develop a sparse and low-rank optimization framework to solve problem $\mathscr{P}_{9.2}$.

9.3. Sparse and low-rank optimization framework

In this section, we provide a sparse and low-rank optimization framework for solving problem $\mathscr{P}_{9.2}$. We adopt a two-step framework to address the sparse objective function to find the maximum number of selected devices and an alternating low-rank optimization approach to address the nonconvex biquadratic constraints.

9.3.1 Two-step framework for sparse objective function

The basic idea of the two-step framework for minimizing sparsity is as follows.

- **Step 1:** Find a sparse solution $\boldsymbol{x}$ that provides the priority of selecting each device.
- **Step 2:** Solve a sequence of feasibility detection problem until finding the maximum number of devices under the MSE requirement.

Here we use the well-known ℓ_1-norm relaxation to induce sparsity in the first step, which is given by

$$\begin{aligned}\mathscr{P}_{9.3.\mathrm{S1}}: \underset{\boldsymbol{x},\boldsymbol{m}}{\text{minimize}} \quad & \|\boldsymbol{x}\|_1 \\ \text{subject to} \quad & (9.18),\ (9.19),\ (9.20).\end{aligned}$$

The kth entry of the solution x_k somehow characterizes the gap between the achievable MSE of device k and the target MSE requirement. Thus we place a high priority of selecting device k if x_k is larger. By arranging x_k in descending order $x_{\pi(1)} \geq \cdots \geq x_{\pi(K)}$ we can find the maximum number of selected devices through solving a sequence of feasibility detection problems

$$\begin{aligned}\mathscr{P}_{9.3.\mathrm{S2}}: \text{find} \quad & \boldsymbol{m}, \boldsymbol{v} \\ \text{subject to} \quad & \|\boldsymbol{m}\|^2 - \gamma_i \left\| \boldsymbol{m}^{\mathsf{H}}(\mathbf{G}\boldsymbol{\Theta}\boldsymbol{h}_i^{\mathsf{r}} + \boldsymbol{h}_i^{\mathsf{d}}) \right\|^2 \leq 0, \ i \in \mathcal{S}^{[k]}, \\ & \|\boldsymbol{m}\|^2 \geq 1, \\ & 0 \leq \theta_n \leq 2\pi, \ n = 1, \ldots, N, \end{aligned} \tag{9.21}$$

for $k = 1, \ldots, K$ and $\mathcal{S}^{[k]} = \{\pi(k), \pi(k+1), \ldots, \pi(K)\}$.

9.3.2 Alternating low-rank optimization for nonconvex biquadratic constraints

To address the nonconvex biquadratic constraints, we can adopt the matrix lifting technique to reformulate it as bilinear constraints and solve the resulting problem with alternating optimization [12]. Alternating optimization is a well-recognized technique for addressing coupled variables in the objective function or constraints of an optimization problem, whose applications include clustering, matrix completion, nonnegative matrix factorization, just to name a few.

Specifically, in the first step of solving problem $\mathscr{P}_{9.3.\mathrm{S1}}$, we will alternatively update $(\boldsymbol{m}, \boldsymbol{x})$ and $\boldsymbol{\Theta}$. Given the phase shifts $\boldsymbol{\Theta}$, we will update $(\boldsymbol{x}, \boldsymbol{m})$ as the solution to

$$\underset{\boldsymbol{x},\boldsymbol{m},\boldsymbol{\Theta}}{\text{minimize}} \quad \|\boldsymbol{x}\|_1$$

$$\text{subject to} \quad \|\boldsymbol{m}\|^2 - \gamma_i \left\| \boldsymbol{m}^{\mathsf{H}} (\boldsymbol{G}\boldsymbol{\Theta}\boldsymbol{h}_i^{\mathsf{r}} + \boldsymbol{h}_i^{\mathsf{d}}) \right\|^2 \le x_i, \forall i, \tag{9.22}$$

$$\|\boldsymbol{m}\|^2 \ge 1, \boldsymbol{x} \succeq \boldsymbol{0}. \tag{9.23}$$

By defining the lifting matrix $\boldsymbol{M} = \boldsymbol{m}\boldsymbol{m}^{\mathsf{H}}$ we can reformulate it as an SDP problem with fixed rank constraint

$$\begin{aligned} \mathscr{P}_{9.3.\mathrm{S1.1}} : \underset{\boldsymbol{x},\boldsymbol{M}}{\text{minimize}} \quad & \|\boldsymbol{x}\|_1 \\ \text{subject to} \quad & \mathrm{Tr}(\boldsymbol{M}) - \gamma_i \mathrm{Tr}(\boldsymbol{M}\boldsymbol{H}_i) \le x_i, \forall i, \qquad (9.24) \\ & \boldsymbol{M} \succeq \boldsymbol{0}, \mathrm{Tr}(\boldsymbol{M}) \ge 1, \mathrm{rank}(\boldsymbol{M}) = 1, \\ & \boldsymbol{x} \succeq \boldsymbol{0}, \qquad (9.25) \end{aligned}$$

where $\boldsymbol{H}_i = (\boldsymbol{G}\boldsymbol{\Theta}\boldsymbol{h}_i^r + \boldsymbol{h}_i^d)(\boldsymbol{G}\boldsymbol{\Theta}\boldsymbol{h}_i^r + \boldsymbol{h}_i^d)^{\mathsf{H}}$.

Note that we have $\boldsymbol{G}\boldsymbol{\Theta}\boldsymbol{h}_i^{\mathsf{r}} = \boldsymbol{G}\mathrm{diag}(\boldsymbol{h}_i^{\mathsf{r}})\boldsymbol{v}$ by denoting $\boldsymbol{v} = \mathrm{diag}(\boldsymbol{\Theta}) \in \mathbb{C}^N$ with $v_n = e^{j\theta_n}$. Thus we can rewrite constraints (9.18) and (9.20) as

$$\|\boldsymbol{m}\|^2 - \gamma_i \left| \boldsymbol{m}^{\mathsf{H}} \boldsymbol{G}\mathrm{diag}(\boldsymbol{h}_i^{\mathsf{r}})\boldsymbol{v} + \boldsymbol{m}^{\mathsf{H}}\boldsymbol{h}_i^{\mathsf{d}}) \right|^2 \le x_i, \forall i, \tag{9.26}$$

$$|v_n|^2 = 1, \ n = 1, \ldots, N. \tag{9.27}$$

By denoting $\boldsymbol{b}_i^{\mathsf{H}} = \boldsymbol{m}^{\mathsf{H}}\boldsymbol{G}\mathrm{diag}(\boldsymbol{h}_i^{\mathsf{r}})$, $c_i^{\mathsf{H}} = \boldsymbol{m}^{\mathsf{H}}\boldsymbol{h}_i^{\mathsf{d}}$ we obtain that

$$|\boldsymbol{m}^{\mathsf{H}}\boldsymbol{G}\mathrm{diag}(\boldsymbol{h}_i^{\mathsf{r}})\boldsymbol{v} + \boldsymbol{m}^{\mathsf{H}}\boldsymbol{h}_i^{\mathsf{d}})|^2 = |\boldsymbol{b}_i^{\mathsf{H}}\boldsymbol{v} + c_i^{\mathsf{H}}|^2 = |\boldsymbol{b}_i^{\mathsf{H}}\boldsymbol{v}e^{j\theta_{N+1}} + c_i^{\mathsf{H}}e^{j\theta_{N+1}})|^2$$

$$= \left| \begin{bmatrix} \boldsymbol{b}_i \\ c_i \end{bmatrix}^{\mathsf{H}} \begin{bmatrix} \boldsymbol{v}e^{j\theta_{N+1}} \\ e^{j\theta_{N+1}} \end{bmatrix} \right|^2 = \mathrm{Tr}(\boldsymbol{R}_i\tilde{\boldsymbol{v}}\tilde{\boldsymbol{v}}^{\mathsf{H}}), \tag{9.28}$$

where

$$\tilde{\boldsymbol{v}} = \begin{bmatrix} \boldsymbol{v}e^{j\theta_{N+1}} \\ e^{j\theta_{N+1}} \end{bmatrix} \in \mathbb{C}^{N+1}, \boldsymbol{R}_i = \begin{bmatrix} \boldsymbol{b}_i\boldsymbol{b}_i^{\mathsf{H}}, & \boldsymbol{b}_i c_i^{\mathsf{H}} \\ c_i\boldsymbol{b}_i^{\mathsf{H}}, & |c_i|^2 \end{bmatrix} \in \mathbb{S}_+^{N+1}. \tag{9.29}$$

Similarly, we adopt the matrix lifting technique, that is, $\boldsymbol{V} = \tilde{\boldsymbol{v}}\tilde{\boldsymbol{v}}^{\mathsf{H}} \in \mathbb{C}^{(N+1)\times(N+1)}$. Given $\boldsymbol{m}$ and $\boldsymbol{x}$, the phase shift matrix $\boldsymbol{\Theta}$ in the first step is updated by solving the following low-rank optimization problem:

$$\begin{aligned} \mathscr{P}_{9.3.\mathrm{S1.2}} : \text{find} \quad & \boldsymbol{V} \\ \text{subject to} \quad & \mathrm{Tr}(\boldsymbol{M}) - \gamma_i \mathrm{Tr}(\boldsymbol{R}_i\boldsymbol{V}) \le x_i, \forall i, \\ & V_{n,n} = 1, \ n = 1, \ldots, N+1, \\ & \boldsymbol{V} \succeq \boldsymbol{0}, \ \mathrm{rank}(\boldsymbol{V}) = 1. \qquad (9.30) \end{aligned}$$

We can compute $\tilde{\boldsymbol{v}}$ through Cholesky decomposition of the rank-one matrix $\boldsymbol{V}$ and then extract $\boldsymbol{v}$ from $\tilde{v} = (\boldsymbol{v}^0, t^0)$ following $\boldsymbol{v} = \boldsymbol{v}^0/t^0$.

Likewise, in the second step, each feasibility detection $\mathscr{P}_{9.3.\mathrm{S2}}$ problem can also be addressed by alternating low-rank optimization. The update of $\boldsymbol{m}$ given $\boldsymbol{\Theta}$ is given by

$$
\begin{aligned}
\mathscr{P}_{9.3.\mathrm{S2.1}}: \text{find} \quad & \boldsymbol{M} \\
\text{subject to} \quad & \mathrm{Tr}(\boldsymbol{M}) - \gamma_i \mathrm{Tr}(\boldsymbol{M}\boldsymbol{H}_i) \leq 0, \ i \in \mathcal{S}^{[k]}, && (9.31)\\
& \boldsymbol{M} \succeq \boldsymbol{0}, \mathrm{Tr}(\boldsymbol{M}) \geq 1, \mathrm{rank}(\boldsymbol{M}) = 1. && (9.32)
\end{aligned}
$$

Given $\boldsymbol{m}$, the update of phase shifts is given by

$$
\begin{aligned}
\mathscr{P}_{9.3.\mathrm{S2.2}}: \text{find} \quad & \boldsymbol{V} \\
\text{subject to} \quad & \mathrm{Tr}(\boldsymbol{M}) - \gamma_i \mathrm{Tr}(\boldsymbol{R}_i\boldsymbol{V}) \leq 0, \ i \in \mathcal{S}^{[k]}, \\
& V_{n,n} = 1, \ n = 1, \ldots, N+1, \\
& \boldsymbol{V} \succeq \boldsymbol{0}, \ \mathrm{rank}(\boldsymbol{V}) = 1. && (9.33)
\end{aligned}
$$

9.3.3 DC program for rank-one constraints

Inducing rank-one solutions are critical for detecting the feasibility of the original biquadratic constraints. Therefore we adopt the exact DC representation for the rank-one constraint of a nonzero PSD matrix as demonstrated in Chapter 7.4.2:

$$
\mathrm{rank}(\boldsymbol{M}) = 1 \Leftrightarrow \mathrm{Tr}(\boldsymbol{M}) - \|\boldsymbol{M}\|_2 = 0 \tag{9.34}
$$

since only the largest singular value is nonzero. Then we use the DC regularization approach to address the rank-one constraint of problem $\mathscr{P}_{9.3.\mathrm{S1.1}}$ in the first step, which is given by

$$
\begin{aligned}
\mathscr{P}_{9.3.\mathrm{S1.1'}}: \underset{\boldsymbol{x},\boldsymbol{M}}{\text{minimize}} \quad & \|\boldsymbol{x}\|_1 + \rho\,(\mathrm{Tr}(\boldsymbol{M}) - \|\boldsymbol{M}\|_2) \\
\text{subject to} \quad & \mathrm{Tr}(\boldsymbol{M}) - \gamma_i \mathrm{Tr}(\boldsymbol{M}\boldsymbol{H}_i) \leq x_i, \forall i \\
& \boldsymbol{M} \succeq \boldsymbol{0}, \mathrm{Tr}(\boldsymbol{M}) \geq 1, \boldsymbol{x} \succeq \boldsymbol{0}, && (9.35)
\end{aligned}
$$

where $\rho > 0$ is a regularization parameter. The DC algorithm is given by successively linearizing the nonconvex part $-\rho\|\boldsymbol{M}\|_2$ of the objective function. The subgradient of spectral norm is given by $\partial\|\boldsymbol{V}\|_2 = \boldsymbol{u}_1\boldsymbol{u}_1^{\mathsf{H}}$, where $\boldsymbol{u}_1$ is the eigenvector corresponding to the largest eigenvalue of $\boldsymbol{V}$.

Likewise, the DC program for problem $\mathscr{P}_{9.3.S1.2}$ is given by

$$\begin{aligned} \mathscr{P}_{9.3.S1.2'}: \underset{\boldsymbol{V}}{\text{minimize}} \quad & \text{Tr}(\boldsymbol{V}) - \|\boldsymbol{V}\|_2 \\ \text{subject to} \quad & \text{Tr}(\boldsymbol{M}) - \gamma_i \text{Tr}(\boldsymbol{R}_i \boldsymbol{V}) \le x_i, \forall i \\ & \boldsymbol{V} \succeq \boldsymbol{0}, V_{n,n} = 1, \ n = 1, \ldots, N+1. \end{aligned} \tag{9.36}$$

In the second step of detecting feasibility, problem $\mathscr{P}_{9.3.S2.1}$ is addressed by the DC program

$$\begin{aligned} \mathscr{P}_{9.3.S2.1'}: \underset{\boldsymbol{M}}{\text{minimize}} \quad & \text{Tr}(\boldsymbol{M}) - \|\boldsymbol{M}\|_2 \\ \text{subject to} \quad & \text{Tr}(\boldsymbol{M}) - \gamma_i \text{Tr}(\boldsymbol{M}\boldsymbol{H}_i) \le 0, \ i \in \mathcal{S}^{[k]} \\ & \boldsymbol{M} \succeq \boldsymbol{0}, \text{Tr}(\boldsymbol{M}) \ge 1, \end{aligned} \tag{9.37}$$

whereas problem $\mathscr{P}_{9.3.S2.2}$ is addressed by

$$\begin{aligned} \mathscr{P}_{9.3.S2.2'}: \underset{\boldsymbol{V}}{\text{minimize}} \quad & \text{Tr}(\boldsymbol{V}) - \|\boldsymbol{V}\|_2 \\ \text{subject to} \quad & \text{Tr}(\boldsymbol{M}) - \gamma_i \text{Tr}(\boldsymbol{R}_i \boldsymbol{V}) \le 0, \ i \in \mathcal{S}^{[k]}, \\ & \boldsymbol{V} \succeq \boldsymbol{0}, V_{n,n} = 1, \ n = 1, \ldots, N+1. \end{aligned} \tag{9.38}$$

If the objective values of problems $\mathscr{P}_{9.3.S1.2'}$, $\mathscr{P}_{9.3.S2.1'}$, and $\mathscr{P}_{9.3.S2.2'}$ achieve zero, then the solutions $\boldsymbol{M}$ and $\boldsymbol{V}$ are exact rank-one. We can further extract the receive beamforming vector $\boldsymbol{m}$ from the Cholesky decomposition $\boldsymbol{M} = \boldsymbol{m}\boldsymbol{m}^{\mathsf{H}}$, and extract the phase shift matrix $\boldsymbol{\Theta} = \text{diag}(\boldsymbol{v})$ from the Cholesky decomposition $\boldsymbol{V} = \tilde{\boldsymbol{v}}\tilde{\boldsymbol{v}}^{\mathsf{H}}$ and $\boldsymbol{v} = \boldsymbol{v}^0/t^0$, $\tilde{v} = (\boldsymbol{v}^0, t^0)$.

The overall procedure of the alternating DC algorithm is concluded in Algorithm 13.

9.4. Simulation results

In this section, we demonstrate the advantages of RIS for on-device distributed federated learning via numerical experiments.

Consider the three-dimensional (3D) coordinate system, where the BS located in $(0, 0, 0)$ has uniformly distributed $M = 6$ antennas in a linear array, and the RIS located in $(0, 100, 0)$ has $N = 40$ reflecting elements in a uniform rectangular array. $K = 20$ single-antenna mobile devices are randomly located in the area of $[-5 \sim 5, 95 \sim 105, 0]$ around the RIS. The units for all coordinates are in meters. We set the path loss model as $L(d) =$

Algorithm 13: Sparse and low-rank optimization approach for solving problem $\mathscr{P}_{9.2}$.

Output: $\boldsymbol{m}$, $\boldsymbol{\Theta} = \text{diag}(\boldsymbol{v})$, and the set of selected devices $\mathcal{S}^{[k]}$
Step 1: inducing sparsity
Initialize: $\boldsymbol{\Theta}^{[0]}, t = 0$.
while *not converge* **do**
  Fixing $\boldsymbol{\Theta}^{[t-1]}$, obtain $\boldsymbol{M}^t$, $\boldsymbol{x}^t$ by solving problem $\mathscr{P}_{9.3.S1.1'}$ with DC algorithm.
  Fixing $\boldsymbol{M}^t$ and $\boldsymbol{x}^t$, obtain $\boldsymbol{\Theta}^t = \text{diag}\boldsymbol{v}^{[t]}$ by solving problem $\mathscr{P}_{9.3.S1.2'}$ with DC algorithm.
  $t \leftarrow t + 1$.
end
Step 2: detecting feasibility
Arrange $\boldsymbol{x}$ in descending order as $x_{\pi(1)} \geq \cdots \geq x_{\pi(K)}$
$k \leftarrow 1$
while *objective value of either problem* $\mathscr{P}_{9.3.S2.1'}$ *or problem* $\mathscr{P}_{9.3.S2.2'}$ *is not zero* **do**
  $\mathcal{S}^{[k]} \leftarrow \{\pi(k), \pi(k+1), \ldots, \pi(K)\}$
  Initialize $\boldsymbol{\Theta}^{[0]}, t = 0$.
  while *not converge* **do**
    Fixing $\boldsymbol{\Theta}^{[t-1]}$, obtain the solution $\boldsymbol{M}^{[t]}$ to problem $\mathscr{P}_{9.3.S2.1'}$ with DC algorithm.
    Fixing $\boldsymbol{M}^{[t]}$, obtain $\boldsymbol{\Theta}^{[t]} = \text{diag}\boldsymbol{v}^{[t]}$ by solving problem $\mathscr{P}_{9.3.S2.2'}$ with DC algorithm.
    $t \leftarrow t + 1$
  end
  $k \leftarrow k + 1$
end

$T_0 d^{-\alpha}$, where d is the link distance, α is the path loss exponent, and $T_0 = -30$ dB is the pass loss at the reference distance $d = 1$ m. Consider the Rayleigh fading channels

$$\boldsymbol{h}_i^d = \sqrt{L(d_i^{\mathrm{d}})}\boldsymbol{\gamma}^d, L(d_i^{\mathrm{d}}) = T_0 \cdot (d_i^{\mathrm{d}})^{-3.76}, \tag{9.39}$$

$$\boldsymbol{h}_i^r = \sqrt{L(d_i^{\mathrm{r}})}\boldsymbol{\gamma}^r = T_0 \cdot (d_i^{\mathrm{r}})^{-2.2}, \tag{9.40}$$

$$\mathbf{G} = \sqrt{L(d_{\mathrm{IB}})}\boldsymbol{\Gamma} = T_0 \cdot (d^{\mathrm{IB}})^{-2.2}, \tag{9.41}$$

$$\boldsymbol{\gamma}^{\mathrm{d}} \sim \mathcal{CN}(\mathbf{0}, \boldsymbol{I}), \boldsymbol{\gamma}^{\mathrm{r}} \sim \mathcal{CN}(\mathbf{0}, \boldsymbol{I}), \boldsymbol{\Gamma} \sim \mathcal{CN}(\mathbf{0}, \boldsymbol{I}), \tag{9.42}$$

where d_i^{d} is the distance between the BS and device i, d_i^{r} is the distance between the RIS and device i, and d^{IB} is the distance between the BS and RIS. Other parameters are set as $P_0 = 20$ dBm, $\sigma^2 = -80$ dBm, and $\rho = 20$.

9.4.1 Device selection

We first compare the performances of number of selected devices for the following settings/algorithms:

- **"Alternating DC":** We evaluate the performance of the provided alternating DC algorithm (i.e., Algorithm 13) for the model aggregation of RIS empowered federated learning system.
- **"RIS+SDR":** For RIS empowered federated learning system, we apply the SDR technique to address the rank-one constraints of problems $\mathscr{P}_{9.3.\mathrm{S}1.1}$, $\mathscr{P}_{9.3.\mathrm{S}1.2}$, $\mathscr{P}_{9.3.\mathrm{S}2.1}$, $\mathscr{P}_{9.3.\mathrm{S}2.2}$.
- **"SDR without RIS":** In this setting, we remove the RIS and consider the system shown in Chapter 8. We adopt the SDR technique to address the nonconvex quadratic constraints.
- **"DC without RIS":** We adopt the DC approach provided in Chapter 8.5.3 for the on-device distributed federated learning system in Chapter 8.

We use the ℓ_1-norm relaxation to induce sparsity for all approaches above. The simulation results illustrated in Fig. 9.3 demonstrate that the provided approach yields more selected devices compared with the SDR approach

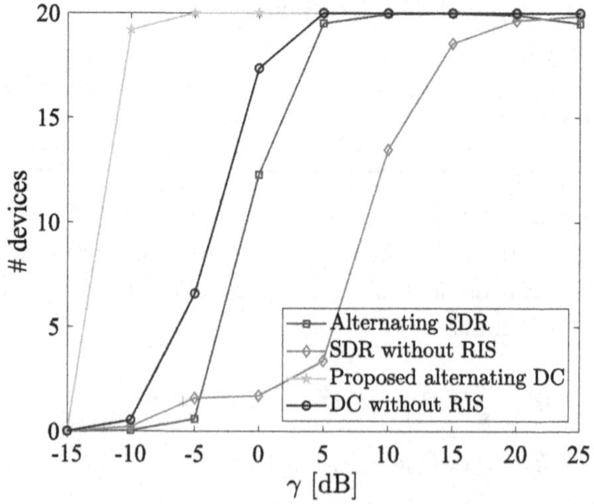

Figure 9.3 Average number selected devices over target MSE.

and considerably improves the performance of model aggregation thanks to the deployment of RIS.

9.4.2 Performance of federated learning

We use the system of 20 mobile devices and a base station to train an SVM classifier with the well-known CIFAR-10 dataset. The dataset is evenly and randomly split and then deployed across 20 mobile devices. We compare the performances of four approaches, "Alternating DC", "RIS+SDR", "SDR without RIS", and "DC without RIS", on the training set and the test set during the training process with FedAvg algorithm. We choose the performance with errorless model aggregation in each communication round as the benchmark. The simulation results are illustrated in Fig. 9.4, where the loss function values on the training set are presented in Fig. 9.4a, and the prediction accuracy is presented in Fig. 9.4b. We conclude that lower training loss and higher prediction accuracy can be achieved with the power of RIS, and the DC algorithm achieves better performance than SDR for the RIS empowered federated learning system.

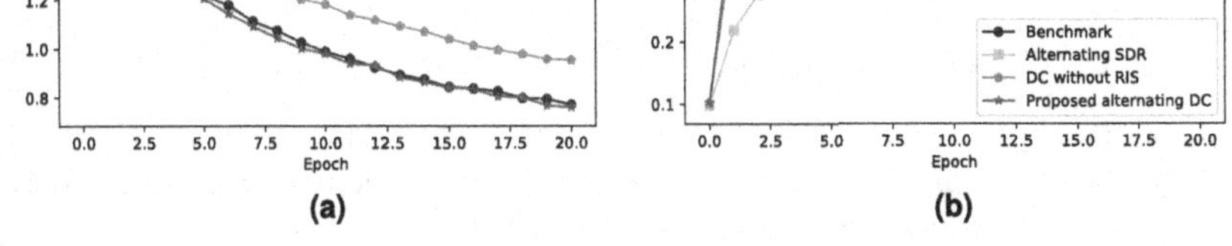

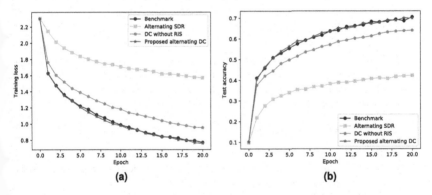

Figure 9.4 Performance comparisons of different algorithms for fast model aggregation in RIS-empowered on-device federated learning. (a) Convergence comparison for FedAvg between different device selection approaches. (b) Relationship between communication rounds and test accuracy.

9.5. Summary

In this chapter, we provided a novel RIS empowered over-the-air computation approach for fast model aggregation of on-device distributed model training to further improve the communication efficiency. The design target was to find the maximum selected devices under the target MSE requirements, which was formulated as a combinatorial optimization problem with nonconvex biquadratic constraints. To address the computational difficulties, we presented a sparse and low-rank optimization framework, which adopted sparse optimization to maximize the number of selected devices and alternating low-rank optimization to address the nonconvex biquadratic constraints. Numerical results demonstrated the advantages of deploying RIS for over-the-air computation-based fast model aggregation approach in federated learning systems.

References

[1] S. Gong, X. Lu, D.T. Hoang, D. Niyato, L. Shu, D.I. Kim, Y.-C. Liang, Toward smart wireless communications via intelligent reflecting surfaces: a contemporary survey, IEEE Commun. Surv. Tutor. 22 (Jun. 2020) 2283–2314.
[2] S.V. Hum, J. Perruisseau-Carrier, Reconfigurable reflectarrays and array lenses for dynamic antenna beam control: a review, IEEE Trans. Antennas Propag. 62 (Jan. 2013) 183–198.
[3] T.J. Cui, M.Q. Qi, X. Wan, J. Zhao, Q. Cheng, Coding metamaterials, digital metamaterials and programmable metamaterials, Light Sci. Appl. 3 (Oct. 2014) e218.
[4] Q. Wu, R. Zhang, Towards smart and reconfigurable environment: intelligent reflecting surface aided wireless network, IEEE Commun. Mag. 58 (Nov. 2020) 106–112.
[5] X. Yuan, Y.-J. Zhang, Y. Shi, W. Yan, H. Liu, Reconfigurable-intelligent-surface empowered 6G wireless communications: challenges and opportunities, preprint, arXiv:2001.00364, 2020.
[6] K. Yang, Y. Shi, Y. Zhou, Z. Yang, L. Fu, W. Chen, Federated machine learning for intelligent IoT via reconfigurable intelligent surface, IEEE Netw. 34 (5) (2020) 16–22.
[7] S. Gong, X. Lu, D.T. Hoang, D. Niyato, L. Shu, D.I. Kim, Y.-C. Liang, Towards smart radio environment for wireless communications via intelligent reflecting surfaces: a comprehensive survey, preprint, arXiv:1912.07794, 2019.
[8] Q. Wu, R. Zhang, Intelligent reflecting surface enhanced wireless network via joint active and passive beamforming, IEEE Trans. Wirel. Commun. 18 (Nov. 2019) 5394–5409.
[9] C. Huang, A. Zappone, G.C. Alexandropoulos, M. Debbah, C. Yuen, Reconfigurable intelligent surfaces for energy efficiency in wireless communication, IEEE Trans. Wirel. Commun. 18 (Aug. 2019) 4157–4170.
[10] M. Fu, Y. Zhou, Y. Shi, K.B. Letaief, Reconfigurable intelligent surface empowered downlink non-orthogonal multiple access, preprint, arXiv:1910.07361, 2019.
[11] Z. Wang, Y. Shi, Y. Zhou, H. Zhou, N. Zhang, Wireless-powered over-the-air computation in intelligent reflecting surface aided IoT networks, IEEE Int. Things J. 8 (3) (2021) 1585–1598.
[12] T. Jiang, Y. Shi, Over-the-air computation via intelligent reflecting surfaces, in: Proc. IEEE Global Commun. Conf. (GLOBECOM), IEEE, 2019, pp. 1–6.

CHAPTER TEN

Blind over-the-air computation for federated learning

10.1. Blind over-the-air computation

Although over-the-air computation presents great promise for facilitating model aggregation of federated learning, the transceivers design relies on instantaneous channel state information (CSI) between each device and the aggregation center. It results in high signaling overhead for federated learning system with massive devices. The signaling overhead reduction [1,2] for acquiring CSI is an extensively studied topic in wireless communication, such as limited-precision CSI, incomplete CSI, statistical CSI, and so on. However, these methods still rely on available CSI in transceiver design. In this chapter, we take the view of blind demixing [3–6]: we directly estimate each transmitted signal and channel vector from the mixed signals. The received signal at the BS can be regarded as the mixing of the convolution between the channel vector and transmitted signal. Therefore we are able to formulate the model aggregation problem through wireless network as a blind demixing problem, and each signal to be aggregated can be estimated simultaneously. Then we can compute the aggregated function based on the estimated results. We call this approach the *blind over-the-air computation*.

In the field of wireless communications, blind demixing is often referred to as an extension of blind deconvolution [7] from a single source to multiple sources and aims to estimate a number of structured unknown signal pairs from the mixing of their convolution. To solve this nonconvex problem, a line of works study convex and nonconvex methods based on low-rank reformulation. Specifically, the convolution of two signals can be rewritten as a linear function of the outer product of two unknown signals in the Fourier domain. Then the outer product can be integrated as a rank-one matrix variable. The convex method [8] adopted the nuclear norm relaxation to induce low-rank structure. The work [5] developed a Riemannian optimization framework to exploit the rank-one structure in blind demixing.

In this chapter, we present nonconvex approaches by directly optimizing all unknown signal pairs from the mix of their convolutions [6]. Since the

Mobile Edge Artificial Intelligence
https://doi.org/10.1016/B978-0-12-823817-2.00021-8

CSI and transmitted signals are complex vectors, we present the Wirtinger flow approach, like the vanilla gradient descent in real field, to solve the nonconvex demixing problem. Instead of using a regularization term to guarantee incoherence [9], the provided approach is regularization free to avoid a tedious tuning of parameters.

10.2. Problem formulation

To present a neat procedure of using blind over-the-air computation for model aggregation, we consider the federated learning system with M mobile devices and a single-antenna BS serving as the fusion center. We focus on the data aggregation procedure of computing

$$\boldsymbol{\theta} = \sum_{i=1}^{S} \boldsymbol{x}_i, \tag{10.1}$$

where S is the number of active devices, and $\boldsymbol{x}_i \in \mathbb{C}^N$ is the symbol vector of model parameters of device i to be aggregated. For the ith mobile device, we denote the precoding matrix as $\boldsymbol{C}_i \in \mathbb{C}^{M \times N}$ over $m > N$ time slots, and the transmitted signal is given by

$$\boldsymbol{f}_i = \boldsymbol{C}_i \boldsymbol{x}_i. \tag{10.2}$$

The signals $\boldsymbol{f}_i \in \mathbb{C}^m$ are assumed to be transmitted through time-invariant channels in the orthogonal frequency division multiplexing (OFDM) system. The impulse response of the channel between the kth mobile device and the base station is given by $\boldsymbol{h}_k \in \mathbb{C}^K$, where K is the maximum delay of $\boldsymbol{h}_k$ measured by the number of samples. Then the received signal at the BS is given by

$$\boldsymbol{p} = \sum_{i=1}^{S} \boldsymbol{f}_i \circledast \boldsymbol{g}_i + \boldsymbol{n}, \tag{10.3}$$

where $\boldsymbol{g}_i = [\boldsymbol{h}_i^\top, \boldsymbol{0}^\top]^\top \in \mathbb{C}^M$ is the zero-padded channel vector, $\circledast$ is the cyclic convolution operator, and $\boldsymbol{n} \in \mathbb{C}^m$ is an additive white complex Gaussian noise. The received signal can be transformed into the Fourier domain as follows:

$$\boldsymbol{y} = \boldsymbol{F}\boldsymbol{p} = \sum_{i=1}^{S} (\boldsymbol{F}\boldsymbol{C}_i\boldsymbol{x}_i) \odot \boldsymbol{B}\boldsymbol{h}_i + \boldsymbol{F}\boldsymbol{n}, \tag{10.4}$$

where $\odot$ denotes the elementwise product, and $\boldsymbol{F} \in \mathbb{C}^{M \times M}$ denotes the unitary discrete Fourier transform (DMT) matrix, that is, the (i, k)th entry of the matrix $\boldsymbol{F}$ is given by $\omega^{ik}/\sqrt{M}$, where $\omega = \exp(-2\pi \mathrm{j}/M)$ with j denoting the imaginary unit. Denote the first K columns of $\boldsymbol{F}$ as the matrix $\boldsymbol{B} = [\boldsymbol{b}_1, \ldots, \boldsymbol{b}_M]^{\mathsf{H}} \in \mathbb{C}^{M \times K}$, where $\boldsymbol{b}_i \in \mathbb{C}^K$ for $1 \leq i \leq M$. Thus we can rewrite the received signal $\boldsymbol{y}$ over M time slots as follows:

$$y_k = \sum_{i=1}^{S} \boldsymbol{b}_k^{\mathsf{H}} \boldsymbol{h}_i \boldsymbol{a}_{ik}^{\mathsf{H}} \boldsymbol{x}_i + \tilde{n}_k \tag{10.5}$$

for $1 \leq k \leq M$, where $\boldsymbol{a}_{ik} \in \mathbb{C}^N$ is the kth column vector of the matrix $(\boldsymbol{F}\boldsymbol{C}_i)^{\mathsf{H}}$, $\tilde{n}_k$ denotes the kth entry of the vector $\boldsymbol{F}\boldsymbol{n}$, which is an independent circularly symmetric complex Gaussian measurement noise.

The target of over-the-air computation is to directly estimate $\boldsymbol{\theta}$ from received signals via concurrent transmissions, instead of concerning individual estimation error for each $\boldsymbol{x}_i$, that is, the estimated value of target function is given by $\boldsymbol{\theta} = \sum_{i=1}^{S} \omega_i \boldsymbol{x}_i$. The relative estimation error of the target function between the estimated $\boldsymbol{\theta}$ and the ground truth $\overline{\boldsymbol{\theta}}$ is given by

$$\mathrm{error}(\boldsymbol{\theta}, \overline{\boldsymbol{\theta}}) = \frac{\| \sum_{i=1}^{S} \omega_i \boldsymbol{x}_i - \sum_{i=1}^{S} \overline{\boldsymbol{x}}_i \|_2^2}{\| \sum_{i=1}^{S} \overline{\boldsymbol{x}}_i \|_2^2}, \tag{10.6}$$

where $\omega_i \in \mathbb{C}$ is an alignment parameter against the ambiguity of $(\frac{1}{\omega_i} \boldsymbol{h}_i, \omega_i \boldsymbol{x}_i)$ in Eq. (10.5), which can be estimated from

$$\omega_i = \arg\min_{\omega_i} \|\omega_i^{-1} \boldsymbol{h}_i - \overline{\boldsymbol{h}}_i\|_2^2 + \|\omega_i \boldsymbol{x}_i - \overline{\boldsymbol{x}}_i\|_2^2. \tag{10.7}$$

To compute a target function over-the-air without knowledge of CSI, we consider the precoding scheme of selecting $\boldsymbol{a}_{ik}$ from i.i.d. circularly symmetric complex normal distribution $\mathcal{CN}(0, \boldsymbol{I}_N)$ for all $1 \leq i \leq S$, $1 \leq k \leq M$. Then we can simultaneously obtain the estimated channel state information $\{\boldsymbol{h}_i\}$ and $\{\boldsymbol{x}_i\}$ for minimizing the relative estimation error by solving

$$\mathscr{P} : \underset{\{\boldsymbol{h}_i\}, \{\boldsymbol{x}_i\}}{\mathrm{minimize}} f(\boldsymbol{h}, \boldsymbol{x}) := \sum_{j=1}^{M} \left| \sum_{k=1}^{S} \boldsymbol{b}_j^{\mathsf{H}} \boldsymbol{h}_k \boldsymbol{a}_{kj}^{\mathsf{H}} \boldsymbol{x}_k - y_j \right|^2. \tag{10.8}$$

Therefore we are able to obtain the estimated target function $\theta = \sum_{i=1}^{S} \boldsymbol{x}_i$ by exploring the signal superposition property of a wireless multiple-access channel without transmitting individual data to the base station. Thus, despite the nonconvexity of problem $\mathscr{P}$, we will provide the Wirtinger flow approach with random initialization in the following.

10.3. Wirtinger flow algorithm for blind over-the-air computation

In this section, we present the overall procedure of the Wirtinger flow algorithm for blind over-the-air computation and the initialization strategies including spectral initialization and random initialization.

10.3.1 Wirtinger flow

The Wirtinger flow is an iterative algorithm with simple gradient descents. The gradients of a real function over complex variables are given by the Wirtinger derivatives [10]. Simplifying the notation, we denote

$$\boldsymbol{z} = \begin{bmatrix} \boldsymbol{z}_1 \\ \cdots \\ \boldsymbol{z}_S \end{bmatrix} \in \mathbb{C}^{S(N+K)} \text{ with } \boldsymbol{z}_i = \begin{bmatrix} \boldsymbol{h}_i \\ \boldsymbol{x}_i \end{bmatrix} \in \mathbb{C}^{N+K}. \tag{10.9}$$

Then the objective function can be represented as $f(\boldsymbol{z}) := f(\boldsymbol{h}, \boldsymbol{x})$, and the Wirtinger derivatives of $f(\boldsymbol{z})$ are given by

$$\nabla_{\boldsymbol{h}_i} f(\boldsymbol{z}) = \sum_{j=1}^{M} \left(\sum_{k=1}^{S} \boldsymbol{b}_j^{\mathsf{H}} \boldsymbol{h}_k \boldsymbol{a}_{kj}^{\mathsf{H}} \boldsymbol{x}_k - y_j \right) \boldsymbol{b}_j \boldsymbol{x}_i^{\mathsf{H}} \boldsymbol{a}_{ij}, \tag{10.10}$$

$$\nabla_{\boldsymbol{x}_i} f(\boldsymbol{z}) = \sum_{j=1}^{M} \left(\sum_{k=1}^{S} \boldsymbol{b}_j^{\mathsf{H}} \boldsymbol{h}_k \boldsymbol{a}_{kj}^{\mathsf{H}} \boldsymbol{x}_k - y_j \right) \boldsymbol{a}_{ij} \boldsymbol{h}_i^{\mathsf{H}} \boldsymbol{b}_j. \tag{10.11}$$

The Wirtinger flow algorithm iteratively applies a gradient descent step with step size $\eta > 0$ via

$$\begin{bmatrix} \boldsymbol{h}_i^{[t+1]} \\ \boldsymbol{x}_i^{[t+1]} \end{bmatrix} = \begin{bmatrix} \boldsymbol{h}_i^{[t]} \\ \boldsymbol{x}_i^{[t]} \end{bmatrix} - \eta \begin{bmatrix} \frac{1}{\|\boldsymbol{x}_i^{[t]}\|_2^2} \nabla_{\boldsymbol{h}_i} f(\boldsymbol{z}^{[t]}) \\ \frac{1}{\|\boldsymbol{h}_i^{[t]}\|_2^2} \nabla_{\boldsymbol{x}_i} f(\boldsymbol{z}^{[t]}) \end{bmatrix}, \ i = 1, \ldots, s. \tag{10.12}$$

10.3.2 Initialization strategies

To get a fast convergence rate and optimality guarantees free of regularization terms, the authors of [4] considered the spectral initialization strategy given by

$$h_i^{[0]} = \sqrt{\|M_i\|_2}\check{h}_i^{[0]}, \; x_i^{[0]} = \sqrt{\|M_i\|}\check{x}_i^{[0]}, \tag{10.13}$$

where $M_i = \sum_{j=1}^{M} y_j b_j a_{ij}^H$, and $\check{h}_i^{[0]}$ and $\check{x}_i^{[0]}$ are the left and right singular vectors of the matrix M_i corresponding to its largest singular value. The statistical optimality guarantees recovering h_i and x_i, and the fast convergence rate of the Wirtinger flow algorithm with spectral initialization is provided under incoherence and robustness conditions.

The work of [6] has considered the model-agnostic random initialization strategy:

$$h_i^{[0]} \sim \mathcal{N}(0, K^{-1}I_K), \; x_i^{[0]} \sim \mathcal{N}(0, N^{-1}I_N), \; i = 1, \ldots, S. \tag{10.14}$$

The random initialization strategy works equally well as the spectral initialization strategy and enjoys a high probability of an exponential decay of the estimation error under some mild conditions. Specifically, there exist a sufficiently small constant $0 \le \gamma \le 1$ and $T_\gamma \sim S\log(\max\{K, N\})$ such that the $\text{error}(\theta, \overline{\theta}) \le \gamma(1 - \frac{\eta}{16\kappa})^{t-T_\gamma}$ with probability at least $1 - c_1 M^{-\mu} - c_1 M e^{-c_2 N}$ for $t \ge T_\gamma$ and some constants μ, c_1, c_2.

10.4. Numerical results

In this section, we evaluate the Wirtinger flow algorithm with extensive numerical results.

We adopt the random initialization strategy to demonstrate the effectiveness and efficiency of the Wirtinger flow for solving problem $\mathscr{P}$. We generate the ground truth $\{h_i, x_i\}$ and initial points $\{h_i^{[0]}, x_i^{[0]}\}$ randomly according to the following distributions:

$$h_i \sim \mathcal{N}(0, K^{-1}I_K), \; x_i \sim \mathcal{N}(0, N^{-1}I_N), \tag{10.15}$$

$$h_i^{[0]} \sim \mathcal{N}(0, K^{-1}I_K), \; x_i^{[0]} \sim \mathcal{N}(0, N^{-1}I_N), \tag{10.16}$$

$i = 1, \ldots, S$. We set $K = N$, $S = 10$, and $m = 50K$. In each iteration the step size $\eta = 0.1$. The convergence rate of the relative error $\text{error}(\theta, \overline{\theta})$ is illustrated in Fig. 10.1. We find that the convergence process can be divided into two stages. In the first stage the relative error is almost flat within dozens of iterations. In the second stage, the relative error decreases exponentially.

Then we then study the effects of noise level on the relative error of the estimated target function. Consider the additive noise $\tilde{n} \in \mathbb{C}^M$ in (10.5)

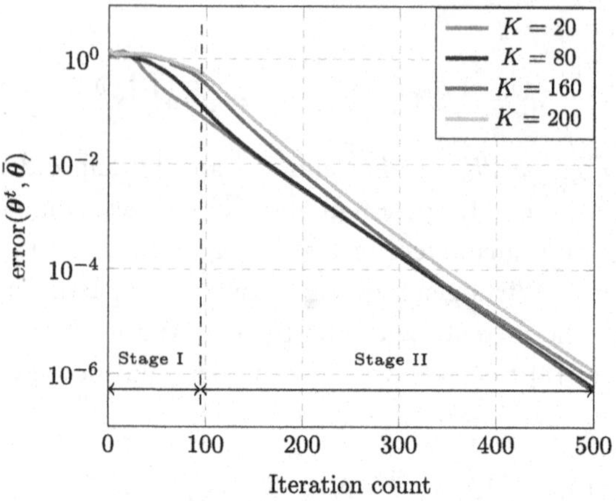

Figure 10.1 Convergence of Wirtinger flow for blind over-the-air computation.

chosen as $\tilde{\boldsymbol{n}} = \gamma \cdot \|\boldsymbol{y}\|_2 \cdot \frac{\boldsymbol{w}}{\|\boldsymbol{w}\|_2}$, where $\boldsymbol{w} \sim \mathcal{CN}(\boldsymbol{0}, \boldsymbol{I}_M)$ is an M-dimensional vector drawn from the standard complex Gaussian distribution. The parameter $\gamma > 0$ equals the signal-to-noise ratio (SNR). We set the encoding matrix as the Hadamard-type encoding matrix given by

$$\boldsymbol{C}_i = \boldsymbol{F}\boldsymbol{D}_i\boldsymbol{H}, \tag{10.17}$$

where $\boldsymbol{F} \in \mathbb{C}^{M \times N}$ is the DFT matrix, $\boldsymbol{D}_i$ is a diagonal matrix whose diagonal elements are independently and randomly chosen from $\{-1, +1\}$, and $\boldsymbol{H} \in \mathbb{C}^{M \times N}$ is a fixed partial Hadamard matrix. We choose $s = 5$ and $K = N = 10$ and stop the Wirtinger flow algorithm if the relative error does not exceed 10^{-15} or the number of iterations exceeds 500. The relationship between the relative error of the estimated target function and SNR averaged over 100 trials is illustrated in Fig. 10.2.

From the numerical results we observe that the blind over-the-air computation approach with Wirtinger flow is able to estimate the aggregation function without considering estimation errors of $\boldsymbol{x}_i$ individually or acquiring instantaneous channel state information.

10.5. Summary

In this chapter, we studied the over-the-air computation approach for model aggregation of federated learning without CSI. This blind over-the-air computation problem was formulated as a blind demixing problem

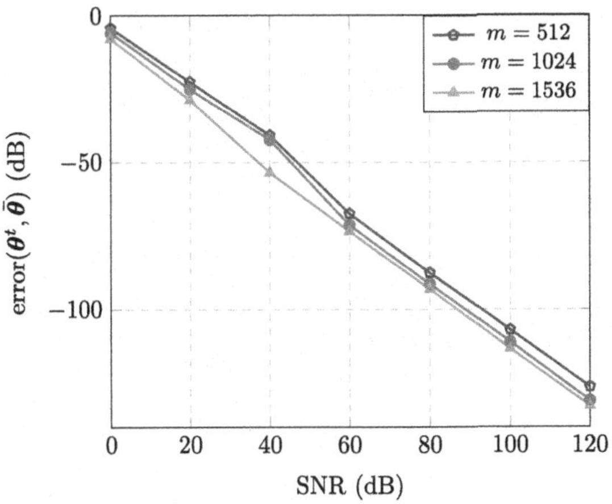

Figure 10.2 Relative error error($\theta, \overline{\theta}$) over σ_W (dB).

from the mixed signal received at the BS. To solve the nonconvex blind demixing problem, we provided the Wirtinger flow algorithm to optimize each channel vector and transmitted signal simultaneously. Theoretically, it has a fast convergence rate, which was also verified through numerical results.

References

[1] B.B. Haile, A.A. Dowhuszko, J. Hämäläinen, R. Wichman, Z. Ding, On performance loss of some comp techniques under channel power imbalance and limited feedback, IEEE Trans. Wirel. Commun. 14 (Aug. 2015) 4469–4481.

[2] Y. Shi, J. Zhang, K.B. Letaief, CSI overhead reduction with stochastic beamforming for cloud radio access networks, in: Proc. IEEE Int. Conf. Commun. (ICC), IEEE, 2014, pp. 5154–5159.

[3] M.B. McCoy, J.A. Tropp, Sharp recovery bounds for convex demixing, with applications, Found. Comput. Math. 14 (Apr. 2014) 503–567.

[4] J. Dong, Y. Shi, Nonconvex demixing from bilinear measurements, IEEE Trans. Signal Process. 66 (Oct. 2018) 5152–5166.

[5] J. Dong, K. Yang, Y. Shi, Blind demixing for low-latency communication, IEEE Trans. Wirel. Commun. 18 (Feb. 2019) 897–911.

[6] J. Dong, Y. Shi, Z. Ding, Blind over-the-air computation and data fusion via provable Wirtinger flow, IEEE Trans. Signal Process. 68 (Jan. 2020) 1136–1151.

[7] A. Ahmed, B. Recht, J. Romberg, Blind deconvolution using convex programming, IEEE Trans. Inf. Theory 60 (Mar. 2014) 1711–1732.

[8] S. Ling, T. Strohmer, Blind deconvolution meets blind demixing: algorithms and performance bounds, IEEE Trans. Inf. Theory 63 (Jul. 2017) 4497–4520.

[9] S. Ling, T. Strohmer, Regularized gradient descent: a non-convex recipe for fast joint blind deconvolution and demixing, Inf. Inference J. IMA 8 (Mar. 2018) 1–49.

[10] E.J. Candes, X. Li, M. Soltanolkotabi, Phase retrieval via Wirtinger flow: theory and algorithms, IEEE Trans. Inf. Theory 61 (4) (Apr. 2015) 1985–2007.

PART FOUR

Final part: conclusions and future directions

CHAPTER ELEVEN

Conclusions and future directions

11.1. Conclusions

In this book, we provided detailed knowledge for mobile edge AI, which is an active area involving AI, optimization, and mobile communication. In the first part, we presented general knowledge on the foundation of mobile edge AI. It began with the motivations and challenges of mobile edge AI and the organization of the book in Chapter 1. In Chapters 1 and 3, we provided primer knowledge on AI and optimization. In Chapter 4, we gave a summary of existing works considering different mobile AI system structures. In the second part, we presented three representative works on edge inference. Specifically, in Chapter 5, we discussed a novel model compression approach to achieve on-device inference. In Chapter 6, we provided an on-device cooperative inference framework with wireless MapReduce structure. In Chapter 7, we provided a cooperative transmission approach for server-based computation offloading edge inference systems. In the third part, we discussed in detail three representative approaches of edge training. In Chapter 8, we provided a novel over-the-air computation approach for fast model aggregation in federated learning, one of the most important area for protecting the data privacy of distributed edge training. The communication efficiency was further improved by deploying reconfigurable intelligent surface in the system, which we presented in Chapter 9. Furthermore, in Chapter 10, we presented a channel blind approach of model aggregation avoiding the heavy communication overhead for acquiring global channel state information.

11.2. Discussions and future directions

Due to the various data availability and system heterogeneity, it becomes almost infeasible to find a unified framework for all mobile edge AI applications. The design of mobile edge AI frameworks relies on interdisciplinary knowledge involving AI, optimization, mobile communication, and so on. There are already some elegant and insightful approaches for certain mobile edge AI applications. We have discussed and presented these works and results to provide the readers with a plethora of the primer and progress

Mobile Edge Artificial Intelligence
https://doi.org/10.1016/B978-0-12-823817-2.00023-1

for mobile edge AI. More importantly, this book is expected to provide insights into the mobile edge AI designs in various scenarios, which motivate more researches and applications in industrial practice.

One of the most important lessons learned from the existing works is that paying more attention to "what to compute" and "what to transmit" can often bring great performance improvements in achieving low-latency and secure AI services for mobile users. This perspective of learning has already motivated the proposal of many approaches to reduce latency, improve energy efficiency, and protect data privacy. Another important line of directions beyond the theoretical designs of mobile edge AI is developing more advanced hardwares and softwares despite the difficulties.

- **Hardware design:** The capabilities of hardware directly determine the physical limits of mobile edge AI. AI hardware is experiencing the process of becoming smaller to support edge AI services, whereas we used to prioritize higher performance in spite of the large size, high power consumption, and high costs. In recent years, there are many efforts on the design of scaled-down AI hardwares. Google has designed the edge TPU (tensor processing unit) for edge inference, which has a smaller size and lower power consumption than cloud TPU. Nvidia has designed Jetson TX2 for efficient AI computing. These hardwares make the training process and inference process at edge servers more applicable.
- **Software platforms:** The hardware of edge computing nodes only gives the physical limits of local computing. With dedicated software design, traditional cloud AI service providers are seeking for embracing the power of edge nodes, especially IoT devices, and trying to make cloud-edge joint system a unified solution for their users. Microsoft Azure IoT,[1] Google Cloud IoT,[2] Amazon Web Services (AWS) IoT,[3] and NVIDIA EGX[4] aim to connect, manage, and intelligentize IoT devices.

[1] https://azure.microsoft.com/en-us/overview/iot/.
[2] https://cloud.google.com/solutions/iot/.
[3] https://aws.amazon.com/iot/.
[4] https://www.nvidia.com/en-us/data-center/products/egx-edge-computing/.

Index

K

L

M

T

U

V

W

Z

Printed in the United States
by Baker & Taylor Publisher Services